1 SPECIAL EDUCA[...] IN TRANSITION

Concepts to Guide the Education of Experienced Teachers

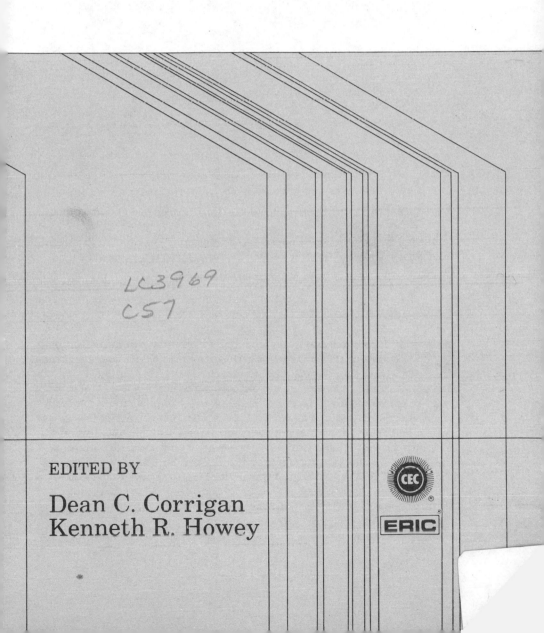

EDITED BY

Dean C. Corrigan
Kenneth R. Howey

A product of the ERIC Clearinghouse on Handicapped and Gifted Children.

Published in 1980 by The Council for Exceptional Children, 1920 Association Drive, Reston, Virginia 22091

Library of Congress Number 80-68281

ISBN 0-86586-109-9

This publication was prepared with funding from the National Institute of Education, US Department of Education, under contract no. 400-76-0119. Contractors undertaking such projects under government sponsorship are encouraged to express freely their judgment in professional and technical matters. Prior to publication the manuscript was submitted to The Council for Exceptional Children for critical review and determination of professional competence. This publication has met such standards. Points of view, however, do not necessarily represent the official view or opinions of either The Council for Exceptional Children, the National Institute of Education, or the Department of Education.

Printed in the United States of America.

Special Education in Transition

A Series Publication of
The Council for Exceptional Children

June B. Jordan, Editor in Chief
Gale S. Adams, Managing Editor

Series Editor: Maynard C. Reynolds

Consulting Editors:

Jack I. Bardon, University of
North Carolina at
Greensboro
Alejandro Benavides, Chicago
Board of Education
Diane Bricker, University of
Oregon
Dean C. Corrigan, University
of Maryland
Julia Davis, University of
Iowa
Stanley L. Deno, University of
Minnesota
Jerry C. Gross, New York
City Public Schools
John Guthrie, International
Reading Association

Reginald L. Jones, University
of California, Berkeley
Barbara K. Keogh, University
of California at Los Angeles
Garry McDaniels, Bureau of
Education for the
Handicapped
Joseph S. Renzulli, University
of Connecticut
Rosemary C. Sarri, University
of Michigan
Judy A. Schrag, Washington
State Department of Public
Instruction
Donald J. Stedman,
University of North
Carolina General
Administration

About the Series

In response to important new social and educational policies, as expressed in Public Law 94-142, for example, the field of special education is in a period of very rapid change. In general, the change is in the direction of more inclusive arrangements in basic institutions; that is, toward expanding the practice of serving exceptional children while they remain in their own homes and neighborhood schools. The result is an enormous challenge to all regular teachers, school principals, and other school staff members who now must participate more fully in programs for exceptional children. Similarly, large numbers of special educators, school psychologists, school social workers, and other specialists employed in the schools are being detached from their specialized work stations and asked to go to work in the mainstream context.

This *Special Education in Transition* series is predicated on the general assumption that the major transformation of the schools now under way, involving the renegotiation of many professional roles and the reorganization of many work stations, requires the development of a corresponding literature. Such a literature ought to be helpful to participants in the change processes through sharing what is learned about what works and what does not work. It also ought to serve as a kind of informal accountability tool by showing what can be achieved and, thus, suggesting to the public at large what it is that can be reasonably expected in various domains of performance.

In this new publications activity it is also planned that all varieties of participants in the change process ought to be reached. There is need for a *shared* literature among teachers of all kinds, school administrators, school psychologists, speech-language pathologists, parents, and others. It is not enough in these busy times to develop separate literatures to be distributed in narrowly defined channels. The challenge today is to study children and to plan educational programs through broad, interprofessional, and family related dialogue. This view led us to the formulation of a broadly representative group of consulting editors to guide plans in the development and marketing of the reports.

Several specific assumptions have also been made in the development of these reports. First, the typical journal article is often too short and the traditional book too long and formal for the communication of essential ideas in a period of rapid change. Second, recognition should be given to the description and analysis of emerging programs as well as to reports of traditional research. Third, reports of difficulties and failures, as well as successes, in efforts of change are valuable. And, finally, reports ought to be published rapidly while they are still fresh from important experience.

Each book will have its own editor(s). Individuals interested in preparing a manuscript for the series are invited to write to the Series Editor. The Board of Consulting Editors will assist the Series Editor in evaluating each proposal and manuscript.

Maynard C. Reynolds

Contents

About the Authors

Audrey S. Anderson, Coordinator for Deans' Grants Programs, College of Education, University of Maryland, College Park, Maryland.

Louise M. Berman, Professor and Associate Dean, College of Education, University of Maryland, College Park, Maryland.

Charles W. Case, Dean, College of Education and Human Services, University of Wisconsin-Oshkosh, Oshkosh, Wisconsin.

Dean C. Corrigan, Dean, College of Education, University of Maryland, College Park, Maryland.

Elizabeth Dillon-Peterson, Director, Staff Development, Lincoln, Nebraska Public Schools, Lincoln, Nebraska.

Martin Haberman, Dean, Urban Outreach, University of Wisconsin-Milwaukee, Milwaukee, Wisconsin.

Kenneth R. Howey, Professor, College of Education, University of Minnesota, Minneapolis, Minnesota.

David W. Johnson, Professor, College of Education, University of Minnesota, Minneapolis, Minnesota.

Roger T. Johnson, Associate Professor, College of Education, University of Minnesota, Minneapolis, Minnesota.

Sally K. Mertens, Assistant Professor, School of Education, Syracuse University, Syracuse, New York.

Lois T. Sprinthall, Associate Professor, Department of Teacher Development, St. Cloud State University, St. Cloud, Minnesota.

Norman A. Sprinthall, Professor, Department of Psychoeducational Studies, University of Minnesota, Minneapolis, Minnesota.

Sam J. Yarger, Professor, School of Education, Syracuse University, Syracuse, New York.

Foreword

This publication is a product of one of the projects supported by the Dean's Grant Program of the Bureau of Education for the Handicapped. During the past five years BEH has supported more than one hundred projects conducted by deans of education. The specific purpose of these grants has been to help administrators and faculties of schools, colleges, and departments of education to reexamine teacher education in the light of P.L. 94-142, The Education for All Handicapped Children Act. In 1978, BEH also placed resources with the American Association of Colleges for Teacher Education to help launch a nationwide program in the same line. The projects now operating under the auspices of the Dean's Grant Program tend to draw deans of education and other teacher education leaders into concerns for the education of handicapped students. They also give special education leaders contact points for supportive activities.

The Education for All Handicapped Children Act, P.L. 94-142, calls for the development of new educational practices in schools, colleges, and universities across the country. The Act is based on principles that educators have long espoused:

- The right to a free, appropriate public education.
- Individualized programing in the least restrictive environment.
- Parental involvement.
- Nondiscriminatory testing and evaluation.
- Due process.
- Comprehensive systems of personnel development.

As educators across the nation attempt to implement this legislative mandate, the relationships between special education and general education are being renegotiated. Policies and procedures for providing educational services for the handicapped now require that schools design programs for children according to their needs as learners. The least restrictive environment principle calls for an end to the exclusion of students and placing them in segregated educational settings. The principle of providing "appropriate education for all children" has created a demand to prepare all educators to respond competently to a variety of individual differences. In the end, training for this approach can help all children, not just those with the nine handicapping conditions defined in the law.

P.L. 94-142 has far reaching implications for education personnel development programs. The process of compliance calls for preservice and inservice teachers and other school personnel to become knowledgeable about the law and the principles upon which it is based. All new as well as currently employed educators in colleges as well as schools must be appropriately and adequately prepared.

The law helps to define what needs to be done in the area of preservice and inservice education. The law does *not* provide direction in terms of *how* training is to be provided or what constitutes good preservice and inservice training. This task falls to the education profession.

This publication, prepared by an outstanding group of educators, is exactly the kind of professional response this project intended to achieve. The authors' purpose is to present a set of concepts that can guide those who are responsible for designing programs for the education of experienced teachers. It should be especially useful to administrators of deans' grants and college faculties, as well as school based teacher educators and others responsible for the development of effective comprehensive systems of personnel development in all parts of the United States.

Thomas R. Behrens
Branch Chief, Eastern Region
Bureau of Education for the Handicapped
US Office of Education

Part 1

PERSPECTIVE

1

Overview

KENNETH R. HOWEY
DEAN C. CORRIGAN

The basic purpose of this book is to advance current thinking about inservice teacher education or staff development, especially as it relates to activities designed to better accommodate children with various handicaps within the regular school setting.

The ideas shared here are based on two premises. First, much of what takes place in inservice teacher education should be focused on changing practice and conditions in specific schools and classrooms. Second, such activities can best be planned and coordinated by a person who spends the majority of his or her time at the school site. For purposes of clarity, we shall refer to this person as a *school based teacher educator*. A number of educational personnel in different positions are now assuming this general role.

We are especially concerned about addressing the following questions: *What are some of the essential knowledge and skills that these school based teacher educators need and how might these best be provided?*

As a backdrop for approaching these problems, in Chapter 2 we shall share what recent research suggests about the current state of the art in inservice teacher education, and then draw implications for needed improvements. One major implication of these data, for example, is a need for more conceptually coherent, comprehensive, and continuing approaches to inservice. In broad brush strokes, we shall attempt to identify some of the more salient characteristics of effective inservice programs. As suggested at the outset, one of our conclusions will be the desirability of having one person identified at the school site who has the capability to interrelate

3

what are too often rather fragmented approaches to staff development and to coordinate a considerable array of diverse educational personnel.

We shall suggest four basic domains of inquiry for school based teacher educator personnel:

1. How adults (teachers) learn and develop.
2. How organizations (schools and classrooms) affect how teachers learn and develop.
3. Knowledge about organizational management and delivery of inservice teacher education.
4. Special education knowledge and skills needed in this school based role.

The book, therefore, is divided into four corresponding selections. Chapters address in turn the following dimensions of a program to prepare school based teacher educators: personal, organizational, teacher education, and special education domains. Our major emphasis will be on looking at the first three of these concerns, in the hope that insights derived therefrom might complement the knowledge base that special education personnel already possess.

THE PERSONAL DIMENSION

In approaching the question of what is known about how adults generally and teachers specifically learn and develop over time, various members of our study group came at the problem from differing perspectives. The insights of Norman and Lois Sprinthall reflect a unique blend of experiences: action research undertaken jointly by a developmental psychologist and a school based teacher educator. The Sprinthalls remind us that cognitive development is a concept that is not only applicable to youngsters. Martin Haberman looks at a related phenomenon that tends to be ignored—sound principles of learning can and should be employed when working with adults as well as with youngsters. He demonstrates that we do know a good deal about how adults learn most effectively. Louise Berman, with her rich experience and background in curriculum, reminds us that one's view of the individual is a fundamental of curriculum planning, whether working with children or adults. She outlines essential personal qualities that must be fostered by those working with teachers, if teachers are in turn to value these same qualities in their own students.

In Chapter 3, Norman and Lois Sprinthall, who for some time have been concerned with generating more adequate conceptions of how adults develop, begin by cautioning us that the knowledge base in adult development is still inadequate, but that initial research efforts in this area have produced provocative findings. The Sprinthalls refer, for example, to David Hunt's studies of teachers in school settings. Hunt found that teachers at advanced stages of conceptual development functioned in more complex and

4

differentiated ways in the classroom than their peers who were at less advanced stages of development. The former were more flexible, tolerant, empathic, responsive to individual differences and employed a greater variety of teaching tactics. Obviously, these traits are highly desirable, if not requisite, for teachers who seek to accommodate adequately various forms of exceptionality in the classroom.

Cited too, is the work of several other developmental theorists, such as Kohlberg, Heath, Loevinger, and Selman, who also suggested that psychological maturity appears to be the most reliable predictor of adult success, as measured by multiple criteria (job performance, family and peer relationships, self fulfillment, respect, status, economic gain). Conversely, several studies have demonstrated that academic achievement is *not* predictive of such success, and has even been found to be inversely correlated with measures of success. Thus, a persuasive case can be made for the desirability of advanced psychological development or maturity.

What are the direct implications of these findings as we consider appropriate experiences for those who work with teachers in schools? First, it seems reasonable that these persons should have some understanding of the various concepts and dimensions of adult development, and of what appears to enhance such development. Quite clearly, academic knowledge alone is not enough to promote such growth.

The Sprinthalls also question the efficacy of traditional psychotherapy, forms of group therapy, and "skills only" training as having contributed much to the achievement of psychological development. Providing some clues for how training programs might be structured by building on the profound insights of John Dewey and his action/reflection model, they state:

> Growth toward more complex levels of cognitive-developmental functioning appears to be most influenced by placing persons in significant role taking experiences. A substantial difference is to be noted between role playing (simulation, games, fantasy trips, etc.) and actual role taking. In the latter case, the person is expected to perform a new, somewhat more complex interpersonal task than his or her own current preferred mode. The experience is direct and active, as opposed to vicarious and indirect. . . . For preservice and inservice teachers, role taking may involve teaching counseling skills and/or supervision skills, or employing new teaching "models." Ryan (1970) suggested the concept of cross role training or role taking for teachers. Although never formally implemented, the idea still seems valid— namely, that educating professionals through direct yet multiple professional roles may act as a stimulus to growth.

While cognizant of the considerable challenge and cautious in their advice, the Sprinthalls nonetheless present a strong argument for a devel-

5

opmental perspective in a well designed program for preparing leadership personnel at school sites.

In Chapter 4, Martin Haberman provides a synthesis of core concepts from disciplines as diverse as the psychology of learning and the sociology of organizations, in a succinct and interrelated set of cogent guidelines for our school based teacher educator. Especially helpful is Haberman's adaptation of basic psychological principles to the unique set of conditions confronting school based teacher educators. His guideline #9, for example, reads:

> Since the most effective learning rewards are those that immediately follow desired behaviors and are, therefore, more likely to be connected with those behaviors, teacher educators, mainstream coordinators, and classroom teachers should have very frequent formal and informal opportunities to share ideas, pass information, signal, or confer in order to immediately connect their praise and support to the specific behaviors they are seeking to influence and strengthen. Distinct advantages are to be gained from engaging in systematic procedures of mutual support by professionals acting in teams and in cooperative relationships.

Historically, principles of learning have been derived from laboratory experiments and then posited for use in K–12 classrooms. Haberman, however, takes account of the actual situations in which teachers work and then adapts appropriate theory and research to fit. In addition to identifying essential conditions for promoting on the job learning by teachers, he addresses a number of other critical concerns.

For example, what essential and requisite attributes and experiences should a person have in order to satisfy minimal *selection* criteria for school based teacher educators? It is likely that educators in several existing roles external to the school will be asked to assume a more school focused staff development posture. While some of these people may pursue additional training, little more in the way of self improvement will be undertaken by others. The rigor of the *selection process* may, therefore, be critical in determining the quality and appropriateness of on site program and staff development personnel.

Haberman presents us with helpful selection criteria. He also addresses critical organizational and structural variables that must be considered in promoting school focused inservice. He addresses the role of the school principal, group relations, and even specific methods of instruction that our school based teacher educator might employ. Although brief, this chapter should not be skimmed. Each of Haberman's guidelines has been distilled from a considerable data base; like fine wine, each must be sipped and savored. As he says, these 33 guidelines are not "discrete rules of conduct" but rather guiding principles, which, if collectively internalized and embraced by a leader at the school site and by the school faculty, should exert a profound effect on teacher behavior.

In Chapter 5, Louise Berman shares rich insights into the complexities of the school curriculum and derives implications from curriculum development for preparing school based teacher educators. Identifying three basic types of curriculum development, she indicates that an *integrated* approach to that field not only involves planning and goal setting, or what we might call intention, but also actualization and, finally, retrospective or analytic information gathered on the spot. The apt choice of such phrases as "moment of now" reflects the preciseness of thought and graphic terminology she employs so well in all of her writings. Vividly, Berman portrays those *personal* qualities a curriculum must foster: "inwardness...curiosity...interaction...and passion for the ethical." Critical analyses and humane, accurate feedback about the transactive process of teaching and learning should be the staples of a self renewing faculty—the very essence of inservice teacher identification. She provides guidelines for studying the school as a setting, with emphasis on how teachers have accommodated students as individuals and learners. Then, she helps us examine whether the school provides conditions for the teacher to grow and develop as well. She always keeps a central place for the individual in the process as she voices her concern that patterns of communication be analyzed:

> If we are concerned about teachers as vital, exciting human beings, then we need to be concerned about communication. Consideration needs to be given to patterns of communication. Who is communicating with whom and for what purpose? With what degree of frequency do teachers interact with each other, with resource teachers? How do people communicate? What kinds of things tend to go in memos? What items are received by teachers, from principals, supervisors, etc.? What happens when somebody intervenes in the life of a teacher? Does the teacher display a negative or positive reaction? What kinds of things seem to annoy teachers? What things seem to give teachers support? What kinds of communication seem to irritate teachers?

Berman's observations appear especially germane for facilitating working relationships among the variety of persons who will come together to better accommodate children with various forms of exceptionality.

THE ORGANIZATIONAL DIMENSION

Although Berman's emphasis has been on the individual in an interactive curriculum, her analysis of the *classroom* setting in terms of promoting student learning and the school setting with respect to enhancing teacher learning provides a logical transition to the second major component of our conceptual framework for preparing school based teacher educators.

The teacher educator should have an understanding of the school as a workplace, and the ability to adapt it to accommodate learning for teachers. Three members of our work group, Charles W. Case, David Johnson, and Roger Johnson, devoted their primary energies to examining relevant concepts and practices from the core discipline of social psychology and the applied studies of social systems analysis and organizational development. First, Case looks at the school and the various systems with which it interacts as the primary unit of analysis; and then the Johnson brothers zero in on the dynamics of the classroom itself.

In Chapter 6, Case stresses the need for more attention to the organizational dimension if the spirit and the intent of P.L. 94-142 are to be achieved:

> P.L. 94-142 affords an excellent example of mandated change that requires major adjustments in organizational and individual purposes, processes, interactions, structure, and accomplishments. Not only does it insure attention to respecting the civil rights of handicapped children and to designing appropriate educational services for them, it also requires interactions among those seeking to accomplish common goals. Business as usual and the continuance of isolated fiefdoms within a school will no longer suffice.

Case also reminds us of a curious paradox that has characterized much of teacher education. Knowledge and skills presented to teachers are assumed to transfer to working with a group of learners, but rarely in the instruction of teachers is emphasis given to the fact that they operate as members of organizations and to the implication of that reality for teaching and learning. Thus, Case suggests that school based educators become familiar with several theoretical concepts from general systems theory. The goal is to help them examine how a number of elements in the school context act together when exposed to simultaneous yet different influences. Readers are cautioned not to confuse systems tools and techniques, which tend to imply linear and sequential planning and management processes, with this larger goal of systems theory, where the emphasis is on interactive and interdependent wholes.

After a concise and lucid review of basic terms and concepts, Case concludes the first portion of Chapter 6 with propositions applicable to systems in general and *open* systems in particular. He then reviews some basic concepts from the field of organizational development, noting several parallels between the growth of organizations and the growth of individuals. The most important changes in schools, he argues, will call not only for changes in individuals but for equally important changes in *relationships*. It is critical, therefore, that we begin to generate desirable futures that are as data based and comprehensive in scope as possible. Case points out that most change efforts in education have been characterized by a desire to oversimplify complex realities and, thus, are focused on changing only a small part of the system.

Much of Case's attention in this chapter is on the ability to diagnose and respond to organizational as well as individual needs. Consistent with the overall posture of the work group, he outlines how the more narrowly defined teacher educator role might be merged with some functions of the organizational development consultant and proposes a descriptor for this new role: "organizational development trainer." In addition to reviewing diagnostic tools and techniques and the generation of alternative scenarios, he also outlines a number of intervention and problem solving strategies. He reminds us that multiple change strategies are called for in many situations and certainly in schools that seriously attempt to accommodate the processes spelled out in P.L. 94-142. In conclusion, Case outlines relevant knowledge and essential skills that persons in this new school based role will need. He breaks these down into three basic domains: conceptual, technical, and human skills.

In Chapter 7, Johnson and Johnson look more specifically at the classroom as a social system. Drawing from the extensive research and development they have engaged in throughout the United States, they build especially upon their innovative efforts in developing cooperative goal structures in the classrooms. Then, they apply these concepts to problems typically encountered in mainstreaming, with focus on two fundamental concerns for the school based teacher educator:

1. In *what* should special education and regular classroom teachers be trained so that mainstreaming has constructive consequences?
2. *How* should special education and regular classroom teachers be trained so mainstreaming has constructive consequences?

An overriding concern of the Johnsons is that constructive peer relationships be established in the classroom. As we all know, simply placing students together (especially students who are different and have been largely separated before, as is the case of many handicapped children) will not guarantee constructive interaction. Although social dynamics of the classroom is often talked about, formal teacher planning for this "hidden curriculum" is rare. The Johnsons have demonstrated in one classroom after another over the years that teachers *can* acquire specific tools and techniques to establish more cooperative social climates. The consequences of providing more collaborative work and play structures for youngsters appear considerable. The following are some of the measured effects that regularly correlate positively with cooperative classroom structures: increased achievement, more effective interpersonal communication, increased problem solving and conflict resolution skills, higher trust among peers, increased respect for peers and school and a greater commitment to learning, decreased fear of failure, and more risk taking behavior.

In summary just about every desirable student behavior appears positively related to classrooms reflecting a high degree of cooperation. Conversely, these desirable behaviors have correlated negatively with classrooms where a disproportionate amount of competitive or highly individualistic activity occurred.

To document the importance of working toward more cooperative social structures, the Johnsons briefly review extensive research on social behavior in the classroom. They share, for example, their findings with respect to motivation:

> Motivation is most commonly viewed as a combination of perceived likelihood of success and the perceived incentive for success. The greater the likelihood of success and the more important it is to succeed, the higher the motivation. Success that is intrinsically rewarding is usually seen as being more desirable for learning than having students believe that only extrinisic rewards are worthwhile. There is a greater perceived likelihood of success, and success is viewed as more important in a cooperative than in a competitive or individualistic learning situation. (Johnson & Johnson, 1975)

Some of their findings relate more directly than others to enhancing mainstreaming. They note that a series of researchers have found that cooperativeness is positively related to the ability to take the emotional perspective of others, while competitiveness is related to egocentrism. Similarly, other experimental evidence suggests that cooperative learning experiences, especially when compared with individualistic ones, result in higher self esteem for all types of students involved.

In the second phase of their chapter, the Johnsons review literature that specifically focuses on attitudes toward handicapped peers. They provide us with insight into how impressions are formed and how stigmatization, categorization, and labeling take place. Analyzing how the processes of both acceptance and rejection evolve, they again relate their findings to the types of social structure and climate existing in the classroom. Once more, the experimental evidence strongly favors more cooperative classroom structures.

The Johnsons conclude their chapter by examining how concepts designed to enhance more collaboration for classroom teachers in their classroom might be used as well by a school based teacher educator in working with teachers. They suggest that a large part of the "what" of the training concerns the application of some of these same cooperative principles to inservice activities. Accordingly, they advocate that some of the inservice engaged in by special education and regular classroom teachers employs collaborative assignments and builds in joint rewards for groups as well as individuals. They also endorse beginning more cooperative types of training activities in preservice training. In summary, the Johnsons provide conceptually clear and empirically derived operating principles for use by our school based teacher educator.

THE TEACHER EDUCATION DIMENSION

Two papers that were developed in our work group incorporate the perspective of persons in teacher education roles. Sam Yarger and his colleague Sally Mertens bring the insights of researcher/teacher educators in higher education who have studied teacher education from a variety of vantage points. Yarger, for example, has conducted national surveys of both preservice and inservice teacher education and was responsible for the first extensive study of teacher centers in this country.

Elizabeth Dillon-Peterson has had responsibility for developing what has proved to be an exemplary program of staff development in a relatively large school district. She has also conducted studies of staff development practices throughout the country. Her vantage point in the local education agency complements Yarger and Mertens' perspective. She has brought to our work group and this publication not only insights about teacher education, but also a necessary reality of school focused practices and problems.

In Chapter 8, Yarger and Mertens remind us of several cautions raised at the outset of this project. The problem of teacher education is not simply one of providing *more* experiences; more serious attempts must be made to conceptualize *continuing* teacher education.

They also note basic economic and political pressures that have provided impetus to school focused inservice. Another caution they voice is that new political, even legal, arrangements might evolve with little if any result in teacher education itself. Perhaps the major concern they share, however, is that highly unrealistic expectations are being attached in some quarters to the evolving role of a school based teacher educator. This concern influenced our group of writers from the beginning. Our strategy has been to provide a school based teacher educator with as much assistance as feasible in terms of understanding the individuals with whom and conditions within which he or she might work. More sophisticated diagnostic and analytic abilities should then allow this educator to better plan for and allocate needed resources.

Yarger and Mertens also remind us that many individuals in different role groups are currently "testing the waters" of school based teacher education (the recent Teacher Center legislation, for example, has promoted such efforts). Commending these "pioneers," they note that these individuals also may contribute to a better delineation of what this role can and should be, but caution:

> On the one hand, those who are actually involved in the transitional efforts will probably have a much better understanding of what is possible. On the other hand, they may short circuit the effort to de-

11

velop truly innovative and better programs. Credit must be given for actually getting out to teachers in schools, but merely extending and modifying traditional roles will not be enough. The problem is like expecting that horses can be modified and further developed for the automobile age. A definite risk exists that these helping roles, in urgent reaction to current pressures, will be extended (and perhaps even institutionalized) without any better understanding of the clients, issues and agendas that should be considered essential to the field.

From their vast knowledge of teacher education, Yarger and Mertens provide the reader with excellent conceptual tools for better interrelating the basic program concerns a teacher educator must address. They begin with a carefully conceived delineation of the various professional stages through which a teacher will progress. We are provided, thereby, with yet another dimension toward developing a general conceptual framework. These two writers go on to identify types of teacher education programs and some critical concerns relative to the delivery of teacher education, such as authority and finances. Finally, they examine "overall program agendas."

At this point, the power of their conception of developmental stages becomes apparent. A series of analytic exercises examine the consonance between stages of teacher career, type of teacher education program and agenda type. Yarger and Mertens well illustrate the complexity of teacher education and provide us with insights into the knowledge base that can be brought to bear on these matters. They conclude their chapter by identifying problems that must be confronted if more viable school based teacher educator roles are to be achieved and that our work group might deal with more fully in the years ahead.

In Chapter 9, Elizabeth Dillon-Peterson further dissects basic issues in the organization and delivery of inservice or staff development, especially those activities concerned with the implementation of P.L. 94-142. She reiterates a common theme that runs throughout this book: special education must necessarily be viewed as having distinctive qualities, but is also similar to the rest of the educational program and should be integrated with it. She begins her chapter by sharing several related assumptions about inservice and special education programing. Another proposition articulated by Dillon-Peterson and embraced by the work group is that effective programing for special education students is more like effective educational programing for all students than it is different.

Her public school perspective is especially valuable in identifying a number of issues relating to P.L. 94-142 that must be attended to if quality staff development is to take place. Examples include the general proliferation of demands upon classroom teachers, some limiting side effects of

categorical regulations, problems associated with certification requirements for personnel who work with the variety of special needs students,
and the generally insufficient attention given to the *personal* needs of
teachers who are expected to assume new responsibilities or move into
modified roles. She suggests that Maslow's hierarchy of needs provides an
excellent framework for responding to individual needs.

On the basis of the assumptions Dillon-Peterson has set forth and the
issues she has identified, she next examines implications for inservice
teacher education. She places a priority on staff development for the building administration, just as Haberman has. Her insights and experience are
demonstrated as she builds upon suggestions made independently by other
members of the work group. She notes the desirability of a team approach,
as the Johnsons have, and the need for comprehensive planning to be built
upon organizational development concepts, as outlined by Case. In detailing
some of the components of an effective inservice program she states:

> Classroom teachers need to acquire a general, nontechnical, mystique
> free understanding of the special needs of the mainstreamed students.
> They also should have highly developed classroom management skills
> and behavior management competence. They must understand cur-
> riculum requirements and have basic skills in curriculum adaptation
> to meet individual needs. Knowledge of mediated materials will help
> them to extend their own capabilities. Human relations skills will
> enable them to assist students in working together with understand-
> ing. Cooperative planning skills will facilitate their collaboration
> with colleagues to find different ways of grouping students to reduce
> the student/teacher ratio. Called for is staff development in teaming,
> differentiating responsibility, and techniques for student diagnosis
> and prescription.

Dillon-Peterson notes that many local school districts can supply much
expertise from within (including classroom teachers as inservice instructors), but that these resources can be substantially assisted through judicious collaboration with and use of outside resources as well. Outlined are
respective responsibilities that a local site team and a cooperative research
team can assume to complement one another. She concludes her chapter
by identifying five primary audiences that must be served in comprehensive
staff development schemes and then outlines five specific phases of inservice as a plan for action.

THE FUTURE DIMENSION

As indicated earlier, the primary concern in our work group has been to
examine what we might bring to bear upon special education concerns from
the field of teacher education and such related lines of inquiry as adult

growth and organizational development. Thus, the members selected to participate in this project largely represented these latter fields of study. Our intent has been to propose a more adequate conceptual base for preparing school focused teacher educators—individuals who would have as their primary concern in most schools at this time more effective and integrated programing for handicapped youngsters. This strategy does not deny the importance of understanding and applying special education concepts and principles but rather speaks to the "what else" that is necessary in addition to special education content.

Currently, a number of different persons assume teacher education roles at school sites and we assume this situation will continue. Certainly special educators will be one type of school based teacher educator. Classroom teachers also will need not only humane and effective inservice strategies but essential skills and knowledge from special education as well. Thus, Chapters 10 and 11 are devoted more specifically to P.L. 94-142, The Education for Handicapped Children Act of 1975, and its implications for reforms needed in schools and teacher education institutions.

In Chapter 10, Audrey Anderson concisely reviews the basic tenets of P.L. 94-142. Then, she examines some implications of that law with special attention to general competencies needed by the classroom teacher. Surveying a variety of efforts to identify these competencies, she summarizes the comprehensive survey conducted by Rader, the inventory of elementary teachers undertaken by Redden and Blackhurst, a checklist developed at the University of Oregon, the Mann Self-Assessment Competency Inventory, and, finally, work engaged in by the Houston Teacher Development Centers. This excellent synthesis should provide tbe school based teacher educator with a variety of means of assessing the special education needs of classroom teachers. Anderson also reviews what have been previously identified as priority needs of teachers with respect to the concept of "mainstreaming."

In Chapter 11, editors Corrigan and Howey state that schools today are not designed to achieve the objectives of P.L. 94-142 and our teachers are not prepared for the responsibilities this legislative mandate expects of them. Such complex educational functions cannot be performed without a high level of professional knowledge and skill and the setting in which to use them. The conditions necessary for professional practice must be created.

The editors present their view of school reforms that are necessary to implement "appropriate" education for all students and then identify selected concepts that can serve as guidelines to those who design educational programs to prepare the kind of experienced teachers who can make these reforms. The reforms implied by P.L. 94-142 must move in both directions. . . to colleges as well as schools.

2

The School Based Teacher Educator: Developing a Conceptual Framework

KENNETH R. HOWEY
DEAN C. CORRIGAN

In this chapter we seek to make a case for planning inservice teacher education in a more conceptually coherent manner. We underscore the need for preparing school based leaders to ensure that such an approach is pursued.

First, we will briefly review what recent research says about current inservice education programs and then contrast the findings with what more ideal forms of inservice would look like. We suggest that at least three basic domains contribute the knowledge and skill needed by the school based teacher educator: adult development and organizational development in general, and teacher education specifically. After illustrating how inservice education will vary according to the emphases given these three interrelated dimensions at different times, we will introduce the reader to our coauthors, who will expand on these concepts in later chapters.

Inservice education or staff development is one of the most criticized but least studied aspects of the educational enterprise. What do we know about this endeavor? How important is it? The fact that considerable resources are devoted to this phase of teacher education suggests that it is *very* important and, at the same time, points to the magnitude of our information needs. There are, for example, almost 50,000 persons in district level line staff positions whose roles would suggest they have some involvement with inservice education. Moreover, approximately 100,000 principals or assistant principals have some responsibility for the continuing education needs of their school faculties. The over 40,000 education professors have obviously been busy as well, especially with credit attached forms of continuing education, as almost half of the over two million teachers in this country possess *at least* a Master's degree.

RESEARCH ON INSERVICE EDUCATION

Most information about inservice education has been in the form of accounts of specific programs, by educators involved in those activities. Thus, survey data derived from large scale sampling helps to portray more accurately both what is happening in inservice as well as what is desired and needed by teachers and teacher educators.

We would like to share briefly highlights from a recent survey conducted by two of our work group members along with Bruce Joyce (Yarger, Howey, & Joyce, in press). They constructed individual survey questionnaires for teachers, teacher educators, and community members respectively. Specific items for these surveys were generated from three major sources: (a) an exhaustive review of the literature; (b) unstructured interviews with almost 1,500 persons, including policy makers, administrators, teacher representatives, and the public at large, as well as many teachers and teacher educators; and (c) the ISTE (Inservice Teacher Education) Reports, a series of position papers and case studies about major inservice issues and efforts.

The preliminary questionnaires were first revised, based on critical analyses of some 20 external reviewers selected for their expertise in either survey research or teacher education. These questionnaires were in turn piloted in several locations throughout the country before final decisions about the survey instruments were made.

Multiple samples were selected for the survey. First, the states of California, Michigan, and Georgia were selected to ensure geographic, ethnic, and socioeconomic diversity. To acquire additional data for comparative purposes, the entire population of the Urban/Rural School Development Program was sampled as well (Joyce, 1978). This program had been conducted at 25 urban or rural sites in economically impoverished areas located throughout tbe United States. Federal monies had been employed over a 5 year period in an attempt to improve schools through community involvement and inservice teacher education. In addition, faculty in institutions of higher education in these states were surveyed. This brief overview of findings will be limited to trends that cut across each of these sample groups.

The following goals were identified for this study:

1. To describe more precisely the various demographic characteristics (age, ethnicity, experience, specialty) of those involved in inservice—both teachers and teacher educators.
2. To describe more precisely the quantity, quality, and diversity of experiences these persons have had relative to inservice education.

16

3. To identify more clearly various legal-political structures (and their interrelationships) for deciding about delivering inservice.
4. To identify more clearly the opinions of the various role groups involved
   in inservice education about basic needs, major issues, and future directions.

Demographic Characteristics of Teachers

No major surprises appeared with respect to the demographic data generated. A large majority of the teacher respondents were well into their 30's;
in fact, the average age in all locations was approximately 40. The limited
number of beginning teachers entering the profession at this time is reflected by the fact that less than 1% of the teachers in these samples was
born after 1955 (i.e., were 22 years of age or younger at the time the data
were collected). Not surprisingly, respondents in higher education were
even older and more experienced. When these inservice data are set along-
side data acquired in a recent preservice study (Howey, Yarger, & Joyce,
1978), the picture is not only one of stability but also of relative homo-
geneity and provincialism. The profile for beginning teachers, which is
probably reflective of their more established colleagues as well, suggests
that they are Caucasian; monolingual; from a small city, suburb, or rural
area; and attended college in their home state—most likely within a
hundred miles of their home.

What does the fact of a maturing, somewhat provincial teaching populace
imply for teacher education? The most recent Rand study of change (Ber
man & McLaughlin, 1975) indicates that experienced teachers frequently
have more difficulty than their younger colleagues in bringing about
change in their own teaching behavior. The pioneer work of some adult
developmentalists suggests that predictable "crises" may recur throughout one's life, such as entering the "40's." The increasingly catalytic
influence of international events on our daily functioning, such as the pressures the OPEC oil countries can exert, presents the need to overcome any
tendency toward provincialism. Thus, the basic demographic profile of
teachers in this survey, while perhaps not surprising, appears to have direct
implications for both the content and the process of inservice.

Quantity, Quality, Diversity

Although the overall health of inservice teacher education is not as bad as
some would make it out to be, it is hardly without problems either. Only
a little more than a quarter of the respondents in California and Georgia
indicated that it was in either good or excellent health, and in Michigan
only 13% (about one in seven teachers) indicated this to be the situation.
Teachers were much more likely to rate the inservice programs they had
participated in as *fair*, this being the case with 40 to 50% of the respondents

17

across all samples. Further, a sizeable minority of teachers perceived inservice education as being in poor or bad condition, ranging from 26% of those responding in Georgia to 42% of those in Michigan.

The studies also considered the question of quantity or adequacy of time for continuing development. Teachers were asked how often they experienced each of the following forms of inservice education: inservice embedded on the job—that is, the type ef activity that would improve skills while teachers are engaged with ongoing duties; "that type which is closely related to the job but does not take place while teaching is going on;" experiences designed to improve general competence but not tailored to meet the specific needs of the job; experiences organized to help one obtain a new credential or prepare for a new role (which some may not consider inservice); and, finally, experiences designed to facilitate personal development and that may contribute to greater effectiveness on the job.

The responses here show the relative infrequency of inservice educational opportunities for the majority of teachers in this study. Most teachers in all samples indicated that they typically engaged in each of these forms of inservice once a year or less. For example, more than three-quarters of tbe teachers in the three states indicated that they experienced job embedded forms of inservice—a central focus of this book—only once a year or less.

However, when teachers were asked whether inservice programs to accommodate these various purposes had any appeal for them, the overwhelming response was that they did indeed. The great majority of teachers in each of the samples indicated considerable support—i.e., each of the five types of inservice was considered either an"excellent" or "good" idea.

Additional problems uncovered in this survey were a lack of followup in the classroom to inservice that takes place outside this setting, little specially designed or concentrated support for the beginning teacher in the critical first year or two of teaching, and an apparent inability to find ways for teachers to engage in inservice at times other than after school or during summer recess.

Some implications of these data for the improvement of inservice programing are obvious. Fundamental concerns that must be addressed include: developing more coherent programs that include more diverse formats and meet a variety of goals, achieving more job embedded and school focused forms of inservice, and providing more inservice opportunities during the instructional day. When inservice is offered externally to the school site, followup support and supervision is needed more often.

The question of who sets program goals gets to the core of the governance process with respect to inservice teacher education. The most common response across all samples in the inservice study was that these decisions are now made by the local district administration. The second most common response was that these decisions are once removed from the district administration; that is, they are made by the local boards of education. Either state legislatures or state education departments were seen as the third most common influence. Teachers were named about as infrequently as building level administrators as a common source of decision making.

The respondents were then asked who *should* make decisions with respect to deciding the goals of inservice teacher education. Perceptions changed dramatically at this point, for the majority of respondents in both higher education and the school sector indicated that teachers should be responsible for deciding these goals. Rarely was any other role group identified as having the primary responsibility. For example, local district administration, the most common source for decisions about inservice at the present time, was identified by only 5% of the respondents as ideally having this authority. Thus, inservice in the future must more fully engage teachers in planning, development, and implementation.

Respondents were also asked to address the problems of cooperative decision making about inservice, or in today's parlance, "collaborative" governance. After being presented with five potential obstacles to cooperative decision making, the respondents were asked to indicate if these were, in fact, problems and, if so, to what degree. All role groups (teachers, professors, administrators, and parents) perceived cooperation in decisions about inservice as highly desirable, notwithstanding the deference to teachers as the preeminent voice; yet each role group reported that each of the five potential problems identified were, in fact, significant obstacles to cooperation between such parties as local education agencies and institutions of higher education.

Thus, these data again suggest several problems that will have to be attended to if we are to move beyond rhetoric about cooperative ventures in inservice and better ensure that a variety of perspectives are brought into planning. These include not only those of the teacher and the school administration but also those of the external and relatively objective scholar, as well as those of parents and other community members.

Overall then, major improvements in the continuing education of teachers are clearly needed. However, despite a verbal willingness on the part of some to work together and to move in new and desired directions, we find little behavioral evidence of such commitment in many places. We have undoubtedly underestimated both what it will take for teachers to internalize and incorporate more complex curricular and instructional strategies into their classrooms or to alter normative school structures and expectations that may allow this to happen. More coherent and intensive forms of inservice appear needed, and individuals who have the capacity to plan or organize such programs must be developed.

A COMPREHENSIVE APPROACH TO INSERVICE EDUCATION

Data from this recent survey call for more conceptually coherent and comprehensive programs of inservice education. We believe that such systematic approaches are consistent with the training goals of the Bureau of

19

Education for the Handicapped—especially as related to P.L. 94-142. A critical federal responsibility is to ensure quality and accountability in the training efforts supported. At this point, we would like to review some characteristics of a comprehensive approach to inservice education, in the hope that this will be helpful to BEH and to those interested in staff development. Since members of our work group will address several of these components in more detail in later chapters of this book, we review these components of inservice only briefly here.

A logical way to begin is by defining terms. It is relatively easy to identify some common characteristics of inservice and to explicate certain related concepts. In other respects, however, our definitional problem is difficult; controversy, change, and conflicting perceptions have contributed to making it so. For example, while nearly everyone interviewed in Phase I of the Inservice Teacher Education Study stressed the inadequacies of present practice, they offered little precision in defining this enterprise or in providing direction for how these problems should be resolved.

Inservice education can readily be differentiated from *preservice* as that developmental activity designed to enhance competence a professional undertakes (singly or with others) after receiving his or her initial license or certificate and after beginning professional practice. Even this distinction is becoming somewhat blurred as a result of increased discussion about a more formal and extended induction period of teacher education for the beginning teacher. This distinction provides few clues as to what characterizes effective practice.

Some would define and approach inservice more narrowly as district sponsored teacher development activities designed to directly improve instruction. Others interpret inservice more broadly. For them, it embraces a variety of purposes (including personal development, and graduate, career and general professional pursuits), takes place in a wide variety of contexts, and has interrelated activities planned for a range of educational personnel.

The regulations attached to P.L. 94-142 require inservice programs for *all* personnel involved in an education related capacity with handicapped children. The comprehensive approach envisioned in this mandate also calls for a needs assessment, an operational plan, and an evaluation scheme. The regulations state as well that this plan include "provisions for appropriate incentive options to guarantee participation."

Characteristics of Effective Programs

Given these general guidelines, where do we turn for further direction? While research is sparse, what does exist—along with the collective experience of respected practitioners—suggests that the following conditions commonly characterize effective programs of inservice. A good inservice program:

- Is undergirded by an explicit set of assumptions about teaching and learning—especially adult learning and development.
- Explicitly acknowledges the relationship of the training to the job responsibility of the trainee and the school environment.
- Is given direction by a comprehensive needs assessment; that is, multiple reference groups are inventoried about a variety of concerns.
- Is developmental; it entails a series of continuing activities many of which culminate in supervised classroom application.
- Needs a realistic focus for a comprehensive plan—in many cases the school unit. (We have ample evidence of the futility of attempting program revision and reform, such as that implicit in the mainstreaming concept, by focusing too *narrowly* on individual teachers, independent of their immediate colleagues on the one hand, or too *broadly* with district wide plans that do not accommodate the unique characteristics of the individual neighborhoods and schools, on the other.)
- Should make portions of its program not only school focused but also job embedded; that is, planned activities intended to further professional development are integrated within one's normal instructional responsibilities (systematic observations and feedback about teaching would be one form of this, and collegial planning and problem solving another).
- Makes a highly skilled person responsible for its planning and management; ideally this person should be located at the school, as this is a reasonable unit for comprehensive change.

Additionally, we suggest that inservice approaches incorporating the following guidelines will have the greatest potential for success relative to P.L. 94-142:

- They should be approached as a collegial planning and problem solving process, which examines the variety of personnel resources, role types, and skills *collectively* needed to accommodate this extended process of individualizing instruction. (Our research and experience indicate that teachers perceive the primary responsibility for mainstreaming as falling upon their shoulders and as making an already difficult job more difficult.)
- Effective programing for special education students is more like effective programing for all students than it is different. Inservice training, therefore, will look at instructional programing for all students and their relationships one to the other, and not just for children with some form of exceptionality.
- All individuals who work with "regular" children already have many skills applicable to forms of instruction for special education students. A comprehensive inservice program will call for different levels of expertise in working with special education students for different educational personnel. Obviously, classroom teachers cannot be all things to all students.

21

Inservice Problems

Some problems contributing to the current dissatisfaction with inservice were identified earlier in the survey research. Additional problems are spelled out here to emphasize that inservice, if not approached in a more enlightened way than it often has been in the past, is just as likely to exacerbate the problems of teachers as to remedy them. Common problems associated with inservice include:

• Inadequate and inaccurate assessment of what is desired and needed (simply asking teachers what they want is obviously not enough; assessment, as we shall see, is a complex and multifaceted process).
• Unrealistic expectations for *individual* classroom teachers and, thus, a disproportionate amount of training focused upon this target group.
• Inadequate incentives for both trainees (usually teachers) and trainers to participate energetically in the process (perhaps the most obvious problem being the lack of ownership teachers generally have had in activities they have been asked to engage in).
• Fundamental structural or organizational problems, that is, limited diversity in how, when, and where inservice is provided (resulting too often in spectator like activity, having limited transferability to classroom practice).
• Lack of coordination and leadership, especially at the *individual school building level.*
• Inadequate explication of the specific goals of inservice, and, thus, limited evaluation of the effects of training.

We believe that knowledge, resources, and technology exist that can at least alleviate the difficulties noted here. The writers in this book speak to these various problems in some detail. At this time, however, we would like to overview such fundamental processes as needs assessment, governance, incentives, actual instruction, program coordination, and evaluation to illustrate the variety of ways one can approach the current problems of inservice.

Needs Assessment

A comprehensive needs assessment approach uses a variety of informants, information sources, and information collection methodologies. For example, as Dillon-Peterson will suggest in Chapter 9, at least six distinct role groups might be inventoried in a comprehensive inservice approach: planners and policymakers, administrators, instructional staff, support/supervisory staff, teacher trainers and researchers, and parents/community. Inventories, to be useful, must generally move beyond asking teachers *what* they think is needed. Also critical are questions of when, where, for how long, in what way, and with whom inservice is to take place. A more rigorous examination of the rich variety of options for providing inservice should result in the development of more desirable and more effective training formats.

Likewise, the perceptions of teachers are but one source of data. Anecdotal records, test scores, and systematic observation in the classroom provide additional data and a more complete and accurate picture of what needs are and what activities should be planned. Present inservice efforts will be advanced when normative assessment practices are altered from asking teachers what they think is needed to: (a) the validity provided by multiple perspectives and objective firsthand observation, and (b) a fuller consideration of the various ways these needs can be accommodated as well.

Inservice Governance

The governance of inservice education indicates the public and political nature of education in general and of inservice teacher education, specifically. Multiple levels of governance and variant degrees of influence can be exerted by different role groups in a comprehensive inservice program. The inservice study reviewed earlier showed the relationship between different purposes to be served by various inservice endeavors and subsequent differences in decision making responsibilities assumed by parties associated with inservice in each instance.

The survey presented the following types of inservice which offer experiences that: (a) can be embedded in the job with the emphasis on "hands on" experience, (b) are closely related to the job, (c) seek to improve general competence but are not tailored to specific needs, (d) are organized to help one obtain a new credential or prepare for a new role, or (e) facilitate personal development, which may be job related.

Given these distinctions, the respondents in the survey clearly differentiated who might most appropriately support the cost of each of these inservice endeavors and also suggested which role groups would be most appropriate as instructors for these different types of inservice.

In summary, present inservice practice will be advanced when collaborative decision making bodies are formalized *as close to the locus of training as possible*—most likely attached to *individual schools* or *school related teacher centers*. These decision making bodies should have representation from all appropriate role groups, with teachers assuming a preeminent voice (majority membership) in those training decisions related most directly to their *individual* situations. However, greater parity in decision making should exist among several role groups in inservice training which is more directly related to district and schoolwide goals.

23

Inducements for Participation in Inservice

Historically, teachers have engaged in a variety of self improvement activities considered essential to maintaining competence. They have also devoted much of their time to such activities as a professional responsibility without recompense. The fundamental reason teachers stated for engaging in inservice is to better provide for their students. This is not to say, however, that teachers neither desire nor deserve additional consideration for their efforts. In fact, teachers have become increasingly adamant about this matter and elements of inservice have become concerns for collective bargaining. Those participating in inservice education are constantly confronted with the pull of the job. In the light of increasingly difficult classroom conditions in many situations today, it is naive to think that teachers will invest even more time and effort for inservice training without more visible benefits than commonly accrued.

Additional credits and nominal financial rewards are increasingly losing what limited appeal they have had, especially for an older and more experienced teaching force. Greater recognition and status, career diversity, mobility, and altered working conditions are closer to the roots of motivation for the classroom teacher to participate in inservice programs. Numerous incentives are feasible in a comprehensive inservice scheme, including *economic, technical* (increased knowledge, skills), *contextual* (alterations in instructional environment and working relationships), and *professional* (enhanced status, autonomy, opportunity) types of benefits. Inservice education will be advanced then when we move beyond the normative practice of token recognition for what is too often token participation.

Inservice Instruction

The limited variation in the instruction of teachers in all phases of teacher education may well be the most fundamental reason it is so widely perceived as a generally ineffective endeavor. The data collected in both the National Preservice Study and the inservice survey reviewed earlier strongly support the prevailing perception that the *most common* and yet often *least preferred* modality of instruction is the lecture-discussion format often embedded in either a course or a workshop. The rich array of other existing instructional modalities and technologies are vastly underused. Among the options are modeling behavior, microteaching, simulation, psychological consultation, clinical supervision, and collaborative problem solving. Again, inservice education will be advanced when we move beyond the normative practice of information sharing with limited modeling of desired skills and minimal classroom follow through.

24

A comprehensive approach to inservice correspondingly calls for a comprehensive scheme of evaluation. Most commonly, evaluation of inservice is limited to the post hoc perceptions of how satisfied the participants are with activities in which they are engaged. Pre-post measures of behavior are infrequent, and efforts to examine impact in the classroom even rarer. This limited evaluation of the training is not enough. For example, the training may indeed have been successful but still highly questionable in terms of its relative importance to begin with. The adequacy of decisions about what should be done and when, in terms of inservice, must be a prior consideration. Yet, such evaluation is often ignored.

Following are outlines of four global types of evaluative methodologies which illustrate dimensions of inservice that are in need of more rigorous evaluation:

1. *Historical analyses.* Especially critical in *externally* supported training efforts, these approaches include attempts to ascertain such fundamental baseline data as what type and level of inservice effort preceded the current plan or proposal, and what the relative magnitude and priority of the funded effort is to other efforts. The inservice program is put into a perspective relative to both present and past activities.

2. *Management analyses.* These examine the efficacy and appropriateness of the host of decisions and communications that go into determining the inservice agenda.

3. *Quantitative analyses.* These look at trainee growth and development in both formative and summative stages and in their most complete form investigate the transfer of teacher behavior to actual instructional settings as well.

4. *Ethnographic analyses.* These study in depth the impact of inservice beyond the primary target (effective instruction by a regular classroom teacher for physically disabled youngsters in the classroom) to the larger ecology of the school or classroom (the effect of this instruction on the quality and quantity of instruction given to other children. . .the attitudes of other children). Inservice will be advanced, then, when more time and attention is given to a comprehensive scheme of evaluation.

THREE BASIC DOMAINS

These then are some key unresolved teacher education concerns. Some of the expertise for resolving problems attendant to inservice resides in the teacher education community, others outside of it. Amply documented, for example, is the lack of transfer of knowledge and abilities teachers acquire in inservice (especially when provided in lecture or laboratory formats) to classroom practice itself. Teacher educators apparently know how to train for certain desired outcomes but cannot ensure the transfer of these behaviors to where it counts.

Research from two different areas of study may explain much of this lack of transfer. First, studies in adult development suggest that some teachers may be able to verbalize or demonstrate elements of more complex instruction outside of the classroom but cannot actually internalize these processes and apply them to practice because their level of psychological development precludes such understanding. Just as students are not ready for certain types of learning experiences, perhaps some teachers are not either. Second, evidence from research on schools as organizations suggests that what may work in focused settings, such as microteaching, may not be feasible in the more complex dynamics of the classroom itself. Conventional wisdom supports the premise that the interaction between level of adult psychological maturity and complexity of the work situation can negate what appear to be understandings and ability acquired outside the school context.

In addition to what is known about how to provide quality inservice training, the effective teacher educator, therefore, should understand how aspects of adult development and a host of organizational variables interact with desired training goals. Thus, we see those who plan inservice programs as attending to each of the following concerns:

1. Enhancing *adult* cognitive, intra- and interpersonal development, as these relate to teaching effectiveness.
2. Altering *environmental* (school) conditions, as these relate to teaching effectiveness.
3. Improving teaching effectiveness directly, especially focusing upon teacher *instructional* behavior in situ.

At different times, teachers will engage in different forms of inservice that relate to these concerns. Certainly, there are times when inservice must appropriately address the concept of adult psychological development. Adults continue to develop along several dimensions, just as children and adolescents do. "Development" is not something that suddenly stops at age 18. Since one's "stage" or "level" of moral and cognitive development affects how one teaches or at least prefers to teach, and since recent research suggests that not all adults (including teachers) *naturally* progress to "higher stages" of development, well conceived programs of inservice appropriately attempt at times to further basic psychological development, providing teachers with clearer insights into their basic patterns of thinking and belief systems.

Likewise, we can readily see that a variety of organizational factors can considerably influence what teachers do in the classroom. Time, space, numbers of students, role expectations, and lines of communication are all factors that can either enhance effective teaching or constrain it.

The inservice survey referred to earlier documented the relative infrequency of forms of inservice that addressed either of these concerns. For example, less than one in five of the teachers in this study engaged, on any regular basis, in inservice related to the work situation, and even fewer reported opportunities to pursue inservice designed to enrich personal development. Even when inservice is provided externally to the school site with the intent of addressing site specific problems, it is rarely accompanied by on the job follow through. Likewise, when teachers in the survey were queried with respect to a number of possible arrangements for engaging in more inservice during the school day, the great majority viewed most favorably every scheme that would periodically free them for such purposes. Yet, these same teachers reported that they rarely engaged in inservice at other than late afternoon and evening times or during the summer. Change in school *organization* to support such desired practice is simply not a realistic possibility. Thus, we have an acknowledged desire for more inservice that will address personal and organizational concerns and also for organizational modification to facilitate it, but a documented lack of adequate responses to these concerns.

Adult Development

A number of studies have indicated that individuals who are measured as having more abstract or advanced abilities in the relational processing of information (higher conceptual levels) demonstrate greater behavioral flexibility, a wider spectrum of coping behaviors, and a greater tolerance for stress. The inservice goal of adult cognitive development might, thus, be addressed, using Hunt's (1971) theory of conceptual development. According to Hunt, *conceptual level* refers to the degree of interpersonal maturity and of complexity of information processing. The latter can be viewed on a continuum, from concrete, limited interaction with stimuli to abstract adaptation within a changing environment. Interpersonal maturity can similarly be seen on a continuum, from an immature, unsocialized state to autonomous self reliance.

Since low conceptual level individuals appear dependent on external standards and concrete categorical thinking, and since they are generally less capable of generating their own concepts, a more highly structured environment appears desirable for them. Conversely, high conceptual level individuals are more capable of generating their own concepts and can integrate standards on multiple levels. Therefore, they require less structure from the instructor or the material. This theoretical framework provides one basis by which to confront adult cognitive development. Other conceptions of adult development have potential application to inservice programs as well. For example, Kohlberg (1966) and Turiel (1966) discussed adult changes from the perspective of moral development. Chickering (1969) addressed ego identity development and Willie (1977) identified critical life issues. In Chapter 3 of this book, the Sprinthalls elaborate on adult development.

27

Organizational Change

Altering environmental (school) conditions that impinge upon teacher development might be effected via numerous organizational development models. The theoretical constructs of Hersey and Blanchard (1977) allow one to systematically study the growth pattern and level of maturity of an organization. Upon discerning the "culture" of the school, an appropriate leadership style can be adopted. In situational leadership schemes, leaders such as school based teacher educators might reduce their task behavior and in turn increase their relationship behavior until the organization reaches a moderate level of maturity. Then, as the organization moves to higher levels of maturity, leaders might appropriately decrease both task and relationship behavior. The assumption is that an appropriate match between leadership behavior and organizational maturity enhances not only such factors as communication and peer relations, but teaching effectiveness as well.

Another possible approach to organizational development is the Concerns-Based Adoption Model (CBAM) developed by Hall (1975). The CBAM model focuses attention on the dynamics of the individual "innovation user" within the organizational context. Two key dimensions of the innovation user are identified: (a) levels of use of the innovation, ranging from nonuse, up through integration and renewal and (b) stages of concern about the innovation, which range from awareness through collaboration and refocusing. The underlying assumption of this model is that the adoption of innovations is a process rather than an event. Individuals progress in their knowledge regarding the innovation and their skill in using it, as well as progressing through stages of feelings and concern about the innovation. Through the assessment of teacher concerns, a clearer understanding of how various organization conditions should bring altered results, and again influence the actions of teachers.

Other models of organizational management include McGregor's (1960), which stressed assumptions about human nature and Argyris's (1971), which included interpersonal competence. Herzberg (1966) discussed motivation and hygiene factors. Later in this book, both Case and the Johnsons will elaborate on such organizational concepts.

Teacher Training Processes

One of the most common of the numerous approaches to altering teacher instructional behavior is clinical supervision. Goldhammer (1969) developed a prototype of clinical supervision, consisting of the following five stages: (a) pre-observation conference, (b) observation, (c) analysis and strategy, (d) supervision conference, and (e) post conference analysis. This scheme is specifically designed to alter the instructional skills of teachers.

Another framework for altering instructional skills has been developed by Joyce and Weil (1978). They identified three major families of teaching.

which include social, personal, and information processing goals. They also outlined alternative teaching strategies, such as inquiry lessons and non-directive counseling approaches. As stated earlier, many other models ranging from microteaching to focused forms of classroom observation can be employed in attempting to enhance teacher instructional behavior.

The position taken here is that a coherent and comprehensive inservice program must consider *interrelationships* of these various goals and purposes of inservice. Figure 1 shows diagramatically various intersections of the aforementioned goals. The center portion of the diagram represents inservice activities that address simultaneously all three major types of desired change. Obviously, each of these three goals or types of change can be approached independently. Our major concern is that all of them be dealt with.

Earlier, we discussed such teacher education processes as the assessment of needs, design, and selection of appropriate instructional formats to meet these needs, incentives to ensure teacher involvement, and adequate documentation and evaluation for providing feedback. These processes will be elaborated upon further in this book by Yarger, Dillon-Peterson, and Haberman.

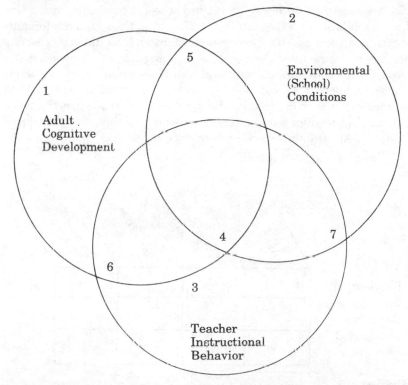

FIGURE 1. Interrelationships of the Goals and Purposes of Inservice

29

As these authors will show, the processes will vary contingent upon the goals of the program. For example, an inservice program stressing changes in instructional or pedagogical behavior might examine specific teaching skills, whereas those attempting to alter adult cognitive or intra- and interpersonal development would attempt to ascertain the development level of individuals and, therefore, conduct a radically different needs assessment. An inservice program directed at altering the school's environmental conditions would take yet another tack—an organizational development approach to assessing needs. Figure 2 illustrates in a simple matrix how basic training processes intersect with different inservice goals.

To illustrate, let us look briefly at assessment. Inservice goals guide the type of assessment conducted. As suggested earlier, it is highly unlikely that a single type of assessment will be adequate to obtain an understanding of inservice needs. Adult cognitive development, for example, has been assessed by using a variety of methods. Hunt's Paragraph Completion Method is a relatively short (15 minutes) innocuous tool by which to assess conceptual complexity (Hunt, Butler, Noy, & Rosser, 1977). A more comprehensive battery of tests (Kohlberg's moral dilemmas or Loevinger's sentence stems for ego development) might also be administered (Kohlberg, 1966; Loevinger, 1970). Ideally, a trained school psychologist, interacting on a regular basis with the staff in a variety of settings, would informally approximate the cognitive development of individuals through observation. Environmental conditions could be assessed using the previously discussed CBAM materials. Needs could also be determined by conducting managerial analysis, as outlined by Hersey and Blanchard (1977) or by using tools later to be outlined in Chapter 6 by Case. Teacher instructional needs can be identified by a variety of systematic observation procedures, a review of past training, specific perceived competencies, or written ques-

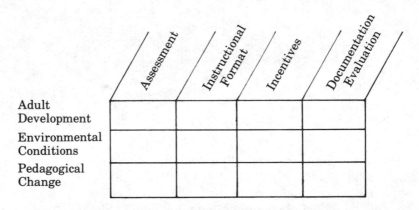

FIGURE 2. Intersection of Basic Training Processes and Inservice Goals

tionnaires. Regardless of what type of assessment is used, Houston et al.'s cautionary counsel is critical:

> A major task in needs assessment is the selection, modification, or development of instruments appropriate for the data to be collected. Two factors related to the task are decisions regarding: 1) the variables associated with the people, programs, and organizational structures which are the data sources for needs assessment; and 2) the instrument formats appropriate for the specific information required (Houston, Faseler, White, Sanders, Senter, & Butts, 1978, p. 207).

One could illustrate, as well, how training techniques, incentive, evaluation strategies, and even governance arrangements and management procedures might vary, depending upon inservice goals. To summarize, inservice is not a simple process. We believe that in order to plan and organize programs that are conceptually coherent, a necessity is a *school based teacher educator,* who has some understanding of teachers and the context within which they work, as well as teacher training expertise. The remainder of this book is designed to help you think through what knowledge and skills this school based leader might need and how these might best be acquired.

References

Argyris, C. *Management and organizational behavior: The path from XA to YB.* New York: McGraw-Hill, 1971.

Berman, P., & McLaughlin, M. W. *Federal programs supporting educational change.* Vol. IV: *The findings in review.* Santa Monica CA: The Rand Corporation, 1975.

Chickering, A. *Education and identity.* San Francisco: Jossey-Bass, 1969.

Goldhammer, R. *Clinical supervision: Special methods for the supervision of teachers.* New York: Holt, Rinehart and Winston, 1969.

Hall, G. E. *The effects of "change" on teachers and professors—theory, research and implications for decision-makers.* Paper presented at the National Invitational Conference on Research on Teacher Effects: An Examination by Policy-Makers and Researchers, Research and Developmental Center for Teacher Education, University of Texas at Austin, November, 1975.

Hersey, P., & Blanchard, K. H. *Management of organizational behavior: Utilizing human resources* (3rd ed.). Englewood Cliffs NJ: Prentice-Hall, 1977.

Herzberg, F. *Work and the nature of man.* New York: World Publishing Co., 1966.

Howey, K. R., Yarger, S. J., & Joyce, B. R. *Improving teacher education.* Washington DC: Association of Teacher Educators, 1978.

Houston, W. R., Faseler, L., White, S. C., Sanders, P., Senter, J., & Butts, W. *Assessing school/college/community needs.* Omaha NE: The Center for Urban Education, 1978.

Hunt, D. E. *Matching models in education.* Toronto: Ontario Institute for Studies in Education, 1971.

Hunt, D. E., Butler, L. F., Noy, J. E., & Rosser, M. E. *Assessing conceptual level by the paragraph completion method.* Toronto: Ontario Institute for Studies in Education, 1977.

Joyce, B. R., (Ed.). *Involvement: A study of shared governance of teacher education.* Syracuse NY: Syracuse University, National Dissemination Center, 1978.

Joyce, B. R., & Weil, M. *Social models of teaching: Expanding your teaching repertoire.* Englewood Cliffs NJ: Prentice-Hall, 1978.

Kohlberg, L. Moral education in the schools: A developmental view. *School Review,* 1966, *74,* 1–30.

Loevinger, J., & Wessler, R. *Measuring ego development I: Construction and use of a sentence completion text.* San Francisco: Jossey-Bass, 1970.

McGregor, D. *The human side of enterprize.* New York: McGraw-Hill, 1960.

Turiel, E. An experimental test of the sequentiality of developmental stages in the child's moral judgments. *Journal of Personality and Social Psychology,* 1966, *3,* 611–618.

Willie, R. *Adult development and continuing professional education.* University of Minnesota/Minneapolis Public Schools, Tenth Cycle Teacher Corps, 1977. (Report)

Yarger, S. J., Howey, K. R., & Joyce, B. R. *Inservice teacher education.* Palo Alto CA: Booksend Laboratories, in press.

Part 2

THE PERSONAL DIMENSION

3

Adult Development and Leadership Training for Mainstream Education

NORMAN A. SPRINTHALL
LOIS THIES SPRINTHALL

How can we use current adult development theory to help prepare adults for new roles as school based teacher educators, who will, in turn, provide leadership for mainstreamed education?

In general, little systematic theory and research is available in the area of normal adult growth and development. Psychology in this country has traditionally focused basic research efforts on children, to a lesser degree on adolescents, and almost not at all on adults. Only in the area of the abnormal has psychology presented much theory or research vis-à-vis adults. Always debatable, of course, is the question of how much the study of the abnormal illuminates the process of normal growth. Much of the research is clinical in nature and, thus, highly speculative.

Case studies, such as those found in the work of Erikson (1959), Levinson (1978), Gould (1972), or Sheehy (1977), provide interesting accounts of adults in crisis. Such a research basis in clinical studies, however, can hardly be considered adequate to justify conclusions of specific adult stages of development. To suggest, as does Erikson, that all adults between the ages of 35 and 50, are confronted by the psychological task of generativity in lieu of self absorption, or that (according to Sheehy) all women face age 35 as a "crossroads" stage, can lead to unsupported generalizations for both theory and practice.

We have great need for requisite basic research concerning adult development, but for now we need to examine other areas for related information and seek to extrapolate practical guidelines. To avoid past errors from other fields, it should prove fruitful to review theory and research derived from previous therapeutic and training models employed with adults. From this review, we may discern promising areas for needed model tryouts, as well as some approaches to avoid lest we replicate previous failures.

THERAPEUTIC AND TRAINING MODELS FOR ADULTS

In the tradition of psychoanalysis, Jersild (1955) suggested some years ago that teachers' successful adult functioning could be stimulated through therapeutic re-education. He held up, as the model for growth and development, a corrective emotional experience through intensive individualized treatment with a psychoanalytically oriented therapist. Adult problems were supposedly derived from infantile, unconscious conflicts. Therapy was regarded as the treatment of choice, the royal road to comprehending one's own intrapsychic struggle. The journey of the id, ego, and superego could be traveled only in the company of a psychotherapist who would serve as guide, transference object uncoverer, and interpreter. Anything less was bound to fail.

Unfortunately, little research data are available to support the psychoanalytic claims. In an exhaustive review of longitudinal studies with children, Kohlberg, LaCrosse, and Ricks (1971) came to starkly pessimistic conclusions: "Put bluntly, there is no research evidence indicating that clinical treatment of emotional symptoms during childhood leads to predictions of adult adjustment ... The best predictors of the absence of adult mental illness are the presence of forms of personal competence and ego maturity during childhood" (p. 1274).

Other researchers investigating the efficacy of adult treatment are no more sanguine. For example, careful reviews of the effects of psychotherapy often concluded that the treatment had become "functionally autonomous" from its original purpose. Bergin (1963) was even more pointed in a review indicating that on the average there was little difference between "treated" groups and control groups. Most importantly, however, he found a differential effect within the treatment groups—about one-third improved, one-third remained the same, and one-third got *worse*. Research studies in counseling and psychotherapy are commonly dismissed as being of poor quality. Indeed, almost any individual study can be soundly criticized on methodological issues. By far the most carefully designed study that has ever appeared in the literature by Volsky, Magoon, Norman, and Hoyt (1965) also reached negative conclusions concerning treatment outcomes.

We could speculate as to why generalized intensive counseling or therapy yields such meager results. For the purpose of this chapter, however, we shall simply conclude that the therapeutic model has little to offer as a procedure for adult growth and development in either the personal or professional domain. In fact, even in clinical psychology graduate training programs, the requirement of psychotherapy for graduate students is optional (Holt & Luborsky, 1958). Only in the most conservative psychoanalytic institutes do we still find that analysts and analysands regularly meet for required treatment. The traditional treatment modalities of one to one psychotherapy seem highly inappropriate to our task of finding a model for adult professional growth, since their effectiveness is highly problematic.

If individual treatment leaves much to be desired as a model, what about treatment in groups? The emergence of a bewildering array of group treatment techniques over the past 20 years makes for genuine difficulties in reviewing overall effectiveness, since many procedures have not even been researched. The reviews that have been accomplished, however, find that supposed advantages of group treatment over individual treatment are problematic. An extensive review by Campbell and Dunnette (1968) found almost no supportive evidence in outcome studies. The more recent review by Yalom (1974) came to conclusions similar to those found in Bergin's work for individual treatment. Yalom found that group treatment, again by trained professionals, yields major within group differences: some get "better," some remain the same, and others get worse. Although highly focused and specific concrete behaviors may be amenable to group treatment (e.g., AA treatment for motivated alcoholics), the general findings are equivocal. Intensive group treatment, which ostensibly simulates a microcosm of society, does not appear to offer much promise as a model for adult professional development. At least part of the problem is that such group treatment aspires toward extremely vague goals, such as personality reconstruction. Conservatively, the therapeutic or remedial focus of such efforts suggests that employing such an intensive and global model as a basis for professional development does not appear justified.

Skills Training

If we discard therapeutic treatment focused on intrapsychic dynamics as a model, what happens if we go to the other extreme? If we want adults to behave differently, why not simply teach new skills? Are adults capable of learning new techniques that might form the basis for higher order professional and/or personal skills? Two somewhat similar approaches or variations represent this model: behaviorism and skills acquisition.

In the highly orthodox behavioristic approach (Skinnerian S-R), one assumes that for humans at any age the change process is the same. A young black box or an old black box can be conditioned with equal facility, as long as we know the appropriate reinforcers. Thus, appropriate skills can be emitted on-call through the ABAB paradigm. Operant behavior is essentially random under normal condition (A). Applying reinforcement principles under condition (B) shapes and directs our behavior. This system has not been tried out in complex systems with normal adults (with the exception of the fantasy in Walden II) but has been employed with mental hospital populations (token economies), with so called "retarded" groups and other "subcultural" or minority populations, prisoners, runaway adolescents, etc.

Generally, the assumptions of behavior modification become highly controversial when applied to such majority populations as adolescents or adults. The amount of control and the need for absolute systematic application of positive reinforcement create technological as well as philosophical problems. And as the majority populations become more aware of such concerns, the employment of such global token economies is increasingly questioned. In addition, basic assumptions of the S-R approach apparently reduce the complexity of the human condition to such a low level that most educators and psychologists would probably agree with Gordon Allport's (1962) description of the total behavioristic approach as so bereft vis-à-vis the human condition that it could only be epitomized as "threadbare or even pitiable." In any case, as a model for adult growth and development, orthodox S-R token economies and the like hold small promise.

Theorists, such as McDonald (1973), have suggested that behaviorism scale down its claims as a technological "fix" for the entire society to a more modest level as an incomplete yet promising instructional method. The fact that some aspects of behaviorism may be important and significant does not, however, justify a total behaviorist approach to the process of development.

A more conservative view suggests that operant conditioning may be a useful tool to complement other instructional approaches for humans at all age ranges. For example, employing so called "precise teaching" to help start the learning process where short term, immediate, concrete feedback is appropriate may be an essential part of any teacher's repertoire. To generalize, however, on such a grand scale as Walden II or to suggest a national or international repository for behavior modification pinpoint charts (Lindsley, 1972) is clearly not justified, either theoretically or practically. From a philosophical standpoint, of course, behavior modification as a way of life raises a series of questions of self determination and freedom versus external control. Those issues are beyond the scope of this book.

A second approach to adult development, without complete allegiance to all of the behavior modification assumptions, has recently emerged—a type of educational skills training programing. Microteaching, microcounseling, and human relations training procedures are common examples of this model. Essentially, such procedures employ a sophisticated instructional strategy that follows a concrete sequence. Complex behaviors are broken into smaller components and discrete skills. The skills are taught through modeling, peer teaching, and then transfer. Much of the instruction is experience based. Usually the programs eschew theory.

38

The primary difficulty with the skills only learning model for adults is that the skills tend to wash out. Commonly, follow up studies find no evidence of skill training from 6 to 12 months later. A comprehensive review by McAuliffe (1974) indicated that learned counseling and active listening techniques disappeared rather quickly in the natural setting followup.

In a recent review of a comprehensive series of such studies in adult teacher training, Joyce (1978) found that the higher order teaching skills deteriorated rather quickly after laboratory instruction.

Transferring complex and comprehensive teaching skills apparently does not hold for long. At least two possibilities may account for such failure. The lack of theoretical information may provide the teacher with no cognitive framework to understand and explain how to select and choose specific procedures for specific situations. Also, the abrupt end of the laboratory training may leave such teachers on the verge of complex skill acquisition. The lack of continued followup and supervision may account for the reversal to "type." In this area, a relatively new one for training, the results are disappointing. However, to write off the micro approach may be premature. Imaginative combinations of skill training in concert with other untried "ingredients" may prove successful. At least, the skills only as a unilateral technique fails the test of transfer and generalization.

Academic Instruction

A third, and in some ways the most traditional, model for adult growth can be derived from academic acquisition as a stimulus for development. If traditional therapy is problematic, behavior modification and skills training too singular, then, perhaps a solution can be found in the classroom and the library in the form of academic content. If we cannot "emote" to growth, nor "do" growth, can we "think" our way to adult growth? Unfortunately, the studies on academic mastery are no more positive than those for the other models, and to some degree are worse.

Generally, the most common finding is that scholastic achievement and/or aptitude *only* predict to scores on the next series of tests. Grade point achievement does not relate to successful adult performance—so called life skills. In fact, a most recent cross cultural and longitudinal study by the highly respected Douglas Heath (1977) found that SAT score was *inversely* related to several hundred indices of adult maturity.

Similarly, Kohlberg (1977) found that success as an adult in "living" resulted from individual ego maturity and moral maturity, and *not* from academic success.

It is hardly surprising to find that tests designed to predict only to success in terms of the arbitrary content and demands of the schools

39

should fail to predict much to later life; there is no psychological or philosophical reason to expect they would. In contrast, assessment of development, like our moral judgment assessment, do predict to life outcomes in job and family (Kohlberg, 1977, p. 28).

Chickering (1969) also suggested that college and post college "adjustment" depend on aspects of psychological maturity rather than achievement. He used the phrase personality "vectors" to connote clusters of psychological variables as determinants of life success. Such concepts as interpersonal maturity, competence, integrity, and managing emotions represent the personality factors associated with effective performance.

McClelland (1973) reviewed a series of studies examining factors associated with specific on the job performance for adults. Although the range of jobs studied varied from the menial (stockroom worker) to the complex (research scientist), the outcomes were similar. Academic achievement did not predict success in any area, but estimates of what he called psychological competence *did* predict. *Competence*, a term developed by White (1969), refers to an intrinsic human drive for mastery and personal efficacy. In this view, formal and informal educational experience (parenting, classrooms, friends) can encourage or discourage the development of this orientation, which then becomes a crucial determinant of adult success. Longitudinal studies of collegiate education and life skills success point directly to similar conclusions. A Brown University/Ford Foundation study (Nicholson, 1970) found that high school grades and SAT scores did not predict to a multiple criteria of success some 16 years later (Who's Who, economic success, graduate school performance, peer nomination, etc.), but estimates of psychological maturity and personal competence ("promise") *were* efficient predictors.

The results of these studies point in two directions. Negatively, the studies clearly indicate that so called academic learning of the type requisite for a high grade point average does not relate to successful adult performance. In other words, academic learning (in a narrow, traditional sense) is as inadequate as a model as are the other models. But from a positive sense, these same studies may point the way to more productive models.

A TENTATIVE SYNTHESIS

With the exception of the psychotherapeutic model, all the others reviewed here share a common weakness. Behavior modification, skills only, and academic learning appear as single variable solutions to multiple variable problems. On the other hand, the psychotherapeutic model is at the other extreme—too vague, generalized, and ambiguous. It seeks to answer everything, yet in fact may effect little. Can we find a synthesis or a middle way from which we may derive an effective model for adult development? Is there an emergent theory that is at least complex enough to respect human diversity and from which we can draw out actual programs that relate directly to the real world of adult teachers?

From our view, we do see significant possibilities for just such an emergence for *both* goals and instructional methods. Tentatively, there is substantial promise in setting out such new directions. Reviewing the past reveals particular inadequacies. At the same time, one major theme emerges. Studies, especially in the academic learning model, point to a series of variables that do predict success as an adult. The names may vary, e.g., ego maturity, psychological maturity, personal competence, allocentrism, integrity, role taking ability, accurate empathy, symbolic processing, interpersonal competence, etc. Nonetheless, the constructs are highly similar. All connote the importance of cognitive-developmental "structures" as significant determinants of life performance. Also, from a historical perspective, these concepts are up to date and empirically cross validated domains embedded in Dewey's (1916) important yet often misunderstood educational philosophy.

Too much space would be required to trace the historical line from Dewey to the modern day developmentalists (Piaget, Kohlberg, Hunt, Loevinger, Heath, Chickering, Selman, and others), but modern day developmental theory rests directly on a basic Deweyian contention. A central goal of education is to promote what Dewey called developmental growth. The last 30 years of theory and research by many of the above mentioned have helped fill in specific stage definitions of such growth, or as we have termed it, psychological maturity. Developmentally mature humans can perform the requisite complex tasks of adulthood. Less mature, less complex, adults process experience and behave less adequately.

In the specific case of adult teachers, the most comprehensive set of validating studies is from Hunt and his associates (1978) at the Ontario Institute. They have been able to document, through natural setting research, that teachers who were classified at more advanced developmental stages were more effective as classroom teachers. Stated simply, teachers at higher stages of development functioned in the classroom at a more complex level, e.g., were more adaptive in teaching style, flexible, and tolerant. Also, such teachers were more responsive to individual differences and most importantly, employed a variety of teaching models, e.g., lectures, small discussions, role plays, indirect teaching strategies. They were also more empathic; that is, such teachers could accurately "read" and respond to the emotions of their pupils. From a theoretical perspective, this behavior is reasonable since at higher stages humans are capable of multiple perspective taking. Their perceptual field is broad or, in Witkin's terms, such teachers are "field-independent" rather than "field-dependent" (Witkin, Moore, Goodenough, & Cox, 1977). In summary, as effective professionals, such teachers provide an abundant learning environment for their pupils.

The teacher's conceptual development level becomes the independent variable, and pupil learning outcomes, the dependent.

Apparently what holds true for teacher performance also applies to the professional effectiveness of school principals as well. A recent study by Silver (1975) found that school principals at high conceptual stages were more adequate as "democratic" educators than those at lower levels. "Higher stage" principals were rated as both more person oriented and more professionally oriented than their "lower stage" colleagues. The latter definition included democratic decision making as well as former variables such as more complex interpersonal environments.

A series of very recent "working papers" from Hunt's group (1978) indicates that similar findings are emerging from studies of effective versus ineffective counseling psychologists. The less mature stage counselors were more ideologically bound to a particular "school" of treatment. Higher stage counselors could more clearly differentiate client needs and apply a greater variety of appropriate therapeutic techniques. In this sense, the results parallel the teacher studies. Higher stage teachers employ more models of teaching and can "read" pupils and "flex" with them. Counselors at higher stages employ a greater variety of counseling strategies (models) and can tailor their responses more in accord with client feedback.

In a related developmental domain, that of stages of moral maturity, similar results are emerging for both teachers and other professionals. In studies of inservice teachers (Sprinthall, N.A. & Bernier, 1978; Oja & Sprinthall, 1978), role taking ability, a requisite for moral maturity, was found to be related to effective teacher performance. In a study of preservice teachers (Sprinthall, L. T., 1979), similar findings were apparent; namely, that student teachers who differ *only* in levels of moral maturity and conceptual level also differ substantially in teaching effectiveness—defined as having a greater repertoire of teaching models.

A study of advanced medical students led to similar conclusions. Candee (1977) found that physicians classified as principled moral "thinkers" on the Kohlberg scale were nonpaternalistic toward patients, could respond to individual differences, role take, place themselves in their patients' shoes, establish colleagueship with patients, etc. In short, even though the medical students were academically homogeneous (a necessity for admission), they showed major differences in role performance by developmental stage, in this case moral maturity.

Klemp (1977) found parallel results for superior versus inferior naval officers, and for social work case officers. Finally, McClelland (1973) reported that role taking ability predicted superior performance among Foreign Service Officers. Such studies point to the significance of aspects of cognitive development as a major determinant of adult "real world" behavior. In other words, more adequate professional functioning does not wash out since such behavior apparently flows from each person's more adequate cognitive development stage.

At the moment, given the fractionated nature of the studies, no single comprehensive developmental theory is available. Each theorist (Piaget, Hunt, Kohlberg, Loevinger, and others) tends to work in isolation, focused mostly on his or her particular domain. The domains, however, are all interrelated. Loevinger (1966) has noted that all developmental theories correlate by definition. The basic assumptions are congruent and significant. Yet (and perhaps fortunately), we are still in the equivalent of a cultural revolution, with a hundred different flowers blooming in the developmental garden. The flowers are different in some content yet highly similar at a process level.

The developmental perspective, incidentally, does hold promise as a possible framework for synthesis vis-à-vis the process of adult growth. What then about promising directions for educational practice? Must we wait 20 or 30 years for more basic research or can we derive incomplete but promising models for instruction? To some degree, of course, such an answer depends on one's own view as to how knowledge is generated. The developmental epistemology suggests that interaction between theory and practice represents the generator.

Following Lewin's (1935) framework, theory and practice are different sides of the same coin and reside in the real world, not the laboratory. Since behavior is a function of the interaction of person and environment (B-P-E), we are not exempt from the same laws. Accordingly, we strongly urge tryouts of a developmental model for adults, even though all the answers are not yet in from basic research. Further, from a developmental perspective, tryout, field based experiments are themselves basic research. Lewin would say that there is nothing so practical as a good theory. By carefully examining actual "best shot" practice, we can more fully illuminate needed theoretical reformulations.

Thus, although heretical, a basic developmental assumption is that we derive practice from theory *and* vice versa; that is, we can derive theory from a careful examination of practice. Practice is not a second class activity for those incapable of armchair abstractions. Rather, interaction means that practice and theory go hand in hand. If we concentrate exclusively on either, both are diminished.

AN INSTRUCTIONAL MODEL

Hunt (1978) noted that the developmental level of a child, adolescent, or adult is not necessarily a permanent classification. Rather, he suggested, we should view it as the current preferred mode of functioning. One of the greatest challenges facing educators, Hunt further stated, is the need to create programs designed to stimulate developmental stage growth. Despite 10 years of research on that question with child and adolescent populations (reviewed by Sprinthall & Ojemann, 1978), for adults we are at the initial entry points. Hunt commented, "We believe that most earlier teacher training, both preservice and inservice, has seriously underestimated teachers' potential for learning new approaches" (1978, p. 244).

On the basis of current study with adult inservice teachers, both at the University of Minnesota and at St. Cloud State University, and extrapolating from studies with elementary and secondary school children, we suggest that a developmental approach include the following elements.

Role Taking Experiences

Growth toward more complex levels of cognitive-developmental functioning appears to be most influenced by placing persons in significant role taking experiences. A substantial difference is to be noted between role playing (simulation, games, fantasy trips, etc.) and actual role taking. In the latter case, the person is expected to perform a new and somewhat more complex interpersonal task than his or her own current preferred mode. The experience is direct and active, as opposed to vicarious and indirect. For example, with teenagers, role taking may involve a pupil in actually learning to counsel a peer or teaching junior high pupils, or coteaching in a nursery school. For preservice and inservice teachers, role taking may involve teaching counseling skills and/or supervision skills, or employing new teaching "models". Ryan (1970) suggested the concept of cross role training or role taking for teachers. Although never formally implemented, the idea still seems valid—namely, that educating professionals through direct yet multiple professional roles may act as a stimulus to growth.

Qualitative Role Taking

A second consideration concerns the qualitative aspects of such experience based role taking. Obviously, as Dewey (1916) noted, major differences are inherent in what anyone can learn from experience. From an experiential point of view, working at the Rub-A-Dub-Dub Car Wash may not be equivalent to teaching a blind retarded child to swim. What we need to chart is the learning potential implicit in particular kinds of experience-role taking that are neither beyond the reach nor below the grasp of an individual learner. Role taking could be a significant educative *or* miseducative activity depending upon the calibration or the experiential "match."

Developmental stage differences imply major differences in the initial ability to role take. For example, in some of the school studies it was clear that the developmentally less mature junior high pupils could not work effectively in a relatively unstructured preschool (Preuss, 1976). On the other hand, children in the same age and stage range could work effectively

44

in a more highly structured cross age teaching assignment in a traditional elementary school (Enright, 1978). Based on clinical evidence, it appears that teachers at modest CL levels have difficulty understanding and accepting why they could employ common counseling techniques for small group instruction for mainstreamed classes. Such a role taking experience may not be appropriate, at least at the outset, for these teachers.

An even clearer case of the negative effects of role taking mismatch has been documented by L. Sprinthall (1979). When low developmental stage school supervisors were mismatched with high developmental stage student teachers, the beginning teachers were evaluated negatively by the supervisors, even though an objective performance rating indicated that the student teachers were performing with substantial effectiveness in the classroom.

Guided Reflection

In addition to "real" experience, we see a genuine need for careful and continuous guided reflection. Again, in a Deweyan sense, unexamined experience misses the point. It appears that an inordinate commitment to this concept is required to make it work. Apparently, the general educational enterprise rarely teaches anyone how to reflect upon real experience. Vocabulary for reflection seems to vary from the minimal to the nonexistent. In a series of secondary schools, most teenagers seemed to believe that "wow," "sad," and "dynamite" represented the complete thesaurus for human emotions! If preservice or inservice teachers are asked to keep a journal, the results are usually meager at best. Teaching how to ask questions, examine experience from a variety of views, etc., seems at least coequal as a growth stimulus to providing real experience. Naturally, there are always some in each group who, for whatever reason, are reflective. Yet, for the majority, structured learning seems requisite to promote rigorous examination.

Guided Integration

Balance is needed then between the real experience and discussion/reflection/teaching. Research with teenagers indicates that tremendous amounts of experience do not have greater impact than more modest amounts. In a peer teaching program, tutoring 2 or 3 hours per week proved as effective as 10 to 12 hours in affecting the level of psychological maturity, *as long as* a weekly seminar was provided. Without the guided reflection, no discernable effect was evident in volunteer tutors (Exum, 1977). A current study (Sprinthall, N. A., & Blum, in press) in elementary schools indicates that with peer teaching ("regular" children and TMR's), the same findings hold to an even greater degree. Under careful and continuous supervision, the regular children develop more effective role taking and empathy skills. Under volunteer only conditions with minimal supervision, the "regular" children become more negative toward and critical of TMR's. Bruininks (1978) also found that under random conditions in most classrooms, "regular" children accorded increasingly lowered social status to mainstreamed children. In some sense, this finding may be only the most recent example that experience by itself may be educative or miseducative. Guided integration appears essential.

Continuity

Programs need to be continuous. Rarely will a single three credit course provide a sufficiently in depth experience to produce significant change. The followup studies noted earlier (McAuliffe's review of human relation training "packages") plus the national study by Howey, Yarger, and Joyce (1978) clearly document the ineffectiveness of brief, episodic, weekend type learning. The time line for significant change probably should extend over at least a 1 year period. In one of our projects (Oja & Sprinthall, 1978), we found that grouping or clustering teachers by school building made it more possible to provide continuous supervision on site when teachers were asked to transfer their newly learned teaching models to their own classrooms.

Miles (1967) has written of the relative isolation of classroom teachers. Such an environmental factor may indeed influence why so little new learning transfers. Without continuity during both the acquisition and transfer phase, new instructional techniques may be placed quickly into desk drawers, atop new curriculum guides. As a result, both new techniques and new content quietly gather dust.

Personal Support and Challenge

Since developmental stage growth represents by definition functioning at a new and more complex level, instruction needs to provide for both personal support and challenge. The general role of the leader must include, at a minimum, the ability to model a variety of teaching modes. By itself, such modeling probably will not be enough. A key Piagetian concept is that development involves the process of upsetting or upending one's current stage (and state of equilibrium), thereby creating dissonance or a state of *equilibration*. The person attempts to incorporate the new into the old without really changing the old.

New learning, in a developmental sense, requires that we actually give up old less adequate, more concrete, less empathic, more stylized systems of thought and action. The stability that a less adequate stage may offer can often become an extremely well entrenched barrier to change. Any effective instructional model must offer major personal support as a direct part of the instruction, not as an indirect service or adjunct "therapy."

46

Separating the person from "old learning" may be similar to the grieving process, for some at least.

Our work with inservice teachers convinces us that significant professional development is often painful. Similarly, Parker and Lawson's (1978) pioneering study of professional adult growth for college level professors clearly suggested the need for careful and continuous support as requisite for change. Their work seems to indicate, at least by inference, that the problems of providing inservice for elementary and secondary teachers pale by comparison with those in doing so for college professors. Higher order skills represent the challenge; interpersonal responsiveness/empathy, the support.

TRAINING/EDUCATIONAL PROGRAM IMPLICATIONS

Given these six points as a start then, we suggest that educational programs designed to train and educate the on site resource trainer incorporate a developmental instructional model. The goals of the model are admittedly broad, yet so are the tasks envisaged.

Throughout this book, the same theme reappears. For example, Case indicates quite correctly that the resource facilitator must possess an array of complex professional competencies vis-à-vis the organization. The facilitator must process at high levels of complexity to view the system as an organic whole, to distinguish between the formal and hidden agendas, and to differentiate between temporary resistance and bottom line barriers. Similarly, Berman stresses that the facilitator needs to view the curriculum not through standard perceptions, formal guidelines, and books but rather must process the total environment at a highly complex cognitive level—characteristics she notes as inwardness, curiosity, interactive knowledge generation, expectancy, and a passion for the ethical.

Dillon-Peterson's on site staff developer must be able to provide differential learning environments to meet different teacher needs, along with such competencies as conflict resolution, problem solving, and consensus building. Similarly, if we review Anderson's competency list, it is immediately apparent that the resource facilitator must manifest a high stage of developmental maturity in order to instruct others successfully in managing mainstream classrooms. Teaching teachers the role taking conflict-resolution skills implicit in the Johnsons' cooperatively organized classrooms represents another obvious parallel. Facilitators, as Haberman notes, need some 33 constructs and skills to successfully operate effective on site staff development. And Yarger and Mertens, although decrying the myth of super teacher, conclude their chapter with very much the same view.

A resource facilitator needs maximum self direction, an abundance of diplomacy, and real theory, plus skills to succeed. Thus, the facilitator's role, no matter how it is phrased, requires that the person function at an advanced stage of psychological maturity. This functioning is not synonymous with academic achievement or norm referenced test scores, nor with any of the usual academic predictors, as we have noted. Instead, advanced psychological development or maturity encompasses a different set of constructs, the ability to role take, to be empathic (allocentric), to process experience from multiple perspectives, to make informed commitments yet remain open to new perspectives, to symbolize experience, to differentiate figure from ground, to be field independent, to be practical and theoretical, etc. Such abilities as these are requisite to the tasks facing the resource facilitator.

Indices of psychological development, therefore, should form an important core of a selection procedure. How these might be assessed could vary all the way from formal development measures, such as Hunt's (1978) C L test, Loevinger's (1966) Ego Development, Kohlberg's (1977) Moral Judgment, to the informal, such as Knight's (1979) open ended interviews in the Vermont project. In any case, successful prior experience in leadership, inner direction, the ability to tolerate stress, complex differentiated perception, and empathy could form the interview domains for judgment and selection. Studies noted earlier clearly indicate that developmentally mature adults function more successfully in complex tasks than do those at more modest levels. Accordingly, a major criterion for selection should be the cognitive developmental characteristics of the prospective resource facilitator.

As to the training program itself, we do not have sufficient space here to present it in detail. However, we would recommend that it follow the format in the six points previously outlined—namely a "learning by doing and reflecting" approach. The institutional model would be heavily oriented to actual role taking as a mechanism for skills acquisition, which would transfer into the real world of on site generalization. Thus, organizational consultation, curriculum and supervision, and facilitative teaching skills could form the core curriculum for resource teacher training.

Naturally, developmental evaluation ought to be a part of such a program, to provide feedback on possible differential training effects, as well as a means of recorrecting and changing the programs themselves. The developmental model offers promise, yet simultaneously requires continued research evaluation. We foresee the need for continued cycles of program tryout and modification, a process of gradual improvement as a means of evolutionary curriculum modification in the service of adult professional development.

CONCLUDING COMMENTS

Our goals in this chapter have been to make a case for a developmental framework as an *aim* of professional growth and to suggest some elements

48

that may form an effective instructional strategy. All the answers are not in, but the system appears promising. The developmental conception of human growth seems to be more broadly based than some conceptions and less grandiose than others. Research appears positive and validating. Implied is a synthesis of many of the old dichotomies: thought *and* action, the real and symbolic, and cognitive and affective. Humans may grow and develop through programs that combine action and reflection, so that (in an oversimplified way) we simultaneously "think, feel, and do" our way to more complex levels of functioning.

Certainly, the problem of leadership training for any area as complex as facilitating the development of a humane mainstream classroom demands that we seek solutions that are at least as comprehensive as the problem. An effective adult school based facilitator will need an educational experience that goes beyond skills acquisition or subject matter mastery.

Our final developmental assumption is that although at any given moment each of us may appear to be functioning as best we can, we can do better. Trying out a developmentally based leadership program may point the way for us all to do better. Effective implementation of the dicta of least restrictive environments and increasing the accommodative capacity of classroom requires that we do.

REFERENCES

Allport, G. Psychological models for guidance. *Harvard Education Review,* 1962, *32*, 373–381.

Bergin, A. The effects of psychotherapy: Negative results revisited. *Journal of Counseling Psychology,* 1963, *10*, 244–250.

Bruininks, V. Actual and perceived peer status of learning-disabled students in mainstreamed program. *Journal of Special Education,* 1978, *12* (1), 51–58.

Campbell, J., & Dunette, M. Effectiveness of T-group experiences in managerial training and development. *Psychology Bulletin,* 1968, *70* (2), 73–104.

Candee, D. Role taking, role conception and moral reasoning as factors in good physicians performance. *Moral Education Forum,* 1977, *2* (2), 14–15.

Chickering, A. *Education and identity.* San Francisco: Jossey-Bass, 1969.

Dewey, J. *Democracy and education.* New York: MacMillan, 1916.

Enright, R. E. Promoting interpersonal and moral growth in elementary schools. *Character Potential,* 1978, *8* (4), 175–181.

Erikson, E. Identity and the life cycle. *Psychological Issues,* 1959, *1* (1), (Entire issue).

Exum, H. Deliberate psychological education: Facilitation of psychological maturity at the junior college level. *Pupil Personnel Services Journal,* 1977, *6* (1), 197–224.

Gould, R. The phases of adult life: A study in developmental psychology. *American Journal of Psychiatry,* 1972, *129,* 521–531.

Heath, D. *Maturity and Competence.* New York: Gardner, 1977.

Holt, R., & Luborsky, L. *Personality patterns of psychiatrists.* New York: Basic Books, 1958.

Howey, K., Yarger, S., & Joyce, B. *Improving teacher education.* Washington DC: Association for Teacher Education, 1978.

Hunt, D. E. In-service training as persons-in relation. *Theory Into Practice,* 1978, *17,* 239–244.

Jersild, A. *When teachers face themselves.* New York: Bureau of Publications, Teachers College, Columbia University, 1955.

Joyce, B. R. *Selecting learning experiences: Linking theory to practice.* Washington DC: ASCD, 1978.

Klemp, G. O. *Three factors of success.* Paper presented at AERA Annual Meeting, Chicago, March 21, 1977.

Knight, M. Personal communication, 1979.

Kohlberg, L. Moral development, ego development, and psychoeducational practice. In D. Miller (Ed.), *Developmental theory.* St Paul: Minnesota Department of Education, 1977.

Kohlberg, L., LaCrosse, R., & Ricks, D. The predictability of adult mental health from childhood behavior. In B. Wolman (Ed.), *Handbook of child psychopathology.* New York: McGraw-Hill, 1971.

Lewin, K. *A dynamic theory of personality.* New York: McGraw-Hill, 1935.

Levinson, D. *The seasons of man's life.* New York: Knopf, 1978.

Lindsley, O. R. From Skinner to precision teaching. In J. B. Jordan & L. S. Robbins (Eds.), *Behavioral principles and the exceptional child.* Arlington Va.: CEC, 1972.

Loevinger, J. The meaning and measurement of ego development. *American Psychologist,* 1966, *21,* 195–206.

McAuliffe, S. *The differential effect of three training models upon acquisition and transfer of interpersonal communication skills.* Unpublished doctoral dissertation, University of Minnesota, 1974.

McClelland, D. Testing for competence rather than for intelligence. *American Psychologist,* 1973, *28* (1), 1–14.

McDonald, F. *A behavior modification view of video playback.* Paper presented at AERA, New Orleans, 1973.

Miles, M. Some properties in schools as social systems. In G. Watson (Ed.), *Change in school systems.* Washington DC: National Education Association, 1967.

Nicholson, E. *Success and admission criterion for potentially successful risks.* Providence RI: The Ford Foundation and Brown University, 1970. (Project Report).

Oja, S., & Sprinthall, N. A. Psychological and moral development for teachers. In N. A. Sprinthall, & P. L. Mosher (Eds.), *Value development as the aim of education.* Schenectady NY: Character Research Press, 1978.

Parker, C., & Lawson, J. From theory to practice to theory: Consulting with college faculty. *Personnel and Guidance Journal,* 1978, *57,* 424–427.

Preuss, J. *Process evaluation in a seminar practicum course to promote psychological development.* Unpublished doctoral dissertation, University of Minnesota, 1976.

Ryan, K. Personal communication, 1970.

Sheehy, G. *Passages.* New York: Bantam, 1977.

Silver, P. Principals' conceptual ability in relation to situation and behavior. *Education Administrator Quarterly,* 1975, *11* (3), 49–66.

Sprinthall, N. A., & Bernier, J. Moral and cognitive development of teachers. *New Catholic World,* 1978, *221* (1324), 179–184.

Sprinthall, N. A. & Blum, L. T. Peer and cross age teaching: Promoting social and psychological development in mainstream classes. In M. Reynolds (Ed.), *Social environment of the schools.* Reston VA: The Council for Exceptional Children, 1980.

Sprinthall, N. A., & Ojemann, R. Psychological education and guidance: Counselors as teachers and curriculum advisors. *Texas Technical Journal of Education,* 1978, *5* (2), 79–99.

Sprinthall, L. T. Supervision: An educative or miseducative process? *Minnesota Association of Teacher Educators: Research Monograph,* 1979, *1* (2), 25–34.

Volsky, T., Magoon, T., Norman, W., & Hoyt, D. *The outcomes of counseling and psychotherapy.* Minneapolis: The University of Minnesota, 1965.

White, R. W. Motivation reconsidered: The concept of competence. *Psychological Review,* 1969, *66,* 297–333.

Witkin, H., Moore, C., Goodenough, D., & Cox, P. Field dependent and field independent cognitive styles. *Review of Education Research,* 1977, *47,* 1–64.

Yalom, I. *The theory and practice of group psychotherapy.* New York: Basic Books, 1974.

4

Principles of Inservice Training for Implementing Mainstreaming in the Public Schools

MARTIN HABERMAN

Implementing Public Law 94-142 will require changing what classroom teachers do. Historically, there have been at least five approaches to causing teacher change. One approach has been directed at changing pedagogy. By advocating new methods of instruction, it is assumed that classroom teachers will test these processes and adopt new methods that prove to be more effective. This approach has been partially successful. Pedagogic patterns, in whole or in part, have been adopted by classroom teachers. At other times, seeking to change instructional methods has had little or no impact.

A second approach attempts to change teachers by focusing on new materials, equipment, or media which are, in effect, teacher proof. The assumption is that new materials will control and force teachers to act in new ways. This is the opposite of the first approach and has also been partially successful. At other times, introducing elaborate equipment such as computers or television has had little impact on teacher behavior.

Third is the effort to change teacher practices through personal development. From elaborate procedures such as psychotherapy to more superficial efforts such as single sessions devoted to values clarification or sensitivity training, this approach has been tested in a variety of ways. Presently, the workshops on teacher burnout are quite popular. There is no question that this approach has been partially effective. There are also numerous examples of how teachers do not transfer their apparent personal growth and development to their teaching behavior.

The fourth approach focuses on changing the settings and, through environmental press, affecting teachers' behavior. The assumption here is that school situations and professional culture control the behavior of teachers significantly more than the teachers' personalities. This approach is supported by concepts derived from organizational theory, sociology, political science, and social psychology. There have been instances where manipulating settings has influenced important teacher changes. There is also an impressive body of knowledge to support the contention that teacher behavior has remained remarkably unchanged regardless of dramatic and radical changes in the larger society. Similarly, sophisticated efforts at changing school environments have frequently been both effective and ineffective at changing teacher behavior.

Fifth has been the curriculum approach which attempts to look at all the elements in school situations: time, classroom organization, materials, subject matter, evaluation procedures, and the nature of teacher-pupil interactions. This approach seeks to change teacher behavior by altering the total set of potential influences. Clearly, there have been notable failures as well as some success in this approach.

This chapter is an eclectic attempt to provide principles of action from all five modalities. It is hoped that this will lead to a higher degree of impact on teacher behavior than using any single approach. These guidelines should be viewed as general principles of inservice teacher education which pertain to teacher change regardless of the content of the new program to be implemented. This is not to say that implementing mainstreaming is the same problem as implementing school integration; there are, however, common elements involved in the problem of changing teacher behavior.

In order to implement P.L. 94-142, preparation should focus on three kinds of personnel. Classroom teachers need retraining. Mainstream coordinators need to be prepared to function in each school building as resource people and facilitators to the classroom teachers. Teacher educators with university affiliations are needed to help educate and consult with the mainstream coordinators. Other personnel are necessary but will be less directly involved: nurses, school psychologists, counselors, administrators, school secretaries, aides, volunteers, and other staff. To the extent that anyone is involved in the change process, these same principles pertain.

While teachers can apply many of these principles in their direct work with students, these principles are intended as guides for use in the inservice education of teachers and mainstream coordinators. The principles are grouped into six areas: selection, learning, organizational setting, group relations, methods of instruction, and evaluation. They seek to apply what we know about adult development, environmental influences, and teacher education to the process of teacher change. The next step in implementing these principles will be to derive the specific policies, performance competencies, and evaluation criteria needed in an actual training program.

54

PART I. TEACHER EDUCATION GUIDELINES

A. Selection

1. Individuals selected for teacher educator roles should have demonstrated effectiveness as facilitators, supervisors, team leaders, or change agents. Classroom teachers who are respected by their peers and who voluntarily seek this role should also be considered.
2. Individuals selected for teacher educator roles should be chosen by panels or teams that include the mainstream coordinators whom they will be training. This process can be expedited by using representatives of those to be supervised—having the panel agree upon selection.
3. Individuals selected as mainstream coordinators should have demonstrated successful classroom teaching experience in schools where they are assigned. Should such an assignment be logistically impossible, or should a promising mainstream coordinator not be capable of switching professional roles in the same school, special assignment to a new school situation should be considered.
4. Individuals selected as mainstream coordinators should be chosen by panels or teams that include the classroom teachers whose work they will facilitate. The process may be facilitated by using representative classroom teachers rather than all teachers. With the agreement of these classroom teachers, others may be added to selection panels, e.g., guidance counselor, administrator, nurse.
5. Selection of teacher educators or mainstream coordinators should not involve criteria such as: college G.P.A.; scores on G.R.E. or Miller Analogies Examination; or profiles from standardized psychological, personality, or occupational preference tests. Where these data are known, they may serve as background information but not as criteria for selection.
6. Selection of teacher educators and mainstream coordinators should be based on knowledge/skills that are openly stated and clearly connected with tasks to be performed. These criteria may include professional experiences, demonstrated competencies, personal interviews, and trial periods of actual performance in the roles. Good communication, peer acceptance, trust, and the ability to work cooperatively are critical criteria. We should not underestimate the impact of a great desire to serve in this role.
7. The process of selecting teacher educators and mainstream coordinators should lead to a clarification of roles to be performed, the mutual expectations of all who will be involved, and the criteria to be used for evaluating all personnel.

B. Learning

8. Since behaviors that are rewarded are most likely to recur and since the best planned learning provides for a continuous cumulation of successful behaviors, teacher educators, mainstream coordinators, and classroom teachers should have very frequent opportunities for demonstrating competencies and receiving praise or recognition. Ultimately, the participants will be motivated predominantly by professional pride and higher levels of self actualization. Credibility with peers and the absence of their criticism will remain an important source of motivation for many.

9. Since the most effective learning rewards are those that immediately follow desired behaviors and are, therefore, more likely to be connected with those behaviors, teacher educators, mainstream coordinators, and classroom teachers should have very frequent formal and informal opportunities to share ideas, pass information, signal, or confer in order to immediately connect their praise and support to the specific behaviors they are seeking to influence and strengthen. Distinct advantages are to be gained from engaging in systematic procedures of mutual support by professionals acting in teams and in cooperative relationships.

10. Since threat and punishment have uncertain effects upon learning, teacher educators, mainstream coordinators, and classroom teachers should be in staff rather than line relationships. Evaluations, whether oral or written, should be open to all concerned.

11. Since practice must be based on feedback to be useful, teacher educators, mainstream coordinators, and classroom teachers should perform and be evaluated on role expectations that are sufficiently clear for self appraisal and for evaluating others. Evaluation should lead to real professional growth and to improved classroom practices. Criteria of evaluation should be regularly reviewed for relevance to practice in order to prevent process from degenerating into paper work.

12. Since readiness for new learning is greatly influenced by expectations of success, teacher educators, mainstream coordinators, and classroom teachers should be given training experiences that emphasize tasks, activities, and specific behaviors to be performed, rather than total immersion in the complexities of mainstreaming and its concomitant problems. Practices and methods must be the starting point; theoretic implications and analysis will be more fruitful later in the program after some success has been achieved.

13. Since reward is the most likely basis for expecting that learning will persist in future situations, it is imperative that the learnings of teacher educators, mainstream coordinators, and classroom teachers be tied to goals and purposes they value. Participants' goals and purposes are sincerely sought, genuinely accepted, and adopted.

14. Since learners progress at individual rates and with a wide range of difference in their learnings, all participants should have their programs individualized both in terms of rate and content. *Individualized* should not be construed to mean that teacher educators, mainstream coordinators, or classroom teachers pay no attention to coordinating the impact of their varied efforts.

C. Organizational Setting

15. Since the single most powerful force for change within the school is the genuine commitment of the administrators who bear responsibility for the program to the public, clear statements of support should be forthcoming from the school board, superintendent, and building principal, as well as the explicit criteria they will use to evaluate and defend the program. These conditions are necessary but not sufficient.

16. Since the success of new programs is dependent, in great measure, on their compatibility with existing programs, especially in regard to the demands for scarce resources, the mainstream program should be able to answer questions regarding the allocation of space, time, personnel, and material and explain why these allocations do not detract from accepted, existing programs. Participants also value existing programs and cannot be put in the position of threatening the success of current offerings.

17. Since successful school change requires the creation of new organizational structures, small task oriented groups should be created to implement the program. A system of reward should be developed to recognize the special contributions of participating teachers. A design whereby building participants continuously plan and evaluate their work should be developed. A linkage process for informing and obtaining reactions from neighborhood/community settings should be put into place. An effective system of communication needs to be established between these organizational structures.

18. Autocratic leadership engenders apathy, defiance, or avoidance. Involvement is associated with greater creativity and initiative. Teacher educators and mainstream coordinators, therefore, should emphasize the involvement of teacher participants in all phases of the program. Informed, structured involvement that does not become a burden or overload will secure positive involvement.

D. Group Relations

19. In groups acting for common goals, cooperative behavior is a more effective process than competition. Personnel should be evaluated as teams, or as task groups wherever possible. This process should not

overlook outstanding individual effort. Group processes require genuine group planning and commitment.

20. Since much learning is accomplished informally, many opportunities should be provided for peer teaching of specific teacher competencies.

21. The relationship between the mainstream coordinators and the classroom teachers will be critical. Their required interactions should be supportive and cooperative rather than judgmental. Directions or expectations should come to both as team members. The evaluation of either should emphasize their mutual responsibilities.

22. Staff development for teacher educators, mainstream coordinators, and classroom teachers should be an intrinsic part of the project and an integral part of the workday teaching load. Scheduling is a key element. Cooperation of those who may not be directly involved in the program may be critical.

23. Teachers are socialized to act on peer concensus. They are uncomfortable when they disagree with their peers, particularly when they are forced to act alone. Therefore, individual classroom teachers must never be put into the position of trying to singlehandedly change a school policy or practice. This principle should not prevent a teacher from stating options, presenting a point of view, or raising questions.

E. Methods of Instruction

24. There are specific stages of adult development during which certain proclivities and capacities appear. The stage of life of teacher educators and mainstream coordinators may be a factor in their development of professional competencies. The extent of professional experience is a factor that may be of equal importance.

25. Since new teaching methods and other required professional skills and understandings are most likely to be applied if they are learned in situations that are most like the situations in which they will be used, the training of all personnel should, wherever possible, be on site, involve the same people, and be subject to the very same situational factors as the application of these learnings.

26. Since new teaching methods and other professional skills and understandings are most likely to be applied if they are learned immediately preceding the time when they are needed and applied, participants should be evaluated, engage in inservice training, or plan next steps prior to any observations of their teaching. This sequence is the reverse of the usual cycle which involves teaching, supervision, and then delay before implementation of criticism.

27. Since people remember more information that confirms their existing attitudes than that which contradicts their belief systems, they are not likely to change in marked shifts but in gradual, step by step phases beginning with ideas that confirm their existing perceptions.

28. People reconsider (think) when they encounter a challenge to a course of action they desire to pursue. The thinking process involves them in testing plausible solutions to problems they deem important. One basic method of instruction, assuming thinking leads to change, should require teacher educators, mainstream coordinators, and classroom teachers to define specific problems and testing alternatives. Because of individual learning styles, people will respond differently to this approach.

29. When people experience too much frustration, their behavior ceases to be rational. They demonstrate rage, discouragement, or withdrawal. The mainstream coordinators and classroom teachers must proceed with courses of study that permit them to receive immediate help when they are blocked.

30. The best method for many to learn and apply a general concept is to experience many examples of the concept in a variety of situations.

31. The best way for many people to learn a particular skill is to practice it with feedback, in the same situation in which it is to be used.

F. Evaluation

32. When the goals of an educational program differ from the tests used, the tests used in evaluating that program become the dominant influence on the curriculum and methods employed. Therefore, competencies and other specially developed criteria of evaluation, rather than norm referenced standardized tests of achievement, should be used to evaluate teaching and learning.

33. People vary in personality as much as in ability. They vary in their response to the same school situation. They vary in the nature and rate of their growth. Therefore, the evaluation of teacher educators, mainstream coordinators, and classroom teachers should state specific performance competencies but allow for variations in the demonstration of these competencies.

PART II. USING THE GUIDELINES

Putting these guidelines into action requires a pattern of day to day operation. It will *not* be possible for a teacher educator, mainstream coordinator, or classroom teacher to use these 33 guidelines as discrete rules of conduct to which they must refer each time they engage in a specific behavior. For these guidelines to become useful principles that exert a genuine effect on teachers' behavior, they need a context—a regular process whereby everyone's mutual expectations are clarified and made predictable. Such a pattern of regularized relationships can be established by prior agreement regarding what it is the classroom teacher will be seeking "help" with, the type of "help" that a mainstream coordinator might provide, and the nature of the "help" that a teacher educator can offer to both of these individuals.

Providing "Help" to Classroom Teachers

Teaching activities for which "help" may be sought by classroom teachers learning to mainstream and the approximate percent of time spent in each activity are discussed by Reynolds and Birch (1977, pp. 303–304; 562–571; 630–636). Table 1 provides a quick summary of their information.

TABLE 1

Teaching Activities for Which "Help" May be Sought by Classroom Teachers Learning to Mainstream

	Approximate Time Spent in Activity, %	Activities
1.	5–10%	Using special materials that are new to the teacher. (Becoming familiar with materials and equipment and being shown how they operate.)
2.	5–10%	Communicating with students who have special handicaps, e.g., hearing, visual. (Receiving straightforward directions.)
3.	5%	Special methods of teaching. Acquiring a *very* small body of special teaching behaviors for working with handicapped students, which teachers can learn through observation and develop through practice, i.e., usual supervisory procedures.
4.	75–85%	Engaging in normal classroom teaching practices that are, in large part, effective with all children.

Unquestionably, the most effective teaching for most handicapped students involves the very same planning methods, materials, evaluation, and forms of teacher-pupil interaction as does effective teaching of students not labeled handicapped.

Table 1 is, in effect, a job description of what the classroom teacher new to mainstreaming will be working on as well as the ways in which the mainstream coordinator will be assisting in that work. For example, in Activity 1, using special materials may involve the classroom teacher in observing how a child's leg brace locks into place. The "supervision" offered by the mainstream coordinator may take the form of simply showing the classroom teacher how the child does this and the help, if any, that may be required.

Similarly, Activity 2 may involve the mainstream coordinator in pointing out that the classroom teacher should face forward when speaking to a class that includes hearing impaired students. Activity 3 might refer to the value of using many concrete examples when teaching the severely retarded.

The obvious conclusion from this role analysis is twofold: that simple telling is a useful and effective way of quickly providing vital information and this will comprise 15 to 25% of the mainstream coordinator's work, but more important, that the overwhelming portion of the classroom teachers', the mainstream coordinators', and the teacher educators' roles will be devoted to improving the regular methods of instruction 75 to 85% and, in this portion, simple telling will not be a satisfactory supervisory process.

Processes Reflecting Effective Instruction

It would be helpful to review those normally desirable processes that reflect the effective teachers' assumptions regarding instruction in general. These ideas are essentially the converse of assumptions offered regarding orthodox teaching (Cantor, 1953, pp. 59–72).

1. *The teacher's job is not to set out what is to be learned and the student's job to learn it.* Much that is to be learned emanates from the students, from the school setting, and from the community. Fortuitous events, resource people, field work, and direct experiences take the content that is learned beyond the control of the teacher. These are not hindrances to the teacher's role but opportunities that should be planned for and used.

2. *Information taken on authority is not in itself educative.* Part I of this chapter sought to offer an elaborate rationale for its proposed guidelines. Genuine knowledge should stand the test of questions such as: how, why, on what basis, who says so, what data, theory, or experience support it. Without such questions and the responses they engender, the knowledge offered as authoritative is rejected and not accepted as the learner's own.

3. *Disconnected subjects do not cumulate into a complete education.* Conceptual problems as well as the life problems to be faced come in interdisciplinary forms. Solutions frequently require knowledge that cannot be neatly categorized into existing disciplines. It is the job of the teachers and not just of the learner to integrate and apply subjects.

4. *Subject matter is not the same to the learner as it is to the teacher.* Students and teachers differ in the degree of importance, the relevance, and the usefulness of subject matters. Students being younger will naturally reflect more modern views of what constitutes communication, music,

61

history, science, etc. The actual stuff—ideas and approach—of a particular field of study is frequently significantly different for teachers and students. An imperative in teaching is gaining the students' perceptions of a subject.

5. *Education is active participation in the present and not preparation for later life.* Daily living experiences are frequently excluded from curriculum as distractions. Discipline problems, energy crises, snowstorms, political campaigns, integration suits are opportunities for effective teaching and learning—not intrusions. It is likely that students will learn, retain, and use the intrusions more than the curriculum they interrupt.

6. *Teachers are not responsible for pupils' acquisition of knowledge.* The teacher is responsible for establishing a readiness for learning, for motivating, for engaging students in interesting activities that cause them to seek further learning, for providing materials and a conducive setting, for encouraging cooperation and interstudent support, for serving as a resource, for helping students see options, for building confidence, for helping to develop evaluative criteria, for answering questions, and for a variety of other critical functions. The actual learning and the amount of learning achieved are the result of the student's actions and reflect many factors—home, siblings, classmates, interest, previous experience, and unknown factors—in addition to teacher's input.

7. *Students cannot be coerced into learning.* In spite of what much of the public would like to believe, individual differences in ability, interests, and life experiences prevent a homogenization and standardization of learning. No first grade or ninth grade or high school curriculum can be guaranteed for all. Perceiving a subject as basic cannot transform coercion into an effective pedagogy.

8. *Knowledge is not more important than learning.* Regardless of one's level, it is involvement with the process of learning that insures growth. Becoming engaged and immersed in processes of inquiry is the best guarantee of continuous achievement. Knowledge taught and accepted as a discrete body has a limiting quality. The perception of promotion or graduation as a terminating exercise reflects this assumption.

9. *Education is not primarily an intellectual process.* It involves a continuous interplay among experience, actions, reflection, valuing, emoting, and imagining. Even the processes of thinking—analyzing, comparing, synthesizing, generalizing, hypothesizing—have equally critical affective and behavioral aspects.

The critical point for the mainstreaming effort is that these nine points are not only true for teaching children. They are equally valid for working with the classroom teachers who will implement mainstreaming. The analogues for teachers are as follows:

1. Mainstream coordinators or anyone else cannot set out what classroom teachers must learn.
2. Classroom teachers will not gain new knowledge by fiat.
3. Disconnected subjects will not give classroom teachers a total pattern of action.
4. Classroom teachers view planning, teaching, and discipline differently than others.
5. Classroom teachers are involved in "now" concerns, not futuristic ones.
6. Teachers are ultimately responsible for their own development.
7. Teachers cannot be coerced into learning.
8. Teachers seek processes for continuous development.
9. Teaching is much more than an intellectual activity.

The foregoing review is intended to serve three purposes. First, much poor teaching offered the handicapped—particularly the retarded—is justified as necessary for "them." Second, our assumption is that 75 to 85% of the work of the classroom teacher (and mainstream coordinator and teacher educator) involves building on sound assumptions for teaching anyone and these beliefs should be stated at the outset *before* teachers become involved in mainstreaming efforts. They should be prepared to work on basic methods not esoteric strategies. Third, in defining a role, we need to be clear about the purposes that role is intended to achieve.

Establishing a Regularized Pattern of Interaction

Now possible is the final task of setting out the regularized pattern of interaction in which the 33 guidelines may be implemented.

The working relationship that will guide the work of teacher educators, mainstream coordinators, and classroom teachers will be an application of the problem solving approach to classroom practices. This process will be an integration of traditional problem solving and action research. Dewey's (1916) original steps of problem solving for pupils can be applied to teachers. The standard components of problem solving as they might apply to classroom teachers are:

1. Teachers must have genuine situations for gaining experience—a continuous activity in which they are interested. (What could be more germane to a teacher than the problems they face!)
2. A genuine problem must develop within this situation as a stimulus to thought.
3. Teachers must possess the information and make the observations needed to deal with the problem. (The mainstream coordinator can help this process.)
4. Suggested solutions will occur to the teacher that he or she will be responsible for implementing. (This process can also be helped along by the mainstream coordinator.)

5. The teachers must have opportunities to test their ideas by application—to discover the validity of their solutions. (Readily accomplished by the teachers in their own classrooms.)

Integrating these five steps and adding some details such as problem definition in Step 3, hypothesizing in Step 4, and trying out and evaluating in Step 5, leads to an approach that might correctly be termed *Action Research*. Classroom teachers, mainstream coordinators, and teacher educators can thereby work in a cooperative, supportive relationship.

Teachers can define classroom problems and, with help, study them and act on tentatively held beliefs. The 33 guidelines will, in effect, support the relationship between all the personnel involved and will increase the likelihood that classroom teachers will learn to mainstream. As classroom teachers experience the problems, as *they* define the problems, as *they* consider options, decide on treatments, try out, evaluate, and start over, *they* will change their behavior.

The usual criticism of this approach is that classroom teachers will not always perceive what they need to learn. Our first response to this position is in Table 1. Limited opportunities (15 to 25%) arise to direct teacher behavior if the students' immediate welfare is involved.

The second response to, "How can we trust teachers to define problems?" is listed in the desirable processes of teaching all children. Teachers cannot be coerced into learning any more effectively than they can coerce their students. The values of building the content of the training program on the perceptions of the classroom teachers is that they will be most actively involved in their own learning.

The goal of our work is to apply what we know about inservice education, in general, to the specific problem of implementing mainstreaming. I propose we try to use the 33 guidelines wherever possible and that the basic pattern of interacting with classroom teachers be a series of on the job activities for implementing *teacher* defined action research projects.

REFERENCES

Cantor, N. *The teaching learning process*. New York: Dryden Press, 1953.
Dewey, J. *Democracy and education*. New York: MacMillan, 1916.
Reynolds, M. C., & Birch, J. W. *Teaching exceptional children in all America's schools*. Reston VA: The Council for Exceptional Children, 1977.

5

A Hard Look at Curriculum Development: Implications for Teacher Development In Situ

LOUISE M. BERMAN

With the passage of P.L. 94-142, diversity of persons increasingly characterizes our country's school systems—perhaps more than ever before in the nation's history. The range of physical, mental, social, and emotional abilities and disabilities found in classrooms or learning areas is often very wide. For example, the hard of hearing child may sit next to a child with sharp vision. The child in a wheelchair may share a room or a pod with an extremely agile individual. The person who acquires concepts slowly may be in the same setting as one who is a leap ahead.

Even as students exhibit variations in abilities and exceptionalities, so educators come with diversities of skills and talents. Schools with principals and teachers have given way to schools with a cadre of administrators, psychologists, "helpers"—aides, volunteers—and oh, yes, teachers!

Shifts in school populations and staffing necessitate changes in curriculum development. Frequently curriculum development takes place within a coterie concerned only about one domain of the curriculum. Mathematics teachers plan mathematics curricula; kindergarten teachers plan for their age group; teachers of the deaf plan for the deaf. Little attention is given to continuity, interrelationships, or realities of specific settings. In light of the complexity of school situations, brought about partially by the range of both students and educators within schools, new ways must be found to facilitate curriculum development that cross age, subject, and ability-disability boundaries. If, then, we are concerned about crossing boundaries for students, we must give attention to *in situ* education of teachers, which enables and facilitates teachers' crossing boundaries among persons, classrooms, schools, and community.

urpose of this chapter is to direct attention to three possible em-
in curriculum development and to highlight the one that seems to
the greatest potential for today's schools. Briefly treated also will be
ications for *in situ* education of teachers. The three approaches dis-
sed are:

1. Curriculum development as intent.
2. Curriculum development as actualization.
3. Curriculum development as intent, actualization, and retrospect.

Lewis and Miel (1972) have thoroughly discussed the first two approaches.
A discussion of the third approach can be found in Berman and Roderick
(1977).

CURRICULUM DEVELOPMENT AS INTENT

When teachers or other curriculum workers intentionally plan goals, purposes, activities, or courses of study for learners, they are intending the
curriculum. They are planning what goals ought to be set, what activities
ought to take place, what evaluation procedures ought to be used. They
may plan one or more of the curricular components. For a fuller treatment
of curricular components, refer to Tyler (1950). The 1960's saw a very
heavy emphasis on such a form of curriculum development, as the various
subject fields developed curricula of intent. Stating objectives in ways that
can be evaluated directly and clearly, planning learning experiences in
advance, and linking various aspects of the curriculum are frequent procedures in curricula of intent.

Posner and Rudnitsky (1978) have written a useful book for teachers
based on this emphasis. Based on the work of Johnson (1967), Posner and
Rudnitsky assist teachers in developing a focus and rationale, refining
learning outcomes, forming and organizing units, developing teaching
strategies, and planning course evaluation.

Emphasis on intent has been the most common mode of curriculum development. Its greatest strength is the logical and rational manner in which
curricula can be planned. It allows the planner to design evaluative procedures clearly in line with intended outcomes. However, when used as the
major or only focus for curriculum development, it presents major problems
in terms of its functional use in classrooms with learners of diverse abilities,
handicaps, strengths, and creative tendencies.

Curriculum development as intent does not easily allow for building upon
serendipitous or unanticipated worthwhile interactions that may occur as
a result of diverse abilities and interests in a classroom. It does not allow
us, whether teachers, aides, or volunteers, to select, from a well developed
repertoire of behaviors, those that will make the "moment of now" a mem-

66

orable, exciting experience. As we educators satisfy our intentions, we may or may not realize the intents of learners.

CURRICULUM DEVELOPMENT AS ACTUALIZATION

Interest in what actually happens in classroom settings has long been a concern of educators, as articulated in an early curriculum text by Caswell and Campbell (1935). A more recent treatment of this point of view might be found in literature dealing with what actually transpires in the classroom or teaching (Rosenshine & Furst, 1973). Although Rosenshine and Furst deal with curriculum as actualization much more systematically than did Caswell and Campbell several decades earlier, both sets of authors use occurrences in the actual interactive situation as the primary emphasis in curriculum development.

Curriculum as actualization frequently causes intent to blur, as what happened becomes the focus for curriculum understanding and change. This reality oriented emphasis allows for discussion of the here and now. Proponents of such a viewpoint are frequently advocates of humanistic and/or democratic values. However, direct relationships between clearly articulated objectives and practice may be difficult to discern. Teachers who have examined their own viewpoints may be able to implement the processes and procedures inherent in this form of curriculum development, but the neophyte may need help in articulating the ideals of the intended curriculum with realities of life in classrooms.

CURRICULUM DEVELOPMENT AS INTENT, ACTUALIZATION, AND RETROSPECT

A third way of viewing curriculum development, perhaps the most fruitful way if we wish to highlight similarities and diversities in students and educators, is to view it multidimensionally, i.e., in terms of *intent* (anticipation), *actualization* (moment of now) and *retrospect*. In other words, curriculum development involves: (a) planning, goal setting, and intention or what we would call anticipation, (b) actualization or the moment of now teaching or instruction, (c) retrospect or analyzing feedback gathered on the spot; considering it in terms of previously designed goals, objectives, or curricular materials; coupling feedback with teachers' goals and best judgments; and planning new arrangements to facilitate new learnings.

Integration of all aspects and incoporation of teaching into the function of curriculum development can best be illustrated if we think in terms of time (see Table 1).

If we accept the integrated approach to curriculum development, according to Berman and Roderick (1977) the following questions are critical:

1. What view(s) of the person is(are) foundational to curriculum planning?

2. In light of the view(s) of the person, what should be the planned or anticipated happenings in the classroom?
3. How do we establish the setting so that students intentionally participate in their knowing and so that unplanned as well as planned events can occur and are accounted for?
4. How do we achieve feedback about what is happening in the classroom?
5. What do we do with the information gathered from answering the above questions? (pp. 26–27)

THE INDIVIDUAL: STARTING POINT FOR CURRICULUM DEVELOPMENT

Any view of curriculum has within it implicit views about the individual. We need to make such views explicit so that congruity or a match exists

TABLE 1

Curriculum Development as Anticipation, Moment of Nowness, and Retrospect

Time	Factor	Curriculum	Teaching
Anticipation	Attending formal and informal curriculum meetings	X	
	Studying curriculum guides	X	
	Writing curriculum guides or other curriculum materials	X	
	Thinking about what one expects to happen	X	
	Thinking about what will probably happen in terms of individuals alone and in groups	X	
Moment of Nowness	Providing learning opportunities for what one wants to happen	X	X
	Accounting for the unexpected	X	X
	Recording what is actually transpiring	X	X
Retrospect	Analyzing on the spot behavior	X	
	Planning new learning opportunities based upon feedback, goals, and purposes	X	

between the qualities deemed important for individuals and the curriculum that can be teased out of these views. What is being suggested is not that all learners should emerge from the schools with the *same* qualities, but that some human qualities are especially desirable, humane, and lead toward higher stages of any developmentalist point of view. These latter qualities, therefore, are critical in terms of schools' attention to them. Since schooling is a moral enterprise, curriculum workers need to give extremely thoughtful attention to this responsibility.

The following are a few personal qualities that the curriculum might seek expressly to develop.

Inwardness

People behave in terms of what makes sense to them. Life is a series of lived experiences, of making sense out of the many daily happenings. Persons constantly construct and arrange their "knowledge of the world in terms of personally relevant interpretational schemata" (Morgan, 1975, p. 127). Individuals develop knowledge as their thought forms are constantly reconstructed during the course of dialogue. A focus on inwardness necessitates each person's giving continuous attention to such questions as "Who am I?" and "Who am I in relation to the world?" (Troutner, 1974, p. 13).

Curiosity

Piqued by an awe of life, individuals have a capacity to be curious, to try new endeavors. They may respond to the natural pricks of the setting by attempting to do something better. The handicapped child may try to sharpen a short story. The teacher may try a research project or experiment on some topic of interest (Bussis, Chittenden, & Amarel, 1976). Curiosity is necessary if fresh and creative learning is to occur.

Interaction

Critical to sharing one's own inner knowing is a simplifying and ordering process (Ruesch, 1975). Also critical to interaction is the seeing of another person or object as worth knowing, caring for, being one with (Buber, 1958). The quality, diversity, and quantity of interaction can have a major effect on the shaping of the individual. The more opportunities for dialogue with others on issues of concern to the individual, the greater the opportunity for quality interior dialogue which in turn enhances quality communication with others. A child engages in meaningful interactions when an adult takes the time to help the child explore a new found interest. A teacher engages in meaningful dialogue when peer and teacher analyze observational data gathered during a few minutes of teaching. A blind person engages in meaningful interaction when opportunities for clarifying information gained through touch are provided.

Knowledge Generation

If we accept the premise that knowledge resides in the knower, then one life task is to find individuals who can help knowers make explicit what seems only dimly undersood. As new insights are gained, knowledge shifts, thus necessitating fresh conceptualizations. Related to the dialogical process is the knowledge generating process which, in concert with others, individuals need to learn. Children can learn to ask questions of their peers so that confusion becomes clarity and new insights are gained. Teachers can learn to reflect back to others what they have said in such a way that the fragmented pieces of a day can meld into a whole. If someone helps link the known to the unknown, hospitalized persons, unable to make sense out of the unknown artifacts found in their room, can begin to see the environment as friendly rather than alien. Indeed, persons of all ages and in all conditions are constantly generating knowledge that has potential for adding richness to life. Individuals can learn to facilitate the knowing and understanding of others.

Expectancy

Hope for the future, transcendence, gratitude for life, love of the world, "morningness," exuberance—these qualities enable a person to have an expectant view of the world (Vandenberg, 1975). Expectancy is critical to a life style marked by generation of knowledge as opposed to absorption of facts, by in depth dialogue as opposed to superficial exchange of banalities, and by curiosity about the unknown as opposed to uncritical acceptance of the familiar.

Passion for the Ethical

Driving emotion or passion for ethical behavior is critical if the freedom inherent in the other qualities is to be wisely used. The word *ethics* is derived from *ethos,* meaning "common abode" or "custom." Our common abode is the earth; thus, ethics is "the task of inhabiting the earth" (Verhoeven, 1972, p. 140). Ethical questions that thoughtful persons must address can be subsumed under one major concern: "How can I best inhabit the earth?" Examples of these questions are: "How shall I show love to my neighbor? What does it mean to be just? Which is a higher good—love or justice? What is the meaning of peace? How shall we recognize different conceptions of beauty?" Responses to these and other ethical questions should be sought with "passionate reasonableness and reasonable passion" (Peters, 1973).

In brief, we have indicated that the curriculum should develop

- Inwardness, so that the person says, "I am a unique person."
- Curiosity, so that the person says, "I can try something new and different."
- Skill in communicating, so that the person feels, "I can share with you."
- Skill in generating knowledge, so that the person says, "I can learn."
- Expectancy, so that the person feels,"I can hope."
- Passion for the ethical, so that the person says, "I can do what is right."*

SETTINGS: PLACES FOR CURRICULUM DEVELOPMENT

Since it is impossible to give adequate attention to the *full* process of curriculum development in a book of this nature, we will highlight the basic importance of analysis of setting. Thinking back to Table 1, we see the setting as the place of the moment of now, of the actualized curriculum, of the merging of curriculum with teaching.

Let us consider first just the setting for students. Then we shall discuss settings for teachers as learners themselves, in terms of the same criteria.

Settings for Students

On page 73 is an instrument entitled "Guidelines for Describing Settings for Students." The comments that follow parallel the headings on the instrument, which presents one way to get a handle on settings in which diversity and openness are prized.

A. Overview

As we enter a building, certain features or combinations of them frequently stand out. Which features seem to be predominant? Is the building colorful or drab? Dirty or clean? Architecturally pleasing or ugly? Does time seem to be used leisurely or is the pacing fast? Are people friendly? Businesslike? Cold?

B. Ideological Context

The curriculum ought to be within an ideological context—rich in worthwhile, powerful ideas derived from a variety of disciplines. Ideas to be included in the setting should intrigue the learner, invite investigation and probing, and at the same time have long range, worthwhile implications.

If we accept the assumption that the ideological context should be rich in worthwhile ideas, then certain other conditions must prevail. For example, learners need opportunities to share their ideas, to develop direc-

---

* I am indebted to Professor Martha Wright, University of Vermont, for the summary of this section (Wright 1979).

tions for dealing with them, to develop materials, to take the initiative in building upon ideas and in carrying them beyond the implied intent.

C. Space

If we are concerned about developing qualities of responsibility, caring, and initiation, then we need to help persons use space in fluid and flexible ways. Students need space for both private reflection and public sharing of new insights. Centers must be located so that interconnection of ideas is invited; noisy areas should be separated from more quiet ones. We need to provide space that evokes varieties of degrees of energy and involvement. We need to study from the perspective of learners so that bewilderment is minimized and wise use of space is fostered.

D. Temporality and Flow of Events

If we accept the assumption that learners can have some control over their own destinies, can be responsible, and can carry out ideas in fruitful ways, then we should allow learners some control over the use of their time. Planning should be shared by both students and teachers. Time needs to be used flexibly so that students can develop means of negotiating between their own body timetables and those timetables necessary because of group living. Days should be marked by some aspects of "dailiness" but also by newness and surprise. Individuals should be able to handle unanticipated and frequent events with enthusiasm and adaptability.

E. Persons

If we believe in the significance of individuals in helping others live qualitative lives, then we need to look at who is in the classroom. Learners need opportunities to interact on a regular basis with persons representing a variety of backgrounds, strengths, weaknesses, and ages. They also need to acquire adeptness in interacting effectively with persons who visit the classroom on an irregular basis—with the unexpected visitor or teacher.

F. Communication

If we accept the assumption of the worthwhileness of the individual, the significance of communication, and the building of a sense of community, then we ought to note communication patterns within the setting. Who is communicating with whom and for what purpose? What is the frequency with which teachers interact with each other? With individual children? With groups of children? What use is made of nonverbal communication such as body language, written communications, oral communications, eye contact, etc.? Of events that seem to evoke intervention on the part of the teacher and what the intervention seems to imply to the learner? Of distractions? What evidence do we find of support or encouragement? What examples are seen of negative communication and what do they seem to do to learners? What does negative communication do to the content of communication?

GUIDELINES FOR DESCRIBING SETTINGS FOR STUDENTS

Following are some questions or guidelines* for describing settings for students. The information derived from the use of this instrument should be helpful in planning for individuals and groups of students.

Here are some suggestions for the use of the instrument. Any one or a combination of the suggestions may be used, depending upon the purpose.

1. Note the letter and number for which you are gathering information.
2. Information may be gathered diary fashion, or a combination of free flowing recording and checklists may be used.
3. Groups of persons may gather information in one setting, each person focusing on one or two categories.
4. One person may gather information on one or two categories over a period of time.
5. Teams of persons may focus on one category.
6. One person or a team may gather information on all categories.
7. With some training, students may help gather information.
8. Other categories may be added if appropriate to the situation.

A. Overview

1. *Outstanding features.* Observe the classroom for 2 to 5 minutes. Describe what seem to be the outstanding features of the setting.
2. *Description.* Record as objectively as possible what you see in the setting. Make a diagram of the room which includes placement of furniture, written directions, windows and doors, etc. Note whether room accommodates children with special needs.

B. The Ideological Context (including materials, directions for use)

1. *Potential for movement.* What is the potential for moving furniture, equipment, games, books, science materials, audiovisual materials from one part of the room to the other? Note whether heavy furniture is on casters, whether there are directions that indicate which materials can be moved, etc.
2. *Interconnecting and interrelating ideas.* Note actual instances when ideas are interconnected, interrelated or carried over from one subject

---

* Originally developed by Louise Berman, Jessie Roderick, Panda Kamara, Diane Lee, and Ron Nichols 12/12/75. Fourth Revision 9/25/78.

or area to another. For example, is an idea discussed in a reading lesson discussed again in a social studies lesson? Are ideas developed at learning centers carried over into other areas of the classroom? Are materials moved from one part of the room to another? Are areas related to the experiences of children?

3. *Directions.* How are directions given relative to the use of materials? Indicate the use of bulletin boards, written memos, teacher-child interaction or child-child interaction in direction giving.

4. *Initiation of ideas.* Who initiates ideas? Do students carry ideas beyond the implied intent? What events precipitate a student's taking initiative?

5. *Origin of materials.* Which ones are commercially produced? School produced by an agent outside the teacher? Child produced for self? Child produced for use by other children? Teacher produced for an individual child? Teacher produced for a group of children?

C. Use of Space

1. *Proximity.* Does the location of centers of interest invite interconnection of ideas?

2. *Compatibility.* Are adjoining interest areas compatible? Are noisy centers separated from ones that require silence?

3. *Physical energy.* How much energy is required to carry out the activities of a given setting?

4. *Understanding or bewilderment.* Note whether a child understands or is bewildered by the expectations of a given area or interest center.

D. Temporality and Flow of Events

1. *Planning.* For whom are individual plans made? Who makes group plans? Who checks whether plans are carried out? Who plans next steps? Who makes schedules for the class?

2. *Flexibility.* What opportunities do children have to carry out a project beyond the scheduled time, to establish their own timetables? Note opportunities for a variety of rhythms in pacing work.

3. *Dailiness.* Note any indicators of regularity of events. What evidence of scheduling for individuals? Small groups? Large groups? Who schedules such events? How are they received by teachers and children?

4. *Infrequent events.* What is the nature of infrequent events? Who plans them? How are they received by teachers and children?

5. *Unanticipated events.* What is the nature of unanticipated events? How are they received by teachers and children?

E. Persons in the Setting

1. *Who.* Who is in the setting? What are the functions or tasks of adults?

Are older or younger children present? For what purpose? Are there children with special needs?

2. *Unexpected persons.* What happens when a person who is not ordinarily part of the setting enters it? For example, what happens when the principal, resource teachers, visitors, parents enter?

F. Communication

1. *Patterns of communication.* Who is communicating with whom? For what purpose? (Note that discussion about ideas is included in B-2). With whom are the children with special needs communicating?
2. *Frequency.* How often do teachers interact with each other? With individual children? With groups of children?
3. *Ways persons communicate.* In what ways do persons communicate? Note body language, written communications, oral communications, directions.
4. *Events and intervention.* What events, scheduled or unscheduled, seem to precipitate teacher intervention? What does a child do immediately following teacher intervention?
5. *Distractions.* What kinds of events or interventions seem to distract children from what they are doing?
6. *Support or encouragement.* Note examples of support or encouragement given by adults or students.
7. *Negative communication.* Note examples of communication that teachers or children use that seem to harm another person.
8. *Content of communication.* What is discussed during the communication process?

G. Other

Teacher Development in Situ

An open setting for learners necessitates conditions in which teachers can show themselves as real, vital, enthusiastic, stimulating, and searching persons. Conditions for teachers can either hinder or foster such qualities. We need to give attention to creating conditions that make teachers the best possible persons that they are and are capable of becoming. What are some of these conditions? Guidelines for Describing Settings for Inservice Teacher Education are found on page 77. The headings parallel the earlier guidelines for students. A brief discussion of each section follows.

A. Overview

Much attention is given to settings for learners, but frequently teachers' needs in terms of their own development are ignored. Settings in which

2. *Interconnecting and interrelating ideas.* Note actual instances when ideas are interconnected, interrelated, or carried over from one subject area, district, classroom, or school to another. Do school personnel use materials earmarked for one type of student with others as well? Do planning procedures vary with different children in the classroom? Do teachers develop ideas used by resource teachers for use with other types of children? Does the leadership personnel make opportunities available for educational personnel within a district to share ideas? Through what vehicles? What opportunities are available for parents and teachers to interconnect and interrelate ideas?

3. *Directions.* How are memos used? From whom or where do they emanate? What percentage are from persons for whom inservice is intended? What percentage are from administrators and supervisors? How are bulletin boards and newsletters used? Who is giving directions in them?

4. *Initiation of ideas.* Who initiates ideas in inservice programs? How are teachers' ideas used? Who establishes the setting so that ideas can be initiated by a number of individuals?

5. *Origin of materials.* Who produces the materials used by teachers? In what ways are teachers encouraged to produce their own materials? What time is given to them to do so? How can commercially produced or central office produced curriculum materials be introduced to teachers? What are teachers' reactions to them? Do teachers produce materials for each other?

C. Use of Space

1. *Proximity.* How does placement of teachers within a school (school system) invite dialogue or opportunites to interrelate ideas? Do centers exist where teachers can find human and material resources?

2. *Compatibility.* Note whether places for inservice are in areas where teachers can be alone, can concentrate, can find human resources with whom to speak. Are "teacher places" set apart so that they are not distracted by the "dailiness" of their classrooms?

3. *Physical energy.* Note the amount of walking the teacher does in the classroom. What other factors within the setting require physical energy? Do teachers seem to possess the energy needed for the tasks? What rearrangements in space might help teachers use less energy?

4. *Understanding or bewilderment.* Do teachers seem bewildered or understanding of expectations of them in given areas? Do they know how to use the various centers established in their classrooms and in spaces developed for their own inservice? Do teachers show competence in the various places they frequent in the course of a day? What factors seem to cause teachers to appear incompetent?

D. Temporality and Flow of Events

1. *Planning.* Who plans inservice for teachers? What part do teachers have in shaping their own inservice programs? How do teachers obtain the necessary information for dealing with special needs of children? To what degree are inservice programs particularized or personalized? To whom do teachers turn when they need help in planning?
2. *Flexibility.* What opportunities do teachers have to establish their own timetables? To work during times of the day congruent with their own "body times"?
3. *Dailiness.* What is regularly scheduled in the day or week of teachers? What opportunities to break out of the routines? What inservice programs are scheduled on a regular basis? Which ones are on an irregular basis?
4. *Unanticipated events.* What is the nature of unanticipated events that influence inservice programs? How are those events seen by teachers?

E. Persons in the Setting

1. *Who.* Who is in the setting? Are persons available who can assist teachers with their various special needs? What kinds of persons are available on a long term basis? On a short term basis?
2. *Unexpected persons.* What happens when an unexpected person enters? How are such persons used? Which persons are seen as "intruders"?

F. Communication

1. *Patterns of communication.* Who is communicating with whom? For what purpose? What types of communication are taking place about children with special needs?
2. *Frequency.* With what degree of frequency do teachers interact with each other? With resource teachers? With principals? With parents?
3. *Ways persons communicate.* In what ways do persons communicate? Note body language. Note written communications such as memos to resource teachers, to principals, etc. Also note communication received by teachers.
4. *Events and intervention.* What events, scheduled or unscheduled, seem to precipitate intervention in the life of a teacher? What does the teacher do immediately following the intervention?
5. *Distractions.* What kinds of events or interventions seem to distract teachers? Seem annoying to teachers?
6. *Support and encouragement.* Note examples of support or encouragement given by teachers to administrators and vice versa, to parents, to other teachers. In other words, who supports whom?
7. *Negative communication.* Note examples of communication which teachers, administrators, etc., use that are harmful to other persons.

teachers learn and grow can be bleak or rich, uncomfortable or inviting, friendly or cold, ideologically rich or barren. Settings can be linked or isolated. What seem to be the outstanding features?

B. Ideological Context

Teachers need opportunities to become excited about the ideological setting in which they live and move. For example, teachers need to interact formally and informally with varieties of persons, such as principals, resource teachers, helping teachers, central office consultants, other teachers; to easily obtain books, audiovisual materials, furniture, equipment; to select from a repertoire of ideas so that they can deal with those substantive areas most appropriate to the learners present; to use procedures and ideas developed for children who have particularized problems; and to develop skill in allowing learners to collaborate in devising directions for classroom management. Teachers need to feel they can initiate ideas that will be used not only in their own classrooms, but also with other teachers and school personnel. They need to create and share materials.

C. Use of Space

If we assume that teachers are vital, live, exciting persons, we then need to help them use space in ways that invite dialogue with varieties of persons. Teachers need centers where they can find human and material resources. They need to find places where they can be alone. They need "retreats" to get away from the dailiness of their own classrooms. Spaces should be available for the restoration of self as well as for the giving of self.

We should arrange spaces so that teachers have the physical energy to carry out their tasks. What rearrangements in space might enable the use of less energy to accomplish similar tasks?

D. Temporality and Flow of Events

If we assume that teachers are responsible and that they wish to do their best for those they teach, then we need to provide time so that they can shape their own inservice programs. Teachers should be able to obtain relatively easily the necessary information for dealing with specialized needs of children; to have available those to whom they can talk when they have problems. Teachers must be free to establish their own timetables so that they can work during parts of the day congruent with their own "body times," so that they are able to break out of the routine, and so that inservice programs are scheduled both on a regular and on an irregular basis. Those programs providing time to deal with the special needs of teachers probably will have more impact than those dealing only with issues deemed important by central office personnel.

E. Persons in the Setting

If we are concerned about teachers being responsible, then we need to be concerned about the persons in the setting. Teachers must have access to others who can help them with special needs, either on a long term or short term basis. Persons who visit infrequently should be seen as possible sources of help and energy rather than as intruders.

F. Communication

If we are concerned about teachers as vital, exciting human beings, then we need to consider patterns of communication. Who is communicating with whom and for what purpose? With what degree of frequency do teachers interact with each other, with resource teachers? How do people communicate? What kinds of things tend to go in memos? What items are received by teachers, from principals, supervisors, etc.? What happens when somebody intervenes in the life of a teacher? Does the teacher display a negative or positive reaction? What kinds of things seem to annoy teachers? What things seem to give teachers support? What kinds of communication seem to irritate teachers?

DESCRIBING SETTINGS FOR INSERVICE TEACHER EDUCATION

Following are some questions or guidelines for describing a setting for inservice education of teachers. Note that the headlines and recommended procedures parallel those of the instrument for students.

A. Overview

1. *Outstanding features.* Observe the setting briefly. Describe the setting for inservice education in terms of its most outstanding features—physical ambience, resource persons, materials, etc.
2. *Description.* Record as objectively as you can all that you see in the setting. You may diagram or describe in narrative form. You may look at an individual room, central office, school, school system.

B. The Ideological Context (including materials, directions for use)

1. *Potential for movement.* What is the potential for moving furniture, equipment, books, audiovisual materials from one part of the setting to another? Note the potential for movement among persons. Do teachers, principals, resource teachers, helping teachers, central office consultants move from one setting to another?

8. *Content of communication.* Note the content of communications. What is included? What is ignored?

G. Other

IMPLICATIONS FOR TEACHER DEVELOPMENT IN SITU

In summary, we have discussed three modes of curriculum development: (a) intent, (b) actualization, and (c) intent, actualization, and retrospect. We developed only the last mode in any detail, since it seemed the most fruitful in terms of valuing diversity in classrooms and of nurturing individual potential. Seeing curriculum development as intent, actualization, and retrospect necessitated a careful look at the qualities we wish to develop in individuals and at settings in which these qualities can emerge. In order to plan carefully, it is important to gather information on site; therefore, we presented instruments that might describe settings both for students and inservice work with teachers, and gave some instruction for their use.

Now, let us assume most teachers have considered the qualities they have tried to develop in students and have gathered information about settings in which the students work. Let us assume also that those responsible for the welfare of teachers have examined where teachers work and have established settings for exploring, questioning, probing, and growing. What are some ways teachers and leadership personnel including building personnel and others responsible for staff development can increase their expertise in curriculum development? Our suggestions (see Table 2) are divided in terms of what teachers can do and what all staff development personnel can do.

TABLE 2

Ways to Increase Expertise in Curriculum Development

Topic	What Teachers Can Do	What Staff Development Personnel Can Do
1. Exploring qualities of the person	1. Attempt to define qualities they feel they should try to develop in their settings.	1. Make available books, resource persons, films that throw fresh insights on the person and encourage discussion of the person.

80

TABLE 2 (Continued)

Ways to Increase Expertise in Curriculum Development

Topic	What Teachers Can Do	What Staff Development Personnel Can Do
2. Developing techniques for recording what happens in settings.	2. Develop new categories in terms of teachers' purposes. Try to use instrument with fellow teacher.	2. Provide materials that encourage teachers to develop fresh categories for observation. Make it possible for teams of teachers to gather information about settings.
3. Sensitizing persons to range of needs in classroom.	3. Try to identify children with special needs.	3. Provide materials—films, texts, resource persons—so that teachers have understanding of persons with special needs.
4. Studying settings and rearranging them in order to accommodate special needs.	4. Study settings and make recommendations about how to make them more serviceable for persons with special needs.	4. Make arrangements for persons to visit settings that accommodate a range of physical and mental abilities and disabilities. Help teachers plan how to use setting so that all can use it well.
5. Developing and sharing ideas.	5. Provide a setting where ideas are exciting, where students have opportunities to develop them,	5. Provide inservice programs where teachers have opportunity to explore and share meaningful ideas

(continued on next page)

81

TABLE 2 (Continued)

Ways to Increase Expertise in Curriculum Development

Topic	What Teachers Can Do	What Staff Development Personnel Can Do
	share them, elaborate on them, communicate them.	with each other and with other knowledgeable, stimulating persons.
6. Developing personal power.	6. Assess one's own strength which seems appropriate to deal with diverse children in classroom. Determine areas where further work is necessary.	6. Provide setting where teachers can come to grips with strengths and limitations, where they have opportunities to show strengths and to develop desired skills.
7. Understanding one's attitudes toward different types of diversity.	7. Discuss with a colleague or record one's feelings about different types of students.	7. Provide settings in which teachers can talk with skilled personnel about feelings toward teaching and individuals within the classroom.
8. Using information gathered through observation to generate hypotheses for testing in classroom.	8. Develop an experimental attitude toward teaching by generating hypotheses as a result of analyzing descriptive information. Test out hypotheses.	8. Provide resource persons skilled in various research procedures to assist teachers in action research.

In conclusion, we believe that school settings can be exciting places where diversity among persons is prized, where teachers learn to perceive richly and fully, where school teams work to generate hypotheses derived from observations, and where all work together to make schooling lively and enriching for all. This can be accomplished when teachers are provided a setting where support is evident, where ideas are prized and probed, and where teachers can receive the help necessary to deal with the complexities of today's schools.

REFERENCES

Berman, L. M., & Roderick, J. A. *Curriculum: Teaching the what, how, and why of living.* Columbus OH: Charles E. Merrill, 1977.

Buber, M. *I and thou* (2nd Ed.). New York: Charles Scribner's Sons, 1958.

Bussis, A. M. Chittenden, E. A., & Amarel, M. *Beyond surface curriculum: An interview study of teachers' undertakings.* Boulder CO: Westview Press, 1976.

Caswell, H. L., & Campbell, D. S. *Curriculum development.* New York: American Book Co., 1935.

Johnson, M., Jr. Definitions and models in curriculum theory. *Educational Theory,* 1967, *17*(2), 127–139.

Lewis, A., & Miel, A. *Supervision for improved instruction.* Belmont CA: Wadsworth Publishing Co.,Inc., 1972.

Morgan, K. Socialization, social models, and the open education movement: Some philosophical considerations. In D. Nyberg (Ed.), *The philosophy of open education.* London: Routledge & Kegan Paul, 1975.

Peters, R. S. *Reason and compassion.* London: Routledge & Kegan Paul, 1973.

Posner, G. J., & Rudnitsky, A. N. *Course design: A guide to curriculum development for teachers.* New York: Longman, 1978.

Rosenshine, B., & Furst, N. The use of direct observation to study teaching. In R. Travers (Ed.), *Second handbook of research on teaching.* Chicago: Rand McNally, 1973.

Ruesch, J. *Knowledge in action: Communication, social operations, and management.* New York: Jason Aronson, 1975.

Troutner, L. F. John Dewey and the existentialist phenomenologist. In D. E. Denton (Ed.), *Existentialism and phenomenology in education.* New York: Teachers College Press, 1974.

Tyler, R. *Basic principles of curriculum and instruction.* Chicago: University of Chicago Press, 1950.

Vandenberg, D. Openness: The pedagogic atmosphere. In D. Nyberg (Ed.), *The philosophy of open education.* London: Routledge & Kegan Paul, 1975.

Verhoeven, C. (M. Foran, Trans.). *The philosophy of wonder.* New York: Macmillan, 1972.

Wright, M. Personal communication, 1979.

Part 3

THE ORGANIZATIONAL DIMENSION

6

Schools as Social Systems: Applying Organizational Development Concepts and Practices to Inservice Education

CHARLES W. CASE

The intent of this chapter is to suggest concepts from social systems analysis and organization development relevant to preparing inservice education leaders. More specifically, applications will be made for those working with school personnel and others to make necessary changes for fulfilling the spirit and intent of Public Law 94-142, The Education of All Handicapped Children Act.

P.L. 94-142 affords an excellent example of a mandated change that requires major adjustments in organizational and individual purposes, processes, interactions, structures, and accomplishments. Not only does it ensure attention to respecting the civil rights of handicapped children and to designing appropriate educational services for them, it also requires interactions among those seeking to accomplish common goals. Business as usual and the continuance of isolated fiefdoms within a school will no longer suffice.

Our underlying assumption will be that organizations are in many ways similar to individual persons: they grow and behave within certain limitations, have differentiating personality characteristics, have parts that must be interdependent if common goals are to be achieved, and must change if they are not to become obsolete.

SOCIAL SYSTEMS ANALYSIS

General Systems Theory, which seeks to look at the complexities of nature in integrated chunks, provides the conceptual framework for this chapter. In recent years, many persons have advocated and designed "system approaches" that are opposite in intent—recommending linear and sequential planning and management and evaluation techniques, rather than interactive and interdependent wholes. Although these linear and sequential approaches may be "neat and clean," they tend to oversimplify the complexities inherent in social systems.

A systems perspective does not restrict us to one set of relationships as the object of investigation. Some general properties, or isomorphisms, that are applicable to any system make it possible for us to switch levels. We can look at a cell, an organ, a family, a community, an ecology, an economy, a school district, a school, or a classroom as a system.

It is possible to analyze the interactions of many related systems as they influence a certain condition. For example, implementation of P.L. 94-142 could be analyzed by interrelating analyses of the federal, state, community, school, and classroom systems. Federal and state levels will focus on issues of policy, law, and finances; community and school levels will include these matters but be more concerned with actual implementation problems.

Certain general system properties that apply to all systems are relevant to our focus here. In a later section, we will posit organizational interventions as being dependent on a comprehensive and goal oriented view of reality. We will see that such properties are essential for both the initial and ongoing diagnosis of an organization or social system, and that a comprehensive diagnosis is imperative for selection of appropriate intervention strategies. Too often, solutions or techniques are chosen before problems have been defined adequately, resulting in treating a symptom rather than a cause.

Historically, elementary schools in the United States have tended to arrange their many parts in *independent* relationships, for instance the self contained classroom. P.L. 94-142 requires *interdependent* planning, implementation, and evaluation involving more persons than just the classroom teacher.

Inputs

A system receives inputs of material, energy, and information from its environment. Schools receive money, mandates, preferences, technology, cultural norms, attitudes, and persons. A school's immediate or *proximal* environment is the next larger system of which it is a part: its school district and community. Although many school districts and communities exhibit similarities, they are subject to differences in inputs and expectations regarding purposes and accomplishments. The school's *distal* environment consists of its state, nation, and beyond, all of which also provide inputs and have expectations regarding the school's output. Often, too, each level of the system has different expectations for the school.

The inputs into the school as an organization are influenced by its purposes or goals (teleology). Not clearly articulating a purpose or failing to

88

adjust purposes to meet changes in the environment can result in differing and conflicting expectations within and without the school. The inputs are further influenced by the formal structure of the organization, which consists of the functions assigned to different job classifications or positions and the relative status of one position to another. The usually unarticulated role structure of the organization also influences the operations through varying perceptions of responsibility and authority. Again the result is a lack of clarity and consensus, or the maintenance of role expectations that may have been appropriate to the past but not to the changing conditions of the present or future.

Outputs

Eventually, outputs emerge from the organization resulting in productivity related to its purpose, levels of morale, and various degrees of integration between individual needs and system needs (Stogdill, 1959). Much organizational research has confirmed the need to give equal attention to matters of accomplishment, employee morale, and orchestration of matches between individuals' needs and those of the organization. If all three are not attended to, all three decline.

Evaluation of outputs occurs in the system's environment, with feedback occurring in a variety of forms. If this feedback is negative and the system ignores it, the environment may provide the same input or less. Through the interaction of the system and its environment, one or both may adapt and modify purposes, inputs, processes, and outputs. If a system is to remain open and growing, a mutual accommodation must be reached between it and other systems involved; if not, it will die (entropy). The relationship between a system and its environment is interactive; each can influence the other. If a system is to continue, change is inevitable.

Boundaries

Systems have boundaries that distinguish them from their environment, regulating the flow of energy, resources, and information between them. Similarly each system has internal boundaries that distinguish its internal parts, components, subgroups, or departments from one another.

Boundaries can be concrete (such as walls, membership cards, lists, map schedules) or subjective and psychological (such as feelings of cohesion, belongingness, territoriality, background, heritage). Moreover, boundaries differ in permeability. Impermeable boundaries close off interaction, thereby restraining initiative and growth. At the other extreme, ambiguity and chaos will result in disorganization and lack of direction. Along with the need for definition, boundaries must have flexibility; they must change as the system and its environment change. P.L. 94-142 seeks changes in the boundaries around classrooms.

89

If a system ceases to change, status equilibrium and death (entropy) occur. A system that continues to change, while remaining balanced and evolutionary, achieves a dynamic or steady state of equilibrium. The system and its environment, thus, are both in a constant process of change; and, if the relationship between the two is healthy, they participate in mutual accommodation and development.

Schools have tended toward the closed system end of the continuum both internally and in their relationships with their communities. Teachers and specialists have tended to provide services to the same child independently of one another. The typical structure of school organization has reinforced this tendency by not demanding interdependent goal setting and task accomplishment.

Given these isomorphisms, we can suggest some propositions applicable to systems in general and open systems in particular (Kuhn, 1974, pp. 32–46):

1. All closed systems are subject to entropy (death) and a loss-differentiation in purpose and function (chaos). The concept of open and closed systems can be viewed as a continuum. Systems at any point in time tend toward one end of the continuum or the other; over time most systems move toward the closed end.

2. A given final state or goal may be reached from different initial conditions and by different routes (concept of equifinality). If the change processes are based on the individuality of the system, different systems can accomplish similar outcomes.

3. Adaptive behavior is behavior of a system and an environment that seeks to maintain a dynamic equilibrium. A system cannot respond unless it has information about the environment and vice versa. Change requires communication.

4. Developmental change is the result of a system's detecting information about the environment (factual judgment), selecting a behavioral response (value judgment), implementing the behavior selected, receiving feedback on the action from the environment, comparing the feedback with the system's goal, and determining the next response or change. Change requires communications and sensitivity and should be continuous.

5. The individual parts of a system and their interactions produce emergent effects greater than their sum. Outcomes are the summation of parts and the interactions among parts.

6. Over time, repeated behaviors and exposures to them have become externalized as values in the form of customary, preferred configurations.

7. The motivation for change originates in a discrepancy perceived to exist between a desirable state or goal and the actual state of affairs as a

result of objective feedback. Such discrepancies tend to be especially apparent at boundary points.

8. The direction and behavior of a system or an individual is influenced by internal teleology, system structure, external and internal interactions, images of reality, knowledge of alternatives, preferences, skills, and feedback. This complexity cannot be ignored if change-interventions are to be selected that are consistent with the individuality of the system.

These definitions, concepts, principles, and propositions undergird the organizational development concepts and practices discussed in the next section.

ORGANIZATIONAL DEVELOPMENT CONCEPTS

The major objectives of organizational development are to improve the effectiveness of the organization or system and to enhance the welfare of its members. Organizational behavior is *learned* behavior, shaped by the actions and experiences of the members of the organization and those served by it. Parenthetically, preservice and inservice programs for educators focus almost exclusively on knowledge and skill requirements for working with a learner or groups of learners. Usually, little attention is given to needs related to helping educators function as members of an organization.

Further, the assumptions that organizations are static and not amenable to growth and development may in fact create the self fulfilling prophesy labeled *bureaucracy*, wherein an organization's primary goal is to serve itself and its survival.

We can see parallels between organizational learning and individual learning. Change at the individual and system levels represents alterations in the way individuals (or groups of individuals) behave as a result of alterations in how they define a situation. A person or a system changes behavior when a current or emerging situation is perceived as being different, requiring different behavior. *Change* can be defined as learning on the part of an individual or a group in response to newly perceived requirements of a given situation, requiring action and altering in the structure and/or functioning of social systems (Zaltman & Duncan, 1977, pp. 9–10). As noted earlier this definition appears most appropriate to the relationship between P.L. 94-142 and the changes required in the behavior of schools and professionals in the school. Mirvis and Berg (1977, pp. 4–5) noted:

Whereas individuals in an organization are the learners because their cognitive structures define and limit the organization's information-processing capabilities and because their behaviors determine and bound the organization's response capabilities, an organization

91

might properly be called a learning system. When designing its actions, the organization draws on the thinking and experiences of its leaders and members, processing and combining them with information gathered from its environment and external knowledge producers.

Organizational change must focus not only on changes in individuals, but also on altered relationships between them and other individuals, the collective perception of a changing reality, consensus on changing purposes, and new arrangements of interaction and interdependency within the organization and between the organization and external systems. One implication for schools seeking to comply with the spirit and intent of P.L. 94-142 is to recognize and identify where the school (system) is now and where it wants to be, and to conceptualize alternatives possible to get from here to there that will achieve a consensus among the staff and community members, along with a willingness to learn the behaviors and skills necessary to implement the changes.

Along with emphasis on feedback, we suggest equal importance be given to the generation of alternative, desirable futures determined individually and collectively. Blending the two sets of information allows an individual or a system to move toward more preferred states while at the same time maintaining enough harmony with the environment to remain a part of the larger system. The emphasis in General Systems Theory and Organizational Development is on the interactive, the complex, change, and purposeful direction.

Change efforts in education are often characterized by a desire to simplify complex realities. The interventions are then directed toward changing a small part of a system; such simplistic attempts have resulted in the failure of many change efforts. Unfortunately, many persons view the failure as having been one of selecting the wrong goal rather than one of conceptualization. Complex change most often requires comprehensive diagnosis and conceptualization, as well as multiple intervention strategies based on the individuality of the system at hand.

In organizational development, we must appreciate error and failure. Healthy, competent persons structure their activities in order to receive the maximum amount of feedback about what is happening in order to detect and respond to errors or new directions; so should healthy organizations.

In the next section, we will focus on the importance of organizational diagnosis conducted on a collective basis and seek to provide an overview of a general sequence for organizational development activities.

P.L. 94-142 is an environmental signal that requires organizational change and new behavior from teachers, other professionals, and parents.

Many of the attempted changes in schools heretofore have been bereft of any comprehensive description of where the school was and where it wanted to go.

ORGANIZATIONAL DIAGNOSIS

In most organizations, the members of the system are often too much a part of it to diagnose it effectively on a comprehensive basis. Internal group approaches tend either to focus on only an immediate task or on interpersonal communications. In both instances, members of an organization tend to describe it only from their individual perspective.

When individuals try to improve their understanding of one another, they are apt to emphasize interpersonal communications alone, with little attention to other variables, such as changing organizational purposes, environmental changes, and need for new patterns of task interdependency. Similarly, when the emphasis is on the development of new skills, the skills most educators select are those needed by the individual to accommodate changes in immediate task requirements; seldom is attention given to skills needed to be an effective member of the organization.

For example, as one listens to the concerns of "regular" classroom teachers regarding mainstreaming, their attention is primarily on how they alone will handle handicapped children in their classroom. Because of their vast organizational experience, they do not conceptualize how they might use other educators to assist them. The organization has taught them to be islands, and they respond to the new requirements from an isolated and lonely perspective.

The reasons for this are multiple. Teachers' professional preparation and subsequent continuing education has tended to focus on the tasks of the individual in relationship to a student or a group of students that are"their" students. Seldom is training provided for the person's role as a member of an organization or for interdependent roles wherein the individual must work with others to accomplish a goal or task. Demands such as those mandated by P.L. 94-142 require such interdependency. If the total system is to grow and develop, we need to consider more variables: new organizational structures, new patterns of interaction, and new ways of working together. The focus of the system must be on the *child* who will be served by many persons, not on the *teacher*.

Experiences with system change processes and the literature on them have demonstrated the need for participation and consensus by those who are to change in order for the change to occur. The organizational development trainer, whether internal or external, should assist the collective membership of the organization to define the system as it now is, become alert to the environmental signals that call for change, generate alternative desirable futures, design ways to get from here to there, and determine the individual knowledge, skill learning, and the ongoing evaluation system needed.*

The primary methods to accomplish these ends include interviews, group sessions, questionnaires, observation; and the examination of written policies, procedures, job descriptions, performance ratings, and indices of achievement and morale. The trainer's role is to generate valid information, help the client make informed and reasonable choices, and to develop internal commitment to these choices. In this interactive process, the trainer summarizes available information and observations and presents the results to the staff for their modification and verification. Additional information is added as the process progresses and is continually presented to the staff for their verification and modification. Over time a consensus and commitment emerges, on both the current state of the organization and future plans.

Some variables to be considered during the diagnostic stage follow:

- What is the climate of the organization? Human resources should be seen as having primacy; people's talents, skills, and motivation are the organization's most important assets.
- What are the decision making practices? Are the decisions made at the right level with all available information?
- Do communications flow effectively upward, downward, and laterally?
- Are the conditions and relationships in the organization encouraging or discouraging of effective work and initiation?
- Is the organization technologically ready? Are equipment and resources up to date, effective, and well maintained?
- Do people at all levels feel they can influence what is going on?
- What is the normative structure of the members and the organization? Are they congruent?
- Is the required change (for example, a law) antithetical to the basic beliefs and values of the members?
- Is there cultural diversity regarding the meaning of space, time, and talk?

IMPLICATIONS FOR P.L. 94-142

Inherent in the previous considerations are a number of implications for the design and implementation of the intents of P.L. 94-142. As stated earlier, full implementation of P.L. 94-142 requires most schools to move from the isolation of the self contained classroom with a single teacher to

---

* Throughout the rest of this chapter, we focus on the role of the organizational development trainer. As discussed later, this role label reflects the merging of two previous roles: the organizational development consultant and the inservice education trainer. Whether the person (or persons) occupying this role is internal or external to the organization is not critical.

an organizational structure wherein a variety of personnel and technological resources are linked with the specific needs of individual handicapped children. To do so necessitates different work arrangements and patterns for teachers, specialists, and students.

The second set of considerations is concerned with the structure of the organization:

- Are the authority relationships defined so each person knows who can make which decisions when and under what conditions?
- Are roles and positions fluid enough to allow the teaming of persons with certain skills to match with problems or opportunities that require multiple knowledge and skill?
- Is human energy harnessed or do barriers exist that block initiative?
- Are the internal and external boundaries of the organization flexible or rigid?
- Is the organization proactive or crisis oriented?
- If certain types of changes are anticipated, what are potential effects on adjacent and interdependent systems?
- Given a particular change (such as P.L. 94-142), what changes are needed in job content, role relationships, communication, and decision making?
- What is the degree of consensus among the members regarding the goals of the organization?
- Is the organization perpetuating functions no longer needed or dysfunctional to the anticipated changes?

The final set of considerations concerns the potential resistances to change.

- Is incompatibility inherent between a particular cultural trait of the members and the anticipated change?
- Is the group quick to reject outsiders?
- How flexible or rigid is the conformity to norms?
- How is conflict handled?
- Does the anticipated change present a threat to the power influence of some?
- What technological barriers are present?
- What is the degree of belief or commitment to the anticipated change?
- Do the members have experience working as a group?

The organizational development trainer will require an extensive period of time to work with individuals and groups to collect their perceptions and develop his or her own perceptions on the same matters, observe the organization in action, and review available written information and data. The consultant will then prepare a description of the organization as it is and conduct group sessions to validate or modify the description in order

95

to achieve a consensus. The trainer will conduct his or her analysis and observations as well as lead the group through a collective process of examination and redesign, using these independent analyses as a source of probing questions to the group and as a base of information to determine areas of needed technical assistance.

DEVELOPMENTAL STRATEGIES

The next phase of activity involves image generalizing or change visualizing: developing a collective commitment to what all would like the organization to be. Possible alternatives can emerge from the data generated in the diagnostic phase; from an examination and analysis of current or emerging demands from the environment (such as P.L. 94-142); input from others external to the system; and the desires, interests, and perceptions of the members of the organization. Alternative scenarios can then be developed, presented, and discussed, until a consensus is achieved—stretching the system considerably beyond where it is presently without reaching so far into the future that it is perceived as a fantasy. Systems, like individuals, can reach but can also be immobilized by what seem to be impossible dreams. The scenarios should contain elements of trends and factors currently visible and others representing desired and valued items. For example, a school staff might opt to implement individualized education programs (IEP's) for *all* students.

A variety of group process techniques, combined with a Delphi process to achieve a series of successive approximations, can facilitate the activities in this phase. The Delphi process or similar processes, which provide for a series of iterations and progressive summaries, insure equality in decision making participation. Such processes also provide a means for successive decisions rather than discussion that may not lead to decisions. Most collective change should be a constant intertwining of processes of rational decision and facilitative communication. Individual growth and organizational growth should occur simultaneously.

At this stage of the process, the organization has a description of where it is and where it wants to be, and of pressing demands. The next activity should be to analyze the discrepancy among these three factors and begin to detail various possible change objectives inherent in the discrepancy, assessing them in terms of their potential impact. An expeditious and effective means by which to accomplish this analysis is for the trainer to draft the change objectives and their potential impact as seen in the description. This draft is submitted to the members for their individual analysis and collective discussion, being redrafted and rediscussed until they reach consensus regarding what shall be done.

Once consensus is achieved on the short term and long term change objectives, the task requirements of each must be analyzed in relationship to the available expertise within the organization. For example, if P.L. 94-142 is the immediate demand signal with the discrepancy between what is and what is desired, required will be new methods of communications, decision making, role definition, interaction-task patterns, linkages with external systems, as well as the often acknowledged additional knowledge and skill training and attitude change needed for instruction.

Most current mainstreaming efforts look primarily at the additional knowledge and skill needed by regular classroom teachers and, sometimes, at new diagnostic teaming arrangements, but rarely at the important organizational considerations suggested here. Again, forms of organizational structure and processes reinforce or constrain certain types of behavior. If new forms of organizational behavior are desired—for example, cooperative task accomplishment rather than single person task accomplishment—it is necessary to redesign the organization accordingly.

INTERVENTION STRATEGIES

This section will briefly describe some commonly used categories of intervention strategies. Generally, the strategies selected for any particular change will depend on the nature of the change objectives selected and the culture of the organization involved. Strategies should be related to the awareness that the members have of the change target, their degree of commitment, perceived need for change, capacity of members to accept and sustain change, resources available, magnitude of the change sought, anticipated level of resistance, and time requirements (Zaltman & Duncan, 1977, p. 90).

The guiding principles for selecting intervention procedures should include integrating rational, social, and political elements into problem solving strategies that emphasize member owned changes. The selection should be guided by commitment to helping the organization learn how to conduct itself as a learning system. Such strategies help members articulate their own theories and examine their own views of the world as well as those of others.

An organizational development effort merges the consultant's knowledge and skills with the insights and experiences of the members. It synthesizes their theories and subjects them to joint inquiry. The strategies selected must be congruent with the problem and the conditions that create the problem; the interventions selected must be inherently consistent with the nature of the change sought. The interventions selected must address the information, technical and social skills, values, and situation demands of the change objective.

The categories of intervention strategies include facilitative, reeducative, persuasive, and power strategies (Zaltman & Duncan, 1977).

Facilitative Strategies

Let us first assume that the members of an organization recognize a problem, are in general agreement that remedial action is necessary, and are open to assistance and willing to engage in self help. When consensus does *not* exist, the organizational development trainer should attempt multiple approaches in order to facilitate the activities of groups with different perspectives. Awareness of the availability of help must exist in sufficient detail and clarity so that the group members know what is available and where and how assistance may be obtained. This clarification should be a responsibility of the trainer. In a school already strongly committed to the goals of P.L. 94-142, but needing additional knowledge and skill for new organizational and teaching behavior, the facilitative strategy would probably be most appropriate.

Implied is involvement of organizational members in the decision processes, thereby increasing the commitment of members to follow through on possible solutions to problems and generating more varied information to use in the problem solving effort. Facilitative strategies assume recognition of a problem and openness to assistance by the members of the organization.

Reeducative Strategies

To rely on the relatively unbiased presentation of fact intended to provide a rational justification for action assumes that humans are rational beings capable of discerning fact and of adjusting their behavior accordingly when facts are presented to them. This strategy may involve the unlearning of something prior to the learning of the new attitude or behavior. Reeducative strategies do not always point to a particular means for engaging in a new or different behavior.

Most feasible when time is not a pressing factor, such strategies are often used in advance of the actual implementation of a change, especially when it is necessary to identify, for potential adopters, the connection between their needs and wants and the advocated change.

Generally, the stronger the commitment (e.g., attitudinal or behavioral compliance) required, the less effective reeducative strategies will be. Cases in point are situations in which factual ambiguity exists, the advocated change is highly ego involving, active opposition is manifest, and the participants do not possess or do not feel they possess the skills or information necessary to assess for themselves information provided by the trainer. Reeducative strategies can be effective in providing a foundation for future action by establishing an awareness of a need for change. In the most common type of reeducative strategy, the survey feedback problem solving change, the members of the organization analyze data collected through questionnaires, define problems, and generate solutions and plans to resolve problems.

Persuasive Strategies

Some attempt to bring about change partly through bias in the way they structure and present a message, by reasoning, urging, and inducement. Persuasive strategies can be based on rational appeal and can reflect facts accurately or be totally false. The lower the degree of commitment to change among the organizational members, the greater the need for persuasive strategies. Commitment can be enhanced by stressing either the possible benefits of change or the costs of not changing.

A persuasive strategy is indicated when the change is risky, not amenable to limited or small scale trial, is technically complex, has a strong potential impact on interpersonal relations, has no clear or highly salient relative advantage, or originates from a poorly regarded source.

Power Strategies

Use of coercion to obtain compliance takes the form of manipulation or threat of manipulation of the organization's or members' outcomes. The members usually are dependent on the change agent for satisfaction of their goals. The strength of power is related to degree of dependency, which is a function of: (a) the goals controlled by the change agent and the members' motivational investment in those goals, (b) the availability of alternatives to satisfy members' goals, and (c) the cost of alternative modes of goal attainment.

A power strategy will be ineffective if the client group does not have the requisite resources for adopting the change, and the change agency cannot provide them. As an example, many in education perceive legal mandates for change without necessary resource allocations for staff retraining. A power strategy can be effective when various individuals or groups may be favorably disposed to change but one person or group is acting as a barrier. More and more, the courts are being used as a power mechanism to achieve changes under these conditions.

Multiple Strategies

The use of multiple strategies is called for in many change situations. The introduction of a change may begin primarily with a reeducative strategy aimed at those persons most prone to adopting innovations early. As the innovation diffuses among those groups, a more persuasive strategy may be appropriate for the more difficult or less change oriented groups. Independent of which strategy or group is of focal concern at any one time, it may be desirable to pursue next a facilitative strategy, making the innovation more readily available and easier to use.

It is necessary to program the mix and use of strategies. Should a strategy of least resistance or greatest resistance be followed? Should the trainer focus first on those most difficult to change? Should the members of the organization be subdivided into groups that might benefit from differentiated strategies? Is the group committed enough to respond from a rational basis, or will feelings and attitudes need to be attended to first?

Finally, here are additional caveats with regard to the selection of intervention strategies: contrary to popular belief, the physical sciences do not wait for complete verification, but many facts and techniques from education and the social sciences are available and seem to be effective despite little empirical proof.

Common pitfalls occur in many change efforts. Some efforts are too strong on a rationalistic, technocratic, or individual basis. Often the change goals and problems are poorly defined. The data and information sources must rely not only on the intragroup behavior, attitudes, and interpersonal relationships of the members of an organization, but must also take into account intersystem relationships and the systemic properties of the target organization and its environment. Implementation of P.L. 94-142 will usually require readiness in the community as well as in the school. Either separately or collectively with the school, the community should have opportunity to participate in the change process in order to examine their beliefs and feelings and to learn new skills that will facilitate meaningful implementation.

Expectations should be built on reasonable probabilities. Time and effort must be taken to secure an overt commitment from all parties to the change goals. The resources that provide organizational development services should be noncompetitive and supportive of one another. While multiple strategies may be necessary, it is crucial that the strategies be consistent with the goals and not contradict each other. Having a representative steering group may help ensure the continuity and appropriateness of the process over time. Packaged interventions should be avoided; the intervention process should be an outgrowth of the agreed on diagnosis and goals, and be consistent with the individuality of the specific organization. The evaluation process should be continuous with numerous checkpoints, so that changes in the process occur when needed.

IMPACT OF P.L. 94-142

P.L. 94-142 demands major organizational changes if the spirit and intent of the law are to be fulfilled. New interaction is required, not only among teachers, administrators, and special educators, but also among transportation personnel, speech pathologists, psychologists, physical and occupational therapists, medical and counseling personnel, recreation personnel, and parents. These groups, which by and large have operated apart from one another, must now operate as team members, each contributing expertise and energy to a common cause, and preferably without power plays or status hang ups. Characteristically, the use of multidisciplinary teams to implement P.L. 94-142 has most often ignored the need to provide the professionals involved with team building experiences. Tasks, responsibilities, and accountability must be reflected in work patterns wherein individuals cannot complete their responsibility without using the expertise and cooperation of others; interdependence should be structured by new decision making, planning, and evaluation procedures that require cooperation.

Preparation, implementation, and evaluation of individualized education programs (IEP's) call for knowledge and skill that do not currently exist in great abundance. Again, properly done, the IEP requires the expertise of many roles, cooperative team behavior, and accountability. It will not suffice for the teacher or any other individual alone to prepare a plan that requires the understanding and commitment by many to achieve its purposes.

The procedural safeguards section of P.L. 94-142 has already affected the organizational structure and practices of schools, not always with the most favorable outcomes. Too often the interaction patterns called for by the law are inserted into a school whose normal interaction patterns, organizational structure, and normative system are antithetical to the intent of due process.

The final major impact of the law on the school is in the needed changes in attitude and belief of the members as regards handicapped persons. The prevalent covert and overt fear, ignorance, and hostility will not be changed by 1 hour inservice education lectures; a more comprehensive process is required.

KNOWLEDGE AND SKILL IMPLICATIONS FOR TRAINERS

Increasingly, the roles of organizational development consultant and educational trainer are moving toward one another. For many years, the former focused primarily on organizational changes, seeking to increase the productivity and the morale of members of an organization, or on the interpersonal communications of its subgroups. Educational trainers focused primarily on designing and implementing educational programs to increase specific knowledge or skill levels to achieve particular individual or organizational purposes. Recent publications in organizational development now stress the concept of the organization as a learner and the relationship to organizational change, planning, growth, and development. Recent literature in educational training includes some incorporation of organizational development techniques into its methods and a greater realization of the effect of organizational variables on individual learning, growth, and development.

The remainder of this chapter will suggest probable relevant knowledge and skill needed by organizational development trainers (a merging of the two historical roles). We will sort our discussion and suggestions into three categories: conceptual skills, technical skills, and human skills.

101

Conceptual Skills

This chapter has emphasized the importance of General Systems Theory and models of organizational development as a guiding conceptual framework for organizational change. In preparing persons to become organizational development trainers, direct instruction and experience in applying these models are essential. Trainers should also be able to communicate these models in oral and written form to a variety of potential users. In addition, they should understand theories of organizational behavior, adult growth and development, change, learning, motivation, cultural diversity, and ethics.

Technical Skills

Among the technical skills that have been identified or implied in this chapter are research and evaluation skills, including a knowledge of measurement, its techniques, assumptions, and limitations. Also needed are sampling techniques, statistical ability, and instrument design abilities, as well as processes of participant observation, questionnaire design, and interviewing.

Additional skills are called for in the areas of supervision, motivation, and staff development techniques. To provide leadership for team building and to construct tasks that require collaborative behavior also require teaching ability, so that the trainers can not only help others through the organizational development process, but also teach those involved in the process the same skills.

Trainers can learn to assess the various dimensions of organizational health: goal focus, communications patterns, use of resources, cohesiveness, morale, autonomy, and adaptiveness. They should also be able to diagnose organizational and change problems, identify and work around constraints, and select intervention strategies appropriate to the task.

Political finesse is essential so that the trainers can promote change that involves the active cooperation of others. The trainers must be able to identify concerns of various constituencies involved in a change, package the change in terms that address those concerns, and be sensitive to situational undercurrents and tensions. They must know how to deal with resistance and conflict, differing perceptions, and to anticipate sources of resistance and be supportive and appreciative of each individual's worth.

As communicators, trainers should have oral and written language abilities to convert information into a variety of usable forms. They must also serve as fact finders, with ability to identify resources and link them with those who need information.

The final technical skill is in the area of administrative ability. Trainers must organize and attend to detail. Familiarity with organizational policies and procedures can assist in avoiding unnecessary conflicts and delays.

Planning skills, both process oriented and technique oriented, are crucial to many of the trainers' responsibilities and activities.

Human Skills

Trainers' group and interpersonal skills should be viewed not as ends in themselves but as means, in order to make knowledge and processes available in a supportive rather than a demeaning manner. The transparent behavior of "professional groupies" becomes self serving rather than client serving. Trainers should be able to express and explore anxiety.

Desired personal traits of trainers are openness, honesty, ethical behavior, self confidence, and willingness to take risks. Finally, it is critical that they have poise and backbone in the face of resistance and opposition.

Because the individuals training for these roles will enter with a variety of previous experiences and training, a careful assessment should be made of what areas of knowledge and skill they already possess. Programs should then be designed to reinforce or update the knowledge and skill areas already in possession, provide appropriate learning experiences not in a person's command, and provide supervised experiences in organizational development. The supervised experiences might first occur in a team arrangement with another organizational development trainer, and later on a solo basis.

REFERENCES

Kuhn, A. *The logic of social systems*. San Francisco: Jossey-Bass, 1974.

Mirvis, P. H., & Berg, D. N. (Eds.). *Failures in organizational development and change: Cases and essays for learning*. New York: John Wiley & Sons, 1977.

Stogdill, R. M. *Individual behavior and group achievement*. New York: Oxford University Press, 1959.

Zaltman, G., & Duncan, R. *Strategies for planned change*. New York: John Wiley & Sons, 1977.

7

The Classroom as a Social System: Classroom Learning, Structure, and Mainstreaming

DAVID W. JOHNSON
ROGER T. JOHNSON

The purpose of this chapter is to present a brief overview of the classroom as a social system and to answer two questions concerning school based teacher education for effective mainstreaming:

1. In *what* should special education and regular classroom teachers be trained so that mainstreaming has constructive consequences?
2. *How* should special education and regular classroom teachers be trained so that mainstreaming has constructive consequences?

In answer to the first question, we shall discuss the importance of peer relationships for maximal achievement and healthy social development, the creation of positive interdependence among students so that constructive peer relationships are developed and maintained, and the processes of acceptance and rejection that take place when handicapped students are mainstreamed into the regular classroom. In answer to the second question, we shall discuss how positive interdependence can be created between special education and regular classroom teachers during inservice training programs and in their functioning in the mainstreamed classroom.

THE CLASSROOM AS A SOCIAL SYSTEM

What happens within the classroom determines whether mainstreaming results in constructive or destructive outcomes for both handicapped and nonhandicapped students. And it is the regular classroom teachers and special education teachers who largely determine what happens within the classroom in regard to mainstreaming. Whether or not constructive relationships are developed between handicapped and nonhandicapped students depends on the student interdependence that the teachers structure within learning situations. How well regular classroom and special education teachers coordinate their instructional efforts depends largely on whether or not a positive goal and resource interdependence were created during their school based training for mainstreaming, and on how well that interdependence is continued in their collaboration on mainstreaming. In order to discuss mainstreaming from the point of view of the students and the teachers, we need to review briefly the nature of the classroom and school as a social system.

Like all other social systems, the classroom is made up of a network of interpersonal relationships structured to facilitate the achievement of established goals (Johnson, 1979). The classroom can be described as an open system consisting of inputs, a transformational process, and outputs. Its *inputs* consist of students and teachers and other school personnel, materials, information, etc., used to transform students into outputs of more socialized, skilled, trained, and healthy individuals who will enter other classrooms the following year.

In order to *transform* students successfully, the classroom must have:

1. Clear, cooperative goals that teachers are committed to achieve.
2. A network of interpersonal relationships structured by role definitions and norms that define appropriate behavior.
3. Technologies consisting of knowledge about the performance of instructional and organizational tasks and activities that include teaching strategies, curriculum materials, collaborative skills, and so forth.
4. A management process that integrates human and material resources into a total system for achieving the school's goals.

The basic dynamics of the classroom, therefore, are that educational goals are achieved through structured interpersonal relationships and the use of the technology of instruction under the supervision of a manager. The social structure of the classroom determines how students interact with each other and the teacher(s), and these interaction patterns determine what cognitive and affective outcomes result from instruction and general classroom life. Teachers control the structure of the classroom's goals, and the goal structure defines the roles and norms which, in turn, determine student-student, student-teacher, and teacher-teacher interaction patterns. These interpersonal interaction patterns largely determine whether the classroom goals are achieved.

SCHOOLS AS ORGANIZATIONS

Several unique characteristics of schools as organizations enable classroom teachers to make marked changes in their own instructional practices whenever they want and to resist changes that other school personnel, parents, or the community may seek to force on them (Johnson, 1979).

First, the goals of the school (and to a large extent of the classroom) are ambiguous and immeasurable. Although instruction clearly should affect acquisition of verbal information, intellectual skills, cognitive strategies, motor skills, attitudes and values, general socialization, and cognitive and social development, it is often difficult to pinpoint the relative importance of the multitude of educational goals at any one time and the hour by hour actions a teacher should engage in to promote the achievement of the goals. Ambiguous goals lead to ambiguous role definitions and an inability to measure goal achievement.

The second unique organizational characteristic is a relatively low degree of division of labor. Teachers generally teach alone in both elementary and secondary schools. What is taught in the first period of the day does not directly influence what students do during the second period. In most schools, the failure of one teacher to perform competently during a given class period does not directly affect the behavior of any other teacher.

Third, along with the unclear division of labor, comparatively little attention is paid to integrating the different role activities within a school. No one teacher has to integrate his or her actions with those of other teachers, counselors, administrators, clerks, custodians, special education teachers, and other school personnel on an hour by hour or even a day to day basis. Role integration is largely dependent on the overall curriculum and the sequential properties of textbook series.

The fourth organizational characteristic of schools is that the role behavior of any teacher is relatively invisible to other school personnel. It is unusual for other teachers, administrators, counselors, and other staff to know exactly what takes place within any given teacher's classroom.

And fifth, economic and status rewards are commonly given on the basis of criteria other than actual quality of teaching or administrating. Seniority, amount of formal education, and other factors are the basis for salary raises and promotions—not the documented competence in doing one's job. Lacking are economic incentives for actually improving one's competence in doing one's job and accountability for errors and incompetence.

Sixth, the value placed on autonomy means that schools operate independently of one another, promoting inflexibility and restricted communication flow.

Seventh, the school is a tax supported monopoly and, therefore, not pressed to develop new and more effective procedures and methods.

Eighth, because schools are publicly financed, they are vulnerable to control and pressure by communities.

Ninth, communication is often inadequate among teachers and between teachers and other school personnel, especially concerning professional matters.

107

Finally, schools tend to be inbred with administrative positions being staffed by teachers and career veterans, resulting in upper management being composed of people with similar experiences and points of view.

The unique organizational characteristics of classrooms and schools as social systems have large effects on the potential collaboration between special education and regular classroom teachers to promote effective mainstreaming. And the unique organizational characteristics of the classroom greatly affect whether school based teacher training on mainstreaming is a success or a failure. Before dealing specifically with how teachers should be trained to ensure that mainstreaming is effective, we shall first discuss what the content of school based teacher training on mainstreaming should be.

THE IMPORTANCE OF CONSTRUCTIVE PEER RELATIONSHIPS

Experience with peers is not a superficial luxury to be enjoyed by some students and not by others. Student-student relationships are an absolute necessity for maximal achievement and for healthy cognitive and social development. In fact, social interactions with peers may be the primary relationships within which development and socialization take place (Lewis & Rosenblum, 1975). Handicapped students especially need access to highly motivated peers who encourage educational aspirations, achievement, and appropriate social behavior. And it is through nonhandicapped peers that handicapped students gain access to normal life experiences of members of our society, such as going to parties and dances, taking buses, dating, shopping, and so forth.

While the importance of adult-child relations on socialization and development is often emphasized (especially with handicapped students), much less attention has been given to the child's acquisition of competence in encounters with other children and to the child's occupation of a comfortable niche within the peer culture. Peer relationships have contributed in many ways to the cognitive and social development and general socialization of children and adolescents, such as:

1. Contributing to the socialization of values, attitudes, competencies, and ways of perceiving the world.
2. Being prognostic indicators of future psychological health.
3. Providing the context in which children learn to master impulses such as aggression and sex.
4. Helping to develop sex role identity.
5. Contributing to the emergence of perspective taking abilities.
6. Influencing educational aspirations and achievement. (For specific references, see Johnson, 1980 and Hartup, 1978).

108

If peer relationships are to be constructive influences, however, they must promote feelings of belonging, acceptance, support, and caring. The more accepting the peer relationships, the more children and adolescents are willing to engage in social interaction, provide positive social rewards for peers, use their abilities in achievement situations, and behave appropriately in the classroom (Johnson, 1980).

As we will discuss in more detail later, simply placing students in physical proximity to each other does not mean that constructive interaction will take place. To build constructive peer relationships characterized by acceptance and support, students must interact with each other within a context of positive goal interdependence. The major focus of school based teacher education on mainstreaming should be on how to structure positive goal interdependence between handicapped and nonhandicapped students.

PROMOTING CONSTRUCTIVE STUDENT INTERACTION THROUGH GOAL STRUCTURES

During instruction, teachers may structure their approaches to goal interdependence (Deutsch, 1962; Johnson & Johnson, 1975): cooperative (positive), competitive (negative), and individualistic (no goal interdependence). A *cooperative* goal structure exists when students perceive that they can obtain a goal only if the other students with whom they are linked obtain their goals. A *competitive* goal structure exists when students perceive that they can obtain a goal only if the other students with whom they are linked fail to obtain their goals. An *individualistic* goal structure exists when students perceive that their obtaining a goal is unrelated to the goal achievement of other students.

In the ideal classroom, all three goal structures would be appropriately used. All students would learn how to work cooperatively with other students, compete for fun and enjoyment, and work autonomously. Most of the time, students would work on instructional tasks within the goal structure that is most productive for the type of task to be done and for the cognitive and affective outcomes desired.

Teachers decide which goal structure to implement within each instructional activity. The way they structure learning goals determines how students interact with each other and with them. Interaction patterns, in turn, determine the cognitive and affective outcomes of instruction. No aspect of teaching is more important than the appropriate use of goal structures.

Student Interaction

Each goal structure will promote a different pattern of interaction among students. Aspects of student interaction important for learning are accurate communication and exchange of information, facilitation of each other's efforts to achieve, constructive conflict management, peer pressures toward achievement, decreased fear of failure, divergent thinking, acceptance and support by peers, use of other's resources, trust, and emotional involvement in and commitment to learning (Johnson & Johnson, 1975).

A summary of the research findings on the relationships between the three goal structures and these aspects of student interaction is presented in Table 1 (for specific references, see Johnson & Johnson, 1975, 1978). Cooperation provides opportunities for positive interaction among students; on the other hand, competition promotes cautious and defensive student

TABLE 1

Goal Structures and Interpersonal Processes Affecting Learning

Cooperation	Competition	Individualization
High interaction	Low interaction	No interaction
Effective communication	No, misleading, or threatening communication	No interaction
Facilitation of other's achievement: helping, sharing, tutoring	Obstruction of other's achievement	No interaction
Peer influence towards achievement	Peer influence against achievement	No interaction
Problem solving conflict management	Win-lose conflict management	No interaction
High divergent and risk taking thinking	Low divergent and risk taking thinking	No interaction
High trust	Low trust	No interaction
High acceptance and support by peers	Low acceptance and support by peers	No interaction
High emotional involvement in and commitment to learning by almost all students	High emotional involvement in and commitment to learning by the few students who have a chance to win	No interaction
High use of resources of other students	No use of resources of other students	No interaction
Division of labor possible	Division of labor impossible	No interaction
Decreased fear of failure	Increased fear of failure	No interaction

interaction (except under very limited conditions). When students are in an individualistic goal structure, they work by themselves to master the skill or knowledge assigned, without interacting with other students. When teachers wish to promote positive interaction among students, a cooperative goal structure should be used, and competitive and individualistic goal structures should be avoided.

Of special importance for students' influencing each other in regard to achievement, appropriate social behavior, cognitive and social development, and general socialization is the degree to which each goal structure affects the students: (a) perceptions that they are accepted, supported, and liked by their peers, (b) exchange of information, (c) motivation to learn, and (d) emotional involvement in learning.

Acceptance, Support, Liking

Cooperative learning experiences, as compared with competitive and individualistic ones, have been found to result in stronger beliefs that one is liked, supported, and accepted by other students, and that other students care about how much one learns and want to help one learn (Cooper, Johnson, Johnson, & Wilderson, 1980; Gunderson & Johnson, 1980; Johnson, Johnson, & Tauer, 1979; Johnson, Johnson, Johnson, & Anderson, 1976; Tjosvold, Marino, & Johnson, 1977). Cooperative attitudes are related to believing that one is liked by other students and wanting to listen, to help, and do schoolwork with other students (Johnson & Ahlgren, 1976; Johnson, Johnson, & Johnson, 1978).

Individualistic attitudes are related to *not* wanting to do schoolwork with other students, to help other students learn, and to participate in social interaction and with *not* valuing being liked by other students (Johnson, Johnson, & Anderson, 1978; Johnson & Norem-Hebeisen, 1977). Furthermore, Deutsch (1962) and other researchers (Johnson, 1974) found that trust is built through cooperative interaction and destroyed through competitive interaction.

Exchange of Information

The seeking of information and using it in one's learning are essential for academic achievement. In problem solving situations, students working within a cooperative goal structure will *seek* significantly more information from each other than will students working within a competitive goal structure (Crawford & Haaland, 1972). Students working within a cooperative goal structure will make optimal use of the information provided by other students, while students working within a competitive goal structure will fail to do so (Laughlin & McGlynn, 1967). Blake and Mouton (1961) provided evidence that competition biases a person's perceptions and comprehension of other individuals' viewpoints.

A cooperative context, compared with a competitive one, promotes more accurate communication of information, more verbalization of ideas and information, more attentiveness to others' statements, more acceptance of and willingness to be influenced by others's ideas and information, fewer difficulties in communicating with and understanding others, more confidence in one's own ideas and in the value that others attach to one's ideas, more frequent communication, more open and honest communication, and greater feelings of agreement between oneself and others (Johnson, 1974; Johnson & Johnson, 1975).

Motivation

Motivation is most commonly viewed as a combination of perceived likelihood of success and the perceived incentive for success. The greater the likelihood of success and the more important it is to succeed, the higher the motivation. Success that is intrinsically rewarding is usually seen as being more desirable for learning than having students believe that only extrinsic rewards are worthwhile. Success is perceived as more likely and more important in a cooperative than in a competitive or individualistic learning situation (Johnson & Johnson, 1975).

The more cooperative the students' attitudes, the more they see themselves as being intrinsically motivated. The more, too, they will persevere in pursuit of clearly defined learning goals, believing that their own efforts determine their school success, wanting to be good students and get good grades, and believing that ideas, feelings, and learning new ideas are important and positive (Johnson & Ahlgren, 1976; Johnson, Johnson, & Anderson, 1978). These studies also indicate that the more competitive the students' attitudes, the more they see themselves as being extrinsically motivated in elementary and junior high schools. Competitive attitudes are somewhat related to intrinsic motivation, to being a good student, and to getting good marks in senior high school.

Individualistic attitudes tend to be unrelated to all measured aspects of motivation to learn. Being part of a cooperative learning group has been found to be related to a high subjective probability of academic success and continuing motivation for further learning by taking more advanced courses in the subject studied (Gunderson & Johnson, 1980). Experimental evidence also indicates that cooperative learning experiences, compared with individualistic ones, will result in more intrinsic motivation, less extrinsic motivation, and less need for teachers to set clear goals for the students (Johnson, Johnson, Johnson, & Anderson, 1976).

Emotional Involvement in Learning

Students are expected to become involved in instructional activities and benefit from them as much as they can. The more cooperative the students'

112

attitudes, the more they see themselves as expressing their ideas and feelings in large and small classes and as listening to the teacher, while competitive and individualistic attitudes are unrelated to indices of emotional involvement in instructional activities (Johnson & Ahlgren, 1976; Johnson, Johnson, & Anderson, 1978).

Cooperative learning experiences, compared with competitive and individualistic ones, result in greater liking for talking to the class about one's ideas (Johnson, Johnson, Johnson, & Anderson, 1976; Wheeler & Ryan, 1973). Cooperative learning experiences also promote greater willingness to present one's answers and the instructional experience (Garibaldi, 1976; Gunderson & Johnson, 1980), as well as more positive attitudes toward the instructional tasks and subject areas (Garibaldi, 1976; Gunderson & Johnson, 1980; R. Johnson & Johnson, 1979; Johnson, Johnson, & Skon, 1979; Wheeler & Ryan, 1973).

INSTRUCTIONAL OUTCOMES

Many researchers have studied the relationship between cooperative, competitive, and individualistic efforts and the cognitive and affective outcomes of instruction (see, e.g., Johnson & Johnson, 1975, 1978). According to the hundreds of research studies that have been conducted, dramatically different learning outcomes will result from the use of the different goal structures. While space is too short in this chapter to review all of the research, we will discuss the evidence concerning achievement, perspective taking, self esteem, psychological health, liking for other students, and positive attitudes toward school personnel such as teachers and principals.

Achievement

The successful mastery, retention, and transfer of concepts, roles, and principles is higher in cooperatively structured learning than in competitive or individualistic learning (Davis, Laughlin, & Komorita, 1976; Johnson & Johnson, 1975, 1978; Laughlin, 1978). Laughlin and his associates have conducted a series of experiments demonstrating the superiority of cooperative pairs over individuals in concept attainment for a variety of conceptual roles, task difficulty conditions, and interaction formats. Members of cooperative groups evolve superior strategies for conceptual learning, seek and use other's information more effectively, cognitively rehearse and formulate, in their own words, the material being learned, and cover more material in a shorter period of time (Johnson, 1979; Johnson & Johnson, 1975, 1978).

A series of studies using a variety of classroom learning tasks found that on mathematical and verbal drill-review, spatial reasoning and verbal problem solving, pictorial and verbal sequencing, and in tasks involving the comparison of attributes of shape, size, and pattern, or retention of

113

facts, and categorization and retrieval tasks, cooperative learning experiences promoted higher achievement than did either competitive or individualistic learning experiences (Garibaldi, 1976; Johnson, Johnson, & Skon, 1979; Johnson, Skon, & Johnson, 1980; R. Johnson & Johnson, 1979). For simple, mechanical, previously mastered tasks that require no help from other students and that are timed for speed, some (but inconsistent) evidence indicates that competition promotes greater quantity of output than do cooperative or individualistic efforts (Johnson & Johnson, 1975).

Laughlin, Keer, Davis, Haiff, and Marciniak (1975) found that when no member of a group knew the correct answer to a problem, the group would still figure it out about 20 % of the time, indicating that the quality of the group discussion can affect the successful solution of problems even when member expertise is low. Such outcomes do not result in competitive and individualistic situations.

Perspective Taking

An important instructional question is which goal structure is most conducive to promoting the emergence of social perspective taking abilities. A series of studies have found that cooperativeness is positively related to the ability to take the emotional perspective of others and that competitiveness is related to egocentrism (Johnson, 1975a, 1975b, Barnett, Matthews, & Howard, in press). Cooperative learning experiences, furthermore, have been found to promote greater cognitive and emotional perspective taking abilities than either competitive or individualistic learning experiences (Bridgeman, 1977; Johnson, Johnson, Johnson, & Anderson, 1976).

Self Esteem

Schools are concerned with promoting student self esteem for a variety of reasons, including school and postschool achievement and general psychological health and well being. Correlational evidence shows that cooperativeness is positively related to self esteem in students throughout elementary, junior, and senior high school in rural, urban, and suburban settings; competitiveness is generally unrelated to self esteem; and individualistic attitudes tend to be related to feelings of worthlessness and self rejection (Gunderson & Johnson, 1980; Johnson & Ahlgren, 1976; Johnson, Johnson, & Anderson, 1978; Johnson & Norem-Hebeisen, 1977; Norem-Hebeisen & Johnson, 1980).

Experimental evidence indicates that cooperative learning experiences, compared with individualistic ones, result in higher self esteem (Johnson, Johnson, & Scott, 1978), that cooperative learning experiences promote higher self esteem than does learning in a traditional classroom (Blaney, Stephan, Rosenfield, Aronson, & Sikes, 1977; Geffner, 1978), and that failure in competitive situations promotes increased self derogation (Ames, Ames & Felker, 1977).

In a series of studies with suburban junior and senior high students, Norem-Hebeisen and Johnson (1980) examined the relationship between cooperative, competitive, and individualistic attitudes and ways of conceptualizing one's worth from information available about oneself. Four primary ways of deriving self esteem are:

1. Basic self acceptance (a belief in the intrinsic acceptability of oneself).
2. Conditional self acceptance (acceptance contingent on meeting external standards and expectations).
3. Self evaluation (one's estimate of how one compares with one's peers).
4. Real-ideal congruence (correspondence between what one thinks one is and what one thinks one should be).

Attitudes toward cooperation are related to basic self acceptance and positive self evaluation compared to peers, attitudes toward competition are related to conditional self acceptance, and individualistic attitudes are related to basic self rejection.

Psychological Health

The ability to build and maintain cooperative relationships is a primary manifestation of psychological health. Johnson and Norem-Hebeisen (1977) compared the attitudes of high school seniors toward cooperation, competition, and individualism with their responses on the Minnesota Multiphasic Personality Inventory. They found that attitudes toward cooperation were significantly negatively correlated with 9 of the 10 scales indicating psychological pathology. Attitudes toward competition were significantly negatively correlated with 7 of the 10 psychological pathology scales. Attitudes toward individualism were significantly positively related to 9 of the 10 pathology scales.

Since both cooperation and competition involve relationships with other people, while individualistic activities involve isolation from other people, these findings indicate that an emphasis on cooperative involvement with other people and on appropriate competition during socialization may promote psychological health and well being; social isolation, however, may promote psychological illness.

In addition, cooperative attitudes were significantly positively related to emotional maturity, well adjusted social relations, strong personal identity, the ability to resolve conflicts between self perceptions and adverse information about oneself, amount of social participation, and basic trust and optimism. Attitudes toward competition were significantly related to emotional maturity, lack of a need for affection, the ability to resolve conflicts between self perceptions and adverse information about oneself, social participation, and basic trust and optimism. Individualistic attitudes were significantly related to delinquency, emotional immaturity, social maladjustment, self alienation, inability to resolve conflicts between self perceptions

115

and adverse information about oneself, social participation, and basic trust and optimism. Individualistic attitudes were significantly related to delinquency, emotional immaturity, social maladjustment, self alienation, inability to resolve conflicts between self perceptions and adverse information about oneself, self rejection, lack of social participation, and basic distrust and pessimism.

Liking for Other Students

Cooperative experiences, compared with competitive and individualistic ones, result in more positive interpersonal relationships characterized by mutual liking, positive attitudes toward each other, mutual concern, friendliness, attentiveness, feelings of obligation to other students, and desire to win the respect of other students (Johnson & Johnson, 1975, 1978). We also have evidence that cooperative learning experiences promote more positive attitudes toward heterogeneity among peers (Johnson, Johnson, & Scott, 1978), and that cooperativeness is related to liking peers who are smarter or less smart than oneself (Johnson & Ahlgren, 1976; Johnson, Johnson, & Anderson, 1978).

Studies involving students from different ethnic groups, handicapped and nonhandicapped students, and male and female junior high school students indicate that cooperative learning experiences promote more positive attitudes among heterogeneous students (Armstrong, Johnson, & Balow, 1980; Cook, 1978; Cooper, Johnson, Johnson, & Wilderson, 1980; DeVries & Slavin, 1978; Johnson, Rynders, Johnson, Schmidt, & Haider, 1979; Rynders, Johnson, Johnson, & Schmidt, 1980; Slavin, 1978).

Liking for School Personnel

The more favorable the students' attitudes toward cooperation, the more they believe that teachers, teacher aides, counselors, and principals are important and positive; that teachers care about and want to increase students' learning; that teachers like and accept students as individuals; and that teachers and principals want to be friends with students (Gunderson & Johnson, 1980; Johnson & Ahlgren, 1976; Johnson, Johnson, & Anderson, 1978). These findings hold in elementary, junior high, and senior high schools in rural, suburban, and urban school districts.

In suburban junior and senior high schools, student competitiveness becomes positively related to perceptions of being liked and supported personally and academically by teachers. Individualistic attitudes are consistently unrelated to attitudes toward school personnel.

Several field experimental studies also demonstrate that students experiencing cooperative instruction like the teacher better and perceive the teacher as being more supportive and accepting, academically and personally, than do students experiencing competitive and individualistic instruction (Gunderson & Johnson, 1980; Johnson, Johnson, Johnson, & Anderson, 1976; Johnson, Johnson, & Scott, 1978; Johnson, Johnson, & Tauer, 1979; Tjosvold, Marino, & Johnson, 1977; Wheeler & Ryan, 1973).

Summary

Perhaps the most important aspect of instruction a teacher can control is the way learning goals are structured. The structure of learning goals controls how students interact with each other, which in turn greatly affects the cognitive and affective outcomes of instruction. When teachers wish to promote positive interaction among students (characterized by peer acceptance, support, and liking; student exchange of information; motivation to learn; and emotional involvement in learning), a cooperative goal structure should be used and competitive and individualistic goal structures should be deemphasized. The emphasis on positive goal interdependence among students will not only create the supportive, accepting, and caring relationships vital for socialization; it will also promote achievement, perspective taking ability, self esteem, psychological health, liking for peers, and positive attitudes toward school personnel.

MAINSTREAMING

The constructive peer relationships so necessary for maximal achievement and healthy cognitive and social development are promoted when teachers structure students' learning goals cooperatively. A major question when handicapped students are mainstreamed into the regular classroom, however, is whether or not the special education students will be accepted by their nonhandicapped classmates. When handicapped students are first mainstreamed, they may be anxious and fearful concerning how they will be treated by the regular classroom students; the nonhandicapped students may have stigmatized views of their handicapped peers. How teachers structure the interaction between handicapped and nonhandicapped students may have considerable impact on these attitudes.

Attitudes Toward Handicapped Peers

Underlying the movement to integrate handicapped students into the regular classroom are the assumptions that labeling will be reduced when handicapped students are not physically separated from the regular classroom (Flynn, 1974), the stigma attached to handicaps will be reduced (Dunn, 1968), negative stereotyping will be diminished through increased

117

contact between handicapped and nonhandicapped students (Christopolos & Renz, 1969; Fischer & Rizzo, 1974), and handicapped students will have equal access to the social resources required for maximal achievement and healthy social and cognitive development (Johnson, 1979). Whether or not these goals are achieved depends on the pattern of interaction that teachers structure between handicapped and nonhandicapped students.

Much of the traditional research on attitude change has focused on isolated and temporary experiences in which people are exposed to a single communication aimed at influencing them in a certain way. The mainstreaming situation, in which students interact with each other over a period of months and even years, is considerably more complex. Negative attitudes toward handicapped peers exist before mainstreaming begins, and first impressions and the labeling process reinforce such stigmatization. However, the actual interaction between handicapped and nonhandicapped students is what determines whether a process of acceptance or rejection mitigates or strengthens the rejection of handicapped peers.

The process of making social judgments about handicapped peers can be described as follows:

1. Original negative attitudes are based on the general stigmatization of handicaps by society at large.
2. An initial impression is made on the basis of the initial actions and perceived characteristics of the handicapped students.
3. Categories classifying the handicapped students' characteristics are formed with labels being attached to each category.
4. When interaction with the handicapped students occurs, it is of great importance whether that interaction takes place within a context of positive, negative, or no interdependence.
5. Depending on the social context within which interaction takes place, a process of acceptance or rejection occurs.
6. The process of acceptance results from interaction within a context of positive goal interdependence, which leads to promotive interaction and feelings of acceptance and psychological safety; differentiated, dynamic, realistic views of collaborators and oneself; positive cathexis toward others and oneself; and expectations for rewarding future interaction with classmates.
7. The process of rejection results from interaction within a context of negative or no goal interdependence. Negative goal interdependence promotes oppositional interaction and feelings of psychological rejection and threat. No goal interdependence results in no interaction with peers. Both lead to monopolistic, static, and stereotyped views of classmates; negative cathexis toward others and oneself; and expectations for distasteful and unpleasant future interaction with other students.
8. With further interaction, the process of acceptance or rejection may be repeated.

Each of these aspects of making social judgments about handicapped peers is discussed in the next section.

Stigmatization

Goffman (1963) defined a *stigma* as a deeply discrediting attribute of an individual. His work represents the only major theoretical work in the area of stigmatization. He made a distinction between an individual's "virtual social identity," the character imputed to the individual by society, and "actual social identity," which reflects the person's true identity. Virtual social identity carries the discrediting connotation. According to Goffman, there are three types of stigma: physical disabilities, character disorders, and tribal stigmas, such as ethnic membership or religious affiliation, which are transmitted through the family with all members being affected.

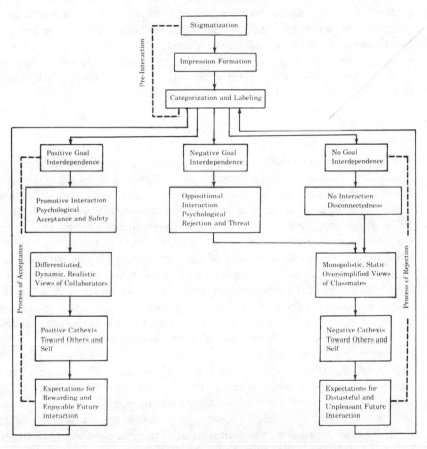

FIGURE 1. Social Judgment Process

When individuals have a highly visible stigma, simple contact with others will cause it to be known. And some stigmas (such as mental retardation) may be viewed by nonhandicapped students as disqualifying handicapped students from certain activities (such as academic work). To the extent that a handicap disqualifies students from major activities in the classroom, it will influence the handicapped students' acceptability to nonhandicapped peers.

Finally, some stigmas may interfere with interaction with nonhandicapped peers (such as deafness, blindness, and being nonambulatory), thus being quite obtrusive and leading to a lack of opportunity to reduce rejection. These three aspects of the visibility of the stigma (readily apparent, disqualifying, and obtrusive) all affect the strength of the feelings of the nonhandicapped students (Abelson, 1976).

When handicapped students are first placed in the regular classroom, nonhandicapped peers will normally have negative attitudes toward them, reflecting the process of stigmatization. A variety of research studies indicates that students who are perceived as handicapped by nonhandicapped students are viewed in negative and prejudiced ways, whether or not the handicapped children and adolescents are in the same or separate classrooms (Goodman, Gottlieb, & Harrison, 1972; Gottlieb & Budoff, 1973; Gottlieb & Davis, 1973; Jaffe, 1966; Johnson, 1950; Johnson & Kirk, 1950; Miller, 1956; Novak, 1975; Rucker, Howe, & Snider, 1969).

Forming Impressions

The second step in making social judgments about handicapped peers begins with the formation of an initial impression as they enter the classroom. The cognitive representations one has of what another person is like are greatly influenced by the first few minutes of contact (Heider, 1958; Kelley, 1973). First impressions can be strong and resistant to change, even with the introduction of contradictory information (Watson & Johnson, 1972). Forming an impression of another person occurs through perceiving initial actions and appearances and generalizing these initial impressions to the total personality of the other person (Asch, 1952). Three important aspects of first impressions should be taken into account: (a) the primary potency of being handicapped, (b) the number of characteristics included in the impression, and (c) the "dynamicness" of the impression.

Some characteristics are more important than others in forming an initial impression. Asch (1952) designated some characteristics as *central* and others as *peripheral*, while Allport (1954) designated the characteristics that overshadow much observed behavior as being of *primary potency*. Even when nonhandicapped students have a great deal of information available about a handicapped peer, the characteristic "handicapped" may dominate initial impressions. And such characteristics as physical attractiveness

120

(Berscheid & Walster, 1974) and perceived similarity to oneself (Taylor & Kowiumake, 1976) have been found to be of primary potency.

Impressions may be classified as either differentiated or monopolistic on the basis of the number of characteristics included in the impression and the way the impression is influenced by the requirements of a given situation. A *differentiated impression* includes many different characteristics, which are weighed differently in one situation compared to another. When only a few characteristics are perceived and when they are weighed the same in all situations, a *monopolistic impression* exists. According to Allport (1954), humans operate under the "principle of least effort," which states that monopolistic impressions are easier to form and maintain than are differentiated impressions.

Finally, differentiated impressions, by their very nature, stay in a dynamic state of change because of their tentativeness and differential weighing of characteristics according to the current situation. Monopolistic impressions, on the other hand, are static due to their rigid weighing of a few characteristics of primary potency, regardless of the demands of the current situation.

As one forms an impression of another person, one will inevitably categorize and then label aspects of the other's appearance and actions. It is to the issues of categorization and labeling that we now turn.

Categorization and Labeling

When nonhandicapped students form an impression of handicapped peers' being mainstreamed, they categorize the handicapped students' characteristics, attach a label to each category, and form a conceptual structure that gives the overall impression organization. Although categorizing and labeling are natural aspects of human learning, thought, and memory (Johnson, 1979), the way nonhandicapped students categorize, label, and organize their impressions of handicapped peers has important influences on mainstreaming. Categorization and labeling may lead to a differentiated, dynamic, and realistic impression, or it may lead to errors based on rigid stereotypes.

Labels are a way of consolidating information in one easily retrievable term. And labels inevitably carry evaluative connotations as well as denotative meanings. Applied to handicapped peers, labels may have negative effects by emphasizing monopolistic categories of primary potency that carry stigmas, by encouraging treatment only in terms of handicaps, and by assigning handicapped students to a low power position.

Combs and Harper (1967) have shown that certain groups such as psychopathic, schizophrenic, and cerebral palsied children were rated more negatively by teachers when labeled than when unlabeled. Teachers also held lower expectations for performance for students labeled culturally deprived or juvenile delinquent (Jones, 1972). Labels, furthermore, often define power relationships between the labeler and the labeled, placing the latter in a low power position.

Interaction Between Nonhandicapped and Handicapped Students

When mainstreaming begins, handicapped students enter the regular classroom, and in the initial proximity nonhandicapped students form an impression of their handicapped classmates. This impression is based on the pre-information received about the handicapped students, the visibility and primary potency of the handicaps, and the labels used to categorize the characteristics of the handicapped students. Being physically, intellectually, and psychologically handicapped does carry a social stigma in our society. Therefore, from the beginning, handicapped students are perceived somewhat negatively in most cases, setting up the strong possibility of nonhandicapped students' rejecting their handicapped classmates.

Physical proximity between handicapped and nonhandicapped students created by placing them in the same classroom is the beginning of an opportunity. However, like all opportunities, it carries a risk of making things worse, as well as the possibility of making things better. Physical proximity does not mean that stigmatization, stereotyping, and rejection of handicapped peers by nonhandicapped students will automatically result, or that handicapped students will automatically be included in the peer relationships with nonhandicapped classmates necessary for maximal achievement and healthy social development.

Several studies indicate that placing handicapped and nonhandicapped students in close physical proximity (e.g., the same classroom) may increase nonhandicapped students' prejudice toward and stereotyping and rejection of their handicapped peers (Goodman, Gottlieb, & Harrison, 1972; Gottlieb & Budoff, 1973; Gottlieb, Cohen, & Goldstein, 1974; Iano, Ayers, Heller, McGettigan, & Walker, 1974; Panda & Bartel, 1972). However, placing handicapped and nonhandicapped students in the same classroom may also result in more positive attitudes of nonhandicapped students toward their handicapped peers (Ballard, Corman, Gottlieb, & Kaufman, 1977; Higgs, 1975; Jaffe, 1966; Lapp, 1957; Sheare, 1975; Wechsler, Suarez, & Mc-Fadden, 1975).

This contradictory evidence is consistent with previous research on ethnic integration which indicates that, while contact between stigmatized and nonstigmatized students may be a necessary condition for reducing prejudice and rejection, it is not a sufficient one (Gerard & Miller, 1975; Harding, Proshansky, Kutner, & Chein, 1969; Shaw, 1973; Watson & Johnson, 1972; Wolf & Simon, 1975).

During the initial interaction between nonhandicapped and handicapped classmates, furthermore, the nonhandicapped students may feel discomfort and show "interaction strain." Siller and Chipman (1967), Whiteman and

122

Lukoff (1964), and Jones (1970) found that physically nonhandicapped persons reported discomfort and uncertainty in interacting with physically handicapped peers. Kleck and his associates provided evidence indicating that nonhandicapped individuals interacting with a physically handicapped person (as opposed to one who is physically nonhandicapped) exhibited greater motoric inhibition (Kleck, 1968); greater physiological arousal (Kleck, 1966); less variability in their behavior; terminated interaction sooner; expressed opinions that were not representative of their actual beliefs; and reported discomfort in the interaction (Kleck, Ono, & Hastorf, 1966); and in the case of a person said to have epilepsy, maintained greater physical distance (Kleck, Buck, Goller, London, Pfeiffer, & Vukcevic, 1968).

Jones (1970) found that nonhandicapped college students who performed a learning task in the presence of a blind confederate (as opposed to a sighted confederate) reported stronger beliefs that they would have performed better on the task if the blind person had not been present, even when the actual performance data indicated that the presence of a blind or sighted person had no significant effects on the college students' achievement. The discomfort many nonhandicapped students seem to feel when initially interacting with a handicapped peer may add to the risk that a monopolistic, static, and overly simplified view of handicapped peers as being stigmatized may dominate relationships between the two groups of students when handicapped students are mainstreamed into the regular classroom.

Whether mainstreaming will result in constructive or destructive peer relationships between handicappped and nonhandicapped students will be largely determined by the type of interdependence teachers structure among students' learning goals. It is the interdependence structured among students' learning goals that defines the social context in which interaction between handicapped and nonhandicapped students takes place. Within any learning situation, teachers can structure positive goal interdependence (i.e., cooperation), negative goal interdependence (i.e., competition), or no goal interdependence (i.e., individualistic efforts) among students (Johnson & Johnson, 1975). These three types of goal interdependence create different patterns of interaction among students which, in turn, create positive attitudes toward and acceptance of classmates regardless of their handicaps (Johnson & Johnson, 1975, 1978).

PROCESS OF ACCEPTANCE

The process of acceptance (described in Figure 1) begins with handicapped and nonhandicapped students' being placed in small, heterogeneous learning groups and given the assignment of completing a lesson as a group, making sure that all members master their assigned work. In other words, a positive interdependence is structured among students' learning goals.

Compared with competitive and individualistic learning situations, working cooperatively with peers will:

1. Create a pattern of promotive interaction, in which there is:
   a. More direct face to face interaction among students.
   b. An expectation that one's peers will facilitate one's learning.
   c. More peer pressure toward achievement and appropriate classroom behavior.
   d. More reciprocal communication and fewer difficulties in communicating with each other.
   e. More actual helping, tutoring, assisting, and general facilitation of each other's learning.
   f. More open mindedness to peers and willingness to be influenced by their ideas and information.
   g. More positive feedback to and reinforcement of each other.
   h. Less hostility, both verbal and physical, expressed toward peers.
2. Create perceptions and feelings of :
   a. Higher trust in other students.
   b. More mutual concern and friendliness for other students, more attentiveness to peers, more feelings of obligation to and responsibility for classmates, and desire to win the respect of other students.
   c. Stronger beliefs that one is liked, supported, and accepted by other students, and that other students care about how much one learns and want to help one learn.
   c. Lower fear of failure and higher psychological safety.
   e. Higher valuing of classmates.
   f. Greater feelings of success. (Johnson & Johnson, 1975, 1978)

Positive goal interdependence creates these patterns of promotive interaction and psychological states, which in turn create (a) differentiated, dynamic, and realistic impressions of handicapped classmates by nonhandicapped students and (b) a positive cathexis toward others and oneself.

Labeled handicaps lose their primary potency when a view of the handicapped peer as a person becomes highly differentiated, dynamic, and realistic. A differentiated, dynamic impression includes many different categories; each category is assigned a weight as to its importance according to the demands of any specific situation, and the weight or salience of each category changes as the requirements of a situation change. New information concerning the handicapped peers is admitted into one's impression as it becomes relevant. Thus, if a peer is visually impaired, this category may be noted when the group is trying to read what the teacher has written on the blackboard, but will be forgotten when the group is discussing the material they are studying. The conceptualization of the handicapped peer stays in a dynamic state of change, open to modification with new information, and takes into account situational factors.

As nonhandicapped students work closely with handicapped peers, the boundaries of the handicap become more and more clear. While handicapped students may be able to hide the extent of their disability when they are isolated, the intensive promotive interaction under positive goal interdependence encourages a realistic as well as a differentiated view of the handicapped students. If a handicapped member of a learning group cannot read or cannot speak clearly, the other members of the learning group become highly aware of that fact. With the realistic perception, however, also comes a decrease in the primary potency of the handicap and a decrease in the stigmatization connected with the handicapped.

A direct consequence of cooperative experiences is a positive cathexis in which (Deutsch, 1949,1962; Johnson & Johnson, 1975, 1978):

1. The positive value attached to another person's efforts to help one achieve one's goals becomes generalized to the person.
2. Students will positively cathect to their own actions aimed at achieving the joint goal and generalize that value to themselves as persons.

In other words, the acceptance of and liking for handicapped peers by nonhandicapped students will increase when interaction takes place within a context of positive goal interdependence, and the self attitudes of handicapped students will become more positive.

PROCESS OF REJECTION

The process of rejection is described in Figure 1. When handicapped students are first placed in the classroom, they carry a social stigma that dominates initial impressions and leads to the formation of monopolistic stereotypes that are static and overshadow much observed behavior. This initial tendency toward rejection of handicapped students by nonhandicapped peers is perpetuated by instructing students to work alone with the purpose of either outperforming their peers (competition) or meeting a set criterion (individualistic efforts).

When interaction between handicapped and nonhandicapped students takes place within a context of negative goal interdependence, compared with cooperative learning activities (Johnson, 1975, 1978), the results are likely to be:

1. A pattern of oppositional interaction in which students:
   a. Have little face to face interaction.
   b. Expect their peers to frustrate the achievement of their learning goals.
   c. Face peer pressure against achievement and appropriate classroom behavior.
   d. Communicate inaccurate information and frequently misunderstand each other.

e. Are closed minded to and unwilling to be influenced by peers.

f. Give each other negative feedback.

g. Express verbal and physical hostility toward peers.

2. Perceptions and feelings of:

a. Distrust for other students.

b. Higher fear of failure and more feelings of failure.

c. Less mutual concern and feelings of responsibility for peers.

d. Being rejected and disliked by classmates.

Negative goal interdependence creates the above patterns of oppositional interaction and psychological states, which in turn create (a) monopolistic, static, and oversimplified impressions of handicapped classmates by non-handicapped students, and (b) a negative cathexis toward others and oneself. In the competitive classroom, two qualities primarily make others or oneself worthwhile: reading ability and competence in spatial reasoning. Those two qualities separate the winners from the losers.

When interaction between handicapped and nonhandicapped students takes place within a context of no goal interdependence, students are instructed to work on their own, without interacting with other students, with their own materials, and on goals that are independent from the learning goals of other students. In such a situation, no interaction takes place among students and no structured interconnectedness with peers. The independence of students during learning activities creates (a) monopolistic, static, and oversimplified impressions of handicapped classmates by non-handicapped students, and (b) a negative cathexis toward others and oneself.

Both competitive and individualistic learning activities provide little or no information about handicapped peers, thus allowing initial stereotypes to continue. What little information is available most likely confirms existing stereotypes that handicapped peers are "losers." The boundaries of the handicap are not clarified.

A direct consequence of competitive experiences is a negative cathexis in which (Deutsch, 1949, 1962; Johnson & Johnson, 1975, 1978):

1. The negative value attached to classmate's efforts to achieve becomes generalized to them as people (because if they "win," you "lose").

2. Students will negatively cathect to their own actions when they lose and generalize that negative evaluation to themselves as persons (and in the usual classroom, achievement hierarchies are relatively stable, leaving the majority of students continually experiencing failure).

Generally, the research does indicate that in comparison with students in cooperative situations, classmates in competitive situations are disliked and self esteem is lower for all but the few "winners." Both self esteem and liking for classmates is lower in individualistic learning situations than in cooperation (Johnson & Johnson, 1975, 1978), although the theoretical rationale for these findings is somewhat unclear.

At any time the process of rejection in the classroom can be replaced by the process of acceptance by structuring cooperative interaction between handicapped and nonhandicapped students.

COOPERATIVE INTERACTION AND MAINSTREAMING

Besides the research on interpersonal attraction on nonhandicapped students discussed previously, five studies have directly compared cooperatively structured learning with competitive and individualistic instruction when handicapped students were mainstreamed into the regular classroom.

In the first study Armstrong, Johnson , and Balow (1980) compared cooperative with individualistic instruction in language arts for 40 fifth and sixth grade students for 90 minutes a day for a 4 week period. Of the sample, 25% (10) were males with learning disabilities. Armstrong and her colleagues found that the regular classroom students in the cooperative learning groups evaluated their learning disabled peers as more valuable and smarter than did the regular classroom students in the individualistic condition. Regular classroom students in the cooperative condition also believed they knew their learning disabled peers better, chose them for friends more often, felt that they had been more frequently helped by their learning disabled peers, and wished for them to be removed from the classroom less frequently. The learning disabled students were far less isolated in the cooperative than in the individualistic condition.

In the second study, 12 second and third grade boys enrolled in a summer swimming program were either taught in cooperative pairs or individually (Martino & Johnson, 1979). Three normal progress and three learning disabled boys were randomly assigned to each condition. In the cooperative condition, a normal progress and a learning disabled boy were randomly assigned to each pair. Observers recorded the number of times the normal progress boys interacted with the learning disabled students during a 15 minute free swim period at the end of each 1 hour class.

Over the 9 days in instruction, in the individualistic condition only one instance was observed of a friendly interaction between a normal progress and learning disabled student. In the cooperative condition, up to 20 daily instances of friendly interactions occurred during the free time between normal progress and learning disabled students, with an average of 10 friendly interactions per day. An average of three hostile interactions between normal progress and learning disabled boys took place each day in the individualistic condition, as opposed to an average of one hostile interaction per day between the two types of students in the cooperative condition.

In a study of seventh graders, Cooper, Johnson, Johnson, and Wilderson (1980) studied the relationships between regular classroom students and learning disabled and emotionally disturbed students in cooperative, competitive, and individualistic science, English, and geography classes. Each class period lasted 60 minutes and the study lasted for 15 instructional days. Students, therefore, received 45 hours of instruction in each condition. The researchers found that far more students reported helping and receiving help from their handicapped peers in the cooperative condition than in the other two. Regular classroom students in the cooperative and competitive conditions chose handicapped peers for friends more frequently than did the nonhandicapped students in the individualistic condition.

In a fourth field experiment, the effects of cooperative, individualistic, and laissez faire goal structures were compared on interpersonal attraction between nonhandicapped junior high school students and severely retarded peers (Johnson, Rynders, Johnson, Schmidt, & Haider, 1979). Students were from a public junior high school, a Catholic junior high school, and a special station school. The retarded students were functioning at a high trainable level. Students participated in a bowling class that met for 1 hour per week for 6 weeks. The results indicate that considerably more positive, supportive, and friendly interaction took place between the nonhandicapped and the retarded students in the cooperative condition than in the other two.

In the fifth field experiment, interpersonal attraction between nonhandicapped junior high school students and Down's syndrome students from a special station school was studied under cooperative, competitive, and individualistic conditions (Rynders, Johnson, Johnson, & Schmidt, 1980). Procedures were identical with those used in the previous bowling study. Considerably more positive, supportive, and friendly interaction took place between the two groups of students in the cooperative condition than in the other two.

APPLICATION TO SCHOOL BASED TEACHER EDUCATION

The classroom, like all other social systems, is a network of interpersonal relationships structured to facilitate the achievement of the school district's goals. When mainstreaming is implemented, the social structure of the classroom must promote constructive peer relationships between handicapped and nonhandicapped students so that a process of acceptance is generated and achievement, social and cognitive development, and socialization occur to the maximal extent possible. Teachers can largely influence the interaction between handicapped and nonhandicapped students through the goal structures they implement in instructional situations.

A major question addressed by this chapter is *how* special education and regular classroom teachers should be trained within their schools so that effective mainstreaming will result. All of the research discussed previously in terms of student learning and socialization is relevant to answering this question. We must pay careful attention to the ways the educational goals of special education and regular classroom teachers involved in mainstreaming are structured so that they interact to facilitate building collaborative and supportive relationships while being trained.

In other words, the educators conducting an inservice program aimed at increasing the effectiveness of mainstreaming must structure cooperative learning activities involving the special education and regular classroom teachers who will work together after the training program is over. Cooperative learning experiences during the inservice training will help build the collaborative relationships necessary for the special education and regular classroom teachers to work together in insuring that mainstreaming results in constructive outcomes for both handicapped and nonhandicapped students. In order for collaborative relationships to transfer from the training program to the classroom, however, clear goal and resource interdependence must be structured between special education and regular classroom teachers.

An example of a possible division of labor resulting from a school based teacher education program on mainstreaming follows:

1. Collaborating special education and regular classroom teachers are trained in the specific strategies and competencies for using heterogeneous cooperative learning groups in the regular classroom to structure constructive peer relationships between handicapped and nonhandicapped students.
2. The training program makes extensive use of collaborative assignments, tests, and projects so that supportive and cooperative relationships are built among teachers as they go through the training program.
3. The collaborating special education and regular classroom teachers work cooperatively in writing IEP's for each mainstreamed student, including social acceptance, social skills, cognitive and social development, self esteem, and achievement as part of the IEP's.
4. The regular classroom teachers structure learning activities cooperatively, placing handicapped and nonhandicapped students in the same learning groups.
5. The special education teachers observe the cooperative learning groups, indentifying problems in cognitive and social functioning of *all* group members, both handicapped and nonhandicapped.
6. The special education teachers engage in such supportive activities as:
   a. Training *all* students in the social skills such as leadership and communication they need in order to function effectively as part of a cooperative learning group.
   b. Giving special tutoring to collaborating pairs of students, one special education and one nonhandicapped, in how to function effectively in their cooperative learning group and how to help the handicapped student learn more and behave more appropriately.

129

c. Providing the regular classroom teachers with guidelines for how much each mainstreamed student can realistically achieve in the regular classroom so that group scores can be adjusted to encourage maximal achievement but not to punish regular classroom students by bringing their group grade down.

d. Being available for other supportive activities the regular classroom teachers might need.

7. At regularly scheduled meetings the special education and regular classroom teachers discuss each student being mainstreamed, referring them for further evaluation when it is warranted and planning interventions to improve the functioning of their cooperative groups when it is needed.

Through procedures such as these, a resource interdependence can be built into the relationships between special education and regular classroom teachers.

The principal is the key to insuring that effective collaboration occurs between special education and regular classroom teachers once the school based teacher education program on mainstreaming is completed. By structuring cooperative goal interdependence between the teachers in a manner similar to the way teachers structure student learning goals cooperatively, the principal can encourage and reward teachers for working collaboratively.

While teachers have traditionally been independent of each other, the special requirements of mainstreaming provide the opportunity to develop day to day collaboration between special education and regular classroom teachers. And while the principal may be able to structure only a few goals cooperatively, some outcomes that might be awarded to successful collaborative efforts are:

1. Team (not individual) evaluations at the end of the year.
2. Released time for planning and helping other teachers develop their skills in working collaboratively with each other and using heterogeneous cooperative groups for instructional purposes.
3. Summer writing time.
4. Favorable evaluation by principal to be placed in teachers' files.
5. Scheduled inservice sessions conducted by the collaborating teachers disseminating information about what they are doing.
6. General recognition by the principal, superintendent, and other significant people that the collaborating teachers are doing an excellent job in managing mainstreaming.

Once effective collaborative relationships are established by special education and regular classroom teachers, the intrinsic rewards of working cooperatively may motivate continued collaboration without any specific rewards being given by the principal.

Most teachers have little specific training in how to function effectively as part of a collaborative effort with their peers. This type of training could begin in the college preservice setting, but it doesn't. College students move through their teacher training programs as individuals, often with a competitive ethic that encourages them to be the "best" in their classes and in student teaching.

Recently, a change was made in the University of Minnesota's elementary education methods classes that could have and effect on preservice teachers' ability to work together. Science, math, and social studies methods classes were"blocked" into a single methods arrangement (as were reading, literature, and language arts). In one of the blocks, students were assigned to base groups at the beginning of the quarter and were not only encouraged to be resources to each other during class periods, but were given quizzes as a group, planned lessons as a group, critiqued each others' lessons which were being taught in the in school practicum part of the course, and were taught the social skills necessary for working together effectively. The results were positive; and many of the base groups continued to function as support and assistance groups during student teaching, even though there was no longer any formal structure requiring collaboration.

To be effective, school based teacher education programs on mainstreaming must train teachers in the procedures for using heterogeneous cooperative groups in order to insure that constructive peer relationships are developed between handicapped and nonhandicapped students; and they must structure positive goal and resource interdependence between special education and regular classroom teachers so that collaborative relationships can be built during the inservice training and be maintained after the school based training has ended. This process is both the *what* and the *how* of school based teacher tranining for mainstreaming.

SUMMARY

Like all social systems, the classroom is made up of a network of interpersonal relationships structured to facilitate the achievement of established goals. The regular classroom and special education teachers largely determine what happens within the classroom in regard to mainstreaming. Through structuring learning goals cooperatively, teachers can insure that handicapped and nonhandicapped students develop constructive relation ships and that a process of acceptance, rather than a process of rejection, is promoted. How well regular classroom and special education teachers can coordinate their efforts to facilitate constructive peer relationships between handicapped and nonhandicapped students depends largely on whether or not a positive goal and resource interdependence were created during their school based training for mainstreaming and on how well that interdependence is continued in their collaboration on mainstreaming.

131

REFERENCES

Abelson, A. Measuring preschool's readiness to mainstream handicapped children. *Child Welfare,* 1976, *55,* 216–220.

Allport, G. *The nature of prejudice.* Cambridge MA: Addison-Wesley, 1954.

Ames, C., Ames, R., & Felker, D. Effects of competitive reward structure and valence of outcome on children's achievement attributions. *Journal of Educational Psychology,* 1977, *69,* 1–8.

Armstrong, B., Johnson, D. W., & Balow, B. Cooperative goal structure as a means of integrating learning-disabled with normal-progress elementary pupils. *Contemporary Educational Psychology,* in press.

Asch, S. *Social psychology.* Englewood Cliffs NJ: Prentice-Hall, 1952.

Ballard, M., Corman, L., Gottlieb, J., & Kaufman, M. Improving the social status of mainstreamed retarded children. *Journal of Educational Psychology,* 1977, *69,* 605–611.

Barnett, M., Matthews, K., & Howard, J. The relationship between competitiveness and empathy in 6 & 7 year olds. *Developmental Psychology,* in press.

Berschied, E., & Walster, E. Physical attractiveness. In L Berkowitz, (Ed.), *Advances in experimental social psychology,* Vol. 7. New York: Academic Press, 1974

Blake, R., & Mouton, J. Comprehension of own and outgroup positions under intergroup competition. *Journal of Conflict Resolution,* 1961, *5,* 304–310.

Blaney, N., Stephan, C., Rosenfield, D., Aronson, E., & Sikes, J. Interdependence in the classroom: A field study. *Journal of Educational Psychology,* 1977, *69,* 139–146.

Bridgeman, D. *Cooperative, interdependent learning and its enhancement of role-taking in fifth grade students.* Paper presented at the American Psychological Association Convention, San Francisco, August, 1977.

Christopolos, F., & Renz, P. A critical examination of special education programs. *Journal of Special Education,* 1969, *3,* 371–380.

Cook, S. Interpersonal and attitudinal outcomes in cooperating interracial groups. *Journal of Research and Development in Education,* 1978, *12,* 97–113.

Cooper, L., Johnson, D. W., Johnson, R., & Wilderson, F. Effects of cooperative, competitive, and individualistic experiences on interpersonal attraction among heterogeneous peers. *Journal of Social Psychology,* 1980, *111,* 243–252.

Combs, R., & Harper, J. Effects of labels on attitudes of educators toward handicapped children. *Exceptional Children,* 1967, *34,* 399–406.

Crawford, J., & Haaland, G. Predecisional information seeking and subsequent conformity in the social influence process. *Journal of Personality and Social Psychology,* 1972, *23,* 112–119.

Davis, J., Laughlin, P., & Komorita, S. The social psychology of small groups: cooperative and mixed-motive interaction. In M. Rosenzweig & L. Porter (Eds.), *Annual Review of Psychology,* 1976, *27,* 501–542.

Deutsch, M. A theory of cooperation and competition. *Human Relations,* 1949, *2,* 129–152.

Deutsch, M. Cooperation and trust: Some theoretical notes. In M. R. Jones (Ed.), *Nebraska Symposium on Motivation*. Lincoln: University of Nebraska Press, 1962.

DeVries, D., & Slavin, R. Teams-games-tournaments: Review of ten classroom experiments. *Jounal of Research and Development in Education*, 1978, *12*, 28–38.

Dunn, L. Special education for the mildly retarded—Is much of it justifiable? *Exceptional Children*, 1968, *35*, 5–22.

Fischer, C., & Rizzo, A. A paradigm for humanizing special education. *Journal of Special Education*, 1974, *8*, 321–329.

Flynn, T. Regular-class adjustment of EMR students attending a part-time special education program. *Journal of Special Education*, 1974, *8*, 167–173.

Garibaldi, A. *Cooperation, competition, and locus of control in Afro-American Students*. Doctoral dissertation, University of Minnesota, 1976.

Geffner, R. *The effects of interdependent learning on self-esteem, inter-ethnic relations, and intra-ethnic attitudes of elementary school children: A field experiment*. Unpublished doctoral dissertation, University of California at Santa Cruz, 1978.

Gerard, H., & Miller, N. *School desegregation*. New York: Plenum Press, 1975.

Goffman, E. *Stigma*. Englewood Cliffs NJ: Prentice-Hall, 1963.

Goodman, H., Gottlieb, J., & Harrison, R. Social acceptance of EMR's integrated into a nongraded elementary school.*American Jounal of Mental Deficiency*, 1972, *76*, 412–417.

Gottlieb, J., & Budoff, A. Social acceptability of retarded children in nongraded schools differing in architecture. *American Journal of Mental Deficiency*, 1973, *78*, 15–19.

Gottlieb, J., Cohen, L., & Goldstein, L. Social contact and personal adjustment as variables relating to attitudes toward educable mentally retarded children. *Training School Bulletin*, 1974, *71*, 9–16.

Gottlieb, J., & Davis, J. Social acceptance of EMR children during overt behavioral interaction. *American Journal of Mental Deficiency*, 1973, *78*, 141–143.

Gunderson, B., & Johnson, D. W. Promoting position attitudes toward learning a foreign language by using cooperative learning groups. *Foreign Language Annuals*, 1980, *13*, 39–46.

Harding, J., Proshansky, H., Kutner, B., & Chein, I. Prejudice and ethnic relations. In G. Lindzey & E. Aronson (Eds.), *The handbook of social psychology* (Vol. 5). Reading MA: Addison-Wesley, 1959.

Hartup, W. Children and their friends. In M. McGurk (Ed.), *Childhood social development*. London: Methuen, 1978

Heider, F. *The psychology of interpersonal relations*. New York: Wiley, 1958.

Higgs, R. Attitude formation—Contact or information? *Exceptional Children*, 1975, *41*, 496–497.

Iano, R., Ayers, D., Heller, H., McGettigan, J., & Walker, V. Sociometric status of retarded children in an integrative program. *Exceptional Chil-*

dren, 1974, *40,* 267–271.

Jaffe, J. Attitudes of adolescents toward mentally retarded. *American Journal of Mental Deficiency,* 1966, *70,* 907–912.

Johnson, D. W. Communication and the inducement of cooperative behavior in conflicts: a critical review. *Speech Monographs,* 1974, *41,* 64–78.

Johnson, D. W. Cooperativeness and social perspective taking. *Journal of Personality and Social Psychology,* 1975, *31,* 241–244. (a)

Johnson, D. W. Affective perspective-taking and cooperative predisposition. *Developmental Psychology,* 1975, *11,* 869–870. (b)

Johnson, D. W. *Human relations and your career: A guide to interpersonal skills.* Englewood Cliffs NJ: Prentice-Hall, 1978.

Johnson, D. W. *Educational psychology.* Englewood Cliffs NJ: Prentice-Hall, 1979.

Johnson, D. W. Group processes: Influences of student-student interaction on school outcomes. In J. McMillan (Ed.), *The social psychology of school learning.* New York: Academic Press, 1980.

Johnson, D. W., & Ahlgren, A. Relationship between student attitudes about cooperation and competition and attitudes toward schooling. *Journal of Educational Psychology,* 1976, *68,* 92–102.

Johnson, D. W., & Johnson, F. *Joining together: Group theory and group skills.* Englewood Cliffs NJ: Prentice-Hall, 1975.

Johnson, D. W., & Johnson R. Cooperative, competitive, and individualistic learning. *Journal of Research and Development in Education,* 1978, *12,* 3–16.

Johnson, D. W., Johnson, R., & Anderson, D. Relationship between student cooperative, competitive, and individualistic attitudes and attitudes toward schooling. *Journal of Psychology,* 1978, *100,* 183–199.

Johnson, D. W., Johnson, R., Johnson, J., & Anderson, D. The effects of cooperative vs. individualized instruction on student prosocial behavior, attitudes toward learning, and achievement. *Journal of Educational Psychology,* 1976, *68,* 446–452.

Johnson, D. W., Johnson, R., & Scott, L. The effects of cooperative and individualized instruction on student attitudes and achievement. *Journal of Social Psychology,* 1978, *104,* 207–216.

Johnson, D. W., Johnson, R., & Skon, L. Student achievement on different types of tasks under cooperative, competitive, and individualistic conditions. *Contemporary Educational Psychology,* 1979, *4,* 99–106.

Johnson, D. W., & Norem-Hebeisen, A. Attitudes toward interdependence among persons and psychological health. *Psychological Reports,* 1977, *40,* 843–850.

Johnson, D. W., Skon, L., & Johnson, R. Effects of cooperative, competitive, and individualistic conditions on problem-solving performance. *American Educational Research Journal.* 1980, *17,* 83–94.

Johnson, G. A study of the social position of mentally handicapped children in the regular grades. *American Journal of Mental Deficiency,* 1950, *55,* 60–89.

Johnson, G., & Kirk, S. Are mentally handicapped children segregated in the regular grades? *Exceptional Children,* 1950, *55,* 60–89.

Johnson, R., & Johson, D. W. Type of task and student achievement and attitudes in interpersonal cooperation, competition, and individualization. *Journal of Social Psychology*, 1979, *108*, 37–48.

Johnson, R., Johnson, D. W., & Tauer, M. Effects of cooperative, competitive, and individualistic goal structures on students' achievement and attitudes. *Journal of Psychology*, 1979, *102*, 191–198.

Johnson, R., Rynders, J., Johnson, D.W., Schmidt, B., & Haider, S. Producing positive interaction between handicapped and nonhandicapped teenagers through cooperative goal structuring: implications for mainstreaming. *American Educational Research Journal*, 1979, *16*, 161–168.

Jones, R. Learning and association in the presence of the blind. *The New Outlook*, 1970 (December), 317–329.

Jones, R. Labels and stigma in special education. *Exceptional Children*, 1972, *38*, 553–564.

Kelley, H. The processes of causal attribution. *American Psychologist*, 1973, *28*, 107–128.

Kleck, R. Emotional arousal in interaction with stigmatized persons. *Psychological Reports*, 1966, *19*, 1226.

Kleck, R. Physical stigma and nonverbal cues emitted in face-to-face interaction. *Human Relations*, 1968, *21*, 19–28.

Kleck, R., Buck, P., Goller, W., London, R., Pfeiffer, J., & Vukcevic, D. Effect of stigmatizing conditions on the use of personal space. *Psychological Reports*, 1968, *23*, 111–118.

Kleck, R., Ono, H., & Hastorf, A. The effects of physical deviance upon face-to-face interaction. *Human Relations*, 1966, *19*, 425–436.

Lapp, E. A study of the social adjustment of slow learning children who were assigned part-time to regular classes. *American Journal of Mental Deficiency*, 1957, *62*, 254–262.

Laughlin, P. Ability and group problem solving. *Journal of Research and Development in Education*, 1978, *12*, 114–121.

Laughlin, P., Keer, N., Davis, J., Haiff, H.,,(Marciniak, K. Group size, member ability, and social decision schemes on an intellective task. *Journal of Personality and Social Psychology*, 1975, *31*, 522–535.

Laughlin, P., & McGlynn, R. Cooperative versus competitive concept attainment as a function of sex and stimulus display. *Journal of Personality and Social Psychology*, 1967, *7*, 398–402.

Lewis, M., & Rosenblum, L. (Eds.). *Friendship and peer relations*. New York: Wiley, 1975.

Martino, L., Johnson, D. W. The effects of cooperative vs. individualistic instruction on interaction between normal-progress and learning-disabled students. *Journal of Social Psychology*, 1979, *107*, 177–183.

Miller, G. The magical number of seven, plus or minus two: Some limits on our capacity for processing information. *The Psychological Review*, 1956, *63*(2), 81–97.

Norem-Hebeisen, A., & Johnson, D. W. *The relationship between cooperative, competitive, and individualistic attitudes and differentiated aspects of self-esteem.* University of Minnesota, mimeographed report, submitted for publication, 1980.

Novak, D. Children's responses to imaginary peers labeled as emotionally disturbed. *Psychology in the Schools,* 1975, *12,* 103–106.

Panda, K., & Bartel, N. Teacher perception of exceptional children. *Journal of Special Education,* 1972, *6,* 261–266.

Rucker, C., Howe, C., & Snider, B. The acceptance of retarded children in junior high academic and non-academic regular classes. *Exceptional Children,* 1969, *35,* 617–623.

Rynders, J., Johnson, R., Johnson, D., & Schmidt, B. Effects of cooperative, competitive, and individualistic goal structures on interaction between handicapped and nonhandicapped adolescents. *American Journal of Mental Deficiency,* in press.

Shaw, M. Changes in sociometric choices following forced integration of an elementary school. *Journal of Social Issues,* 1973, *29,* 143–157.

Sheare, J. *The relationship between peer acceptance and self-concept of children in grades 3 through 6.* Doctoral dissertation, Penn State University, University Microfilms, No. 76-10, 783, 1975.

Siller, J., & Chipman, A. *Attitudes of the nondisabled toward the physically disabled.* New York: New York University, 1967.

Slavin, R. Students teams and achievement divisions. *Journal of Research and Development in Education,* 1978, *12,* 39–49.

Taylor, S., & Kowiumake, J. The perception of self and others: Acquaintanceship, affect, and actor-observer differences. *Journal of Personality and Social Psychology,* 1976, *33,* 403–408.

Tjosvold, D., Marino, P., & Johnson, D. W. The effects of cooperation and competition on student reactions to inquiry and didactic learning. *Journal of Research in Science Teaching,* 1977, *14,* 281–288.

Watson, G., & Johnson, D. W. *Social Psychology: Issues and insights.* Philadelphia: Lippincott, 1972.

Wechsler, H., Suarez, A., & McFadden, M. Teachers' attitudes toward the education of physically handicapped children: Implications for implementation of Massachusetts Chapter 766. *Journal of Education,* 1975, *157,* 17–24.

Wheeler, R., & Ryan, F. Effects of cooperative and competitive classroom environments on the attitudes and achievement of elementary school students engaged in social studies inquiry activities. *Journal of Educational Psychology,* 1973, *65,* 402–407.

Whiteman, M., & Lukoff, I. A factorial study of sighted people's attitudes toward blindness. *Journal of Social Psychology,* 1964, *64,* 339–353.

Wolf, R., & Simon, R. Does busing improve the racial interactions of children? *Educational Researcher,* 1975, *4,* 5–10.

Part 4

THE TEACHER EDUCATION DIMENSION

8

Testing the Waters of School Based Teacher Education

SAM J. YARGER
SALLY K. MERTENS

The value of providing teachers with relevant training experiences in school settings has long been recognized. Relatively new is the idea of developing a cadre of professionals for the specific purpose of training teachers in the schools. Within the past 5 years the idea of "school based teacher educators" has been especially promoted. This chapter will examine the context within which the concept of school based teacher education (SBTE) is currently evolving. Our goal will be to develop a better awareness, understanding, and appreciation of problems and complexities that attend the concept. Specifically, we will seek to delineate certain key issues, to present a model for focusing on key program concepts, and to explore the emerging roles of school based teacher educators.

SBTE: A RENEWED EFFORT TO SOLVE AN OLD PROBLEM

The current press toward school based teacher education is a renewed effort to solve an old problem—how to integrate theory (historically the bailiwick of schools of education's preservice programs) and practice (usually the focus of inservice education offered by school districts). Institutionalized traditions have generated a long history of complaints by school professionals that newly certified beginning teachers do not know how to teach and have resulted in concern that once teachers become involved in school district sponsored inservice programs they lose their ideals.

Typically, the solution for bridging the gap between the theoretical orientation of preservice and the practical orientation of inservice has been to provide more practical experiences in the school for preservice teachers and to encourage additional college course work for inservice teachers. Although the contents of "practical experience" and "course work" have been loosely defined, teacher educators have generally assumed that more is better.

Vigorous good intentions may have propelled these programs; nonetheless, at question is whether either preservice or inservice teachers have actually benefitted from more of anything. Most successful attempts to bridge the gap between the theoretical and applied components of teacher education have been isolated, serendipitous exceptions, rather than examples of carefully developed models for making teacher education more powerful. Perhaps current interest in school based teacher education will result not only in better programing, but also in a reconceptualization of the field.

MAKING TEACHER EDUCATION MORE RELEVANT

Those promoting school based teacher education today are not talking about the need to add more "field or clinical experiences," or "practically oriented" theory courses to otherwise traditional programs. They are focusing instead on the necessity of centering teacher education *in* the schools. The logic of the idea is hard to fault. Contemporary organizational developmentalists view the school building as the basic unit of change and improvement. Inservice theorists cite the need for both job embedded training and classroom follow through. Conventional wisdom suggests that real improvement in teaching children will most likely occur within the context of the world that teachers and children inhabit.

While the need for improved teacher education is obvious, and not a subject for debate, some promoters of SBTE are suggesting that a shift in locus of training will solve most, if not all, of the problems. But the move toward school based teacher education is likely to be an exercise in frustration and futility unless some basic issues and problems are recognized and dealt with. Just changing the geography of teacher education is probably not going to dramatically change or improve traditional programing. Furthermore, teacher educators must be very careful that in attempts to integrate theory and practice, theory not be eliminated (Broudy, 1972).

PRIMARY TARGET: INSERVICE TEACHERS

The notion of SBTE naturally has support from those who have always believed teacher education should be more classroom oriented. But as the concept is currently evolving, it differs significantly from previous efforts to develop applied teacher education programs. Past efforts have been concerned primarily with preparing beginning teachers. The main target of school based teacher education, however, is inservice teachers. So, although the argument for relevance in teacher education has been around for a long time, SBTE is currently evolving within a new context, i. e., recognition of the need for the continuous professional development of teachers.

The idea of providing teachers with opportunities and incentives for engaging in professional development throughout their careers is based on the assumption that all people, teachers included, can continue to learn and improve. Sound though this logic may be, it contradicts the traditional, institutionalized practice of permanently certifying teachers. Consider that in some states hair stylists are required to have more hours of instruction and supervised practice to receive a license than do either elementary or secondary teachers to obtain certification! Despite the fact that many teachers have conscientiously and continuously engaged in activities to upgrade their teaching skills, in many cases upgrading simply does not occur. How many careers have followed the path (a) getting a teaching job, (b) taking 30 to 36 requisite graduate hours (even less is required to teach in many states), (c) putting in 3 to 5 years on the job time (to get teaching tenure), (d) taking a maternity leave, and (e) returning to the teaching ranks as a full fledged "professional," on the way to becoming a long term veteran. For male teachers, one can omit the fourth step; but the pattern remains constant.

The career path to becoming a veteran teacher is open to most except the most blatantly incompetent of teachers. And once a teaching certification has been achieved, a pervasive mentality traditionally supports the notion that a teacher need never again have to bother with what is called "professional development." Some fine teachers *have* emerged from this process; many others *could* have been stretched into becoming better teachers—but have not. Mediocrity has too often been the norm. Under such conditions, often the only avenue open for teachers to engage in professional development has been to leave the teaching ranks and become specialists or principals. The system has channeled many of our best teachers into other professional roles.

School based teacher education, then, represents a renewed large scale effort to address the problem of reform in teacher education. Most important, it says a lot about where the problem will be addressed—directly in the schools. Furthermore, SBTE is perhaps the first attempt to involve career teachers, who historically have been ignored. Much more than logic is required, however, for an idea to generate the type of interest currently being exhibited in SBTE.

For example, we might well ask why schools and colleges of education are displaying a sudden interest in teacher education in the schools—an enterprise that has historically been anathema to the way they operate. One reason may be that teacher education (undergraduate and graduate) has been the bread and butter of many colleges and universities. With the

141

declining birth rate and the resultant lack of demand for new teachers, many of these institutions have had to face declining revenues from their teacher education programs. In addition, the decline in the need for new teachers has been paralleled by a much lower turnover rate in the schools. Thus, teachers who are employed tend to be highly degreed and credentialed. The resultant effect on schools and colleges of education has been a distinct decline in the demand for traditional graduate and advanced certification programs.

Thus, the appeal of SBTE is understandable. If the idea of permanent professional competence can be successfully challenged, then a large group is in need of continuous teacher education. A number of schools of education may find that their very existence depends on the concept of continuous professional development for teachers.

The support for school based teacher education that is coming from teacher organizations, by contrast, appears to be generated more by political than economic concerns. If the locus of teacher education comes to reside in the schools, control may prove an issue that will operate against its speedy institutionalization. As schools of education have lost some of their influence, talk about "collaboration" has become very fashionable. A showdown is probably on the horizon with respect to the control of teacher education, however, since all constituencies have an opportunity to gain influence in this increasingly popular endeavor. The important point remains—not only do sound educational reasons support school based teacher education; political pressures do so as well.

THE CHALLENGES OF SBTE

When we say that "the time is right—school based teacher education has finally come of age"—we imply that currently propitious political and economic conditions promote the idea. Translated, that means conditions finally exist for developing programs to meet the ever increasing inservice needs of teachers and schools.

Unfortunately, the potential also exists for operating *only* at the political and economic levels, thus creating the type of programs that John Sawhill (1978/79) feared might become the "Scandal of the 80's." What Sawhill questioned was the nationwide higher education media blitz to create a need for lifelong learning and the lowering of academic standards that may well accompany it. The possibility of this phenomenon occurring in school based programs clearly exists and must be guarded against. As schools and colleges of education make tradeoffs in order to increase the pool of "learners," and as they loosen traditional control, they must take care not to create a situation where the new political arrangements will result in programs that are either no improvement on, or even worse than what traditionally existed.

142

THE SCHOOL BASED TEACHER EDUCATOR THUS FAR

The idea of a school based teacher educator—of a well trained professional who actually works on a day to day basis with teachers in schools—certainly sounds good, especially since traditional teacher educators, whether coming from campus or district administrative offices, have frequently not been well received by teachers. However, it is probably naive at best to argue that putting a teacher educator in a school building will solve all the problems of teacher education. Caution is needed to avoid oversell so that politics and economics do not take over at the expense of careful planning. What is being promoted as a cure all could turn out to be nothing but old wine in new bottles.

Unrealistic Expectations

What if there were an advertisement for a "Super Teacher" with a role description like this:

> Super Teacher to assist staff teachers with an average of 15 years experience in 16 specialties. Super Teacher should be able to assist and promote the professional development of all these teachers in their specialty areas and in 21 specific skills areas, including research and ranging from philosophy of education to leadership training. Two qualifications are necessary: (1) the ability to demonstrate 21 skills in the 16 specialty areas; (2) the ability to assist each staff person in the effort to further develop these skills.

Such a role description would be laughable if it were not for the fact that in teacher education such a creature, in the shape of a school based teacher educator, has actually been proposed.

The stage is being set for unrealistic expectations—and dramatic failure. And the blame cannot be placed on groups external to the enterprise of teacher education. People who should know better, teacher educators themselves, are creating the expectation that one person can be trained to fulfill all the traditional duties of an entire college faculty as well as those of a district inservice and administrative staff. Appealing though this expectation may be to many in this "cost effective" age, it simply is not within the realm of possibility.

Testing the Waters

Teacher education is in a transitional period. Most teachers currently involved in professional development are likely to be engaged in traditional certification, degree, and/or district credit inservice programs. Subtle differences are already evident, however, in thinking about roles of teacher educators. The most notable is that teachers are much more likely to have support and resource personnel (titles vary tremendously) when and where they are needed. Although these personnel may not have received special training as school based teacher educators and tend to function quite independently with varying strengths and areas of expertise, they are testing the waters of school based teacher education.

For example, *media specialists,* probably trained in a previous decade to meet other types of needs, are often designated as key personnel in plans to strengthen resources for teachers; conveniently located and well stocked "teacher resource rooms" are becoming quite common. *Clinical consultants,* traditionally campus based and trained to facilitate the transition of beginning teachers from campus to schools, are also assuming a higher level of visibility and importance in the schools as attempts are made to involve career teachers in professional development. In other approaches to involving teachers in school based professional development, *master teachers,* usually experienced teachers with strong peer respect, are being promoted to positions with titles such as "staff development specialist" or "teacher center coordinator." Less commonly, academic types, traditionally associated with degree and credential programs, are being selected to spearhead the move toward school based teacher education. Even though not destined to spend a great deal of time in schools, they provide a perspective and analytical approach that can be helpful.

Delineating the Role

These professionals, in testing the waters of SBTE, may contribute more to delineating the role expectations of the school based teacher educator than will be contributed by some of the current efforts to come up with a comprehensive and ideal role description.

On the one hand, those actually involved in the transitional efforts will probably have a good understanding of what is possible. On the other hand, they may short circuit the effort to develop truly innovative and better programs. Credit must be given for actually getting out to teachers in schools, but merely extending and modifying traditional roles will not be enough. The problem is like one expecting that horses can be modified and further developed for the automobile age. A definite risk exists that "helping" roles, in urgent reaction to current pressures, will be extended (and perhaps even institutionalized) without any better understanding of the clients, issues and agendas that should be considered essential to the field.

In addition to the new political and logistical problems, SBTE must face inbred teacher education problems. The biggest, of course, is "relevance" of substance. In attempting to be relevant, teacher education has suffered from programs that approach either of two extremes. Having developed in almost total ignorance of the nature of its clients, most programs have been based on the assumption that all teachers can benefit from similar courses. At issue is the belief that teacher education is best provided for by encouraging teachers, of all backgrounds and aspirations, to engage periodically in a relatively stable, academic program of fundamental courses. Other, less traditional programs, which are based on the assumption that all teachers are alike only in that their needs are idiosyncratic, typically mature, and "improve" by developing individualized or personalized courses and experiences to "respond" to identified needs. Prerequisite to understanding the nature of relevance is an understanding of the types of clients to be served.

THE CLIENTS OF TEACHER EDUCATION

A great deal of the work being done in psychology and education today is related to Lewin's deceptively simple notion that human behavior is a function of the interaction between a person and the environment $B = f(PE)$. But interaction between a person and the environment may be extremely complicated. Most work designed to help understand this interaction continues to focus on the person. No productive purpose will be served by attempting to build a case that one factor in the interaction is more important than the other. We suggest that the answer to that question is variable—in some cases the personal characteristics are more important; in others, environmental influences or press contribute most to the interaction.

In teacher education, however, we need to recognize that we can do little to change a teacher's personality. Thus, our focus should be on the environment—which in teacher education means the program. This chapter will not attempt to integrate personal characteristics with environmental factors. To that extent, the work should be considered incomplete. By attempting to develop a more thorough understanding of the environment in which teacher education programs operate, however, we believe that both research and teacher education programs can move the field even closer to that "complete understanding" so clearly needed.

THE CONTINUUM OF TEACHING CAREER STAGES

The teacher educator's challenge is to provide an optimal environment for teacher growth. This environment, the teacher education program, can best be provided if planned and implemented with an understanding that teachers progress through a continuum of career stages. As a beginning, we have identified six. A delineation of these stages may ward off future temptations to consider teachers only idiosyncratically, or even worse, as a homogeneous population. Highlighting the need for different types of programing for teachers at the different stages is a necessary first step in addressing the problems of relevance. Furthermore, delineation of these stages will set some parameters within which professional differences and variations exhibited by individuals can be better comprehended and provided for.

All teachers progress through these stages chronologically and sequentially. Whether or not they develop professionally is a different question. The answer will be primarily determined by the appropriateness of teacher education programing at the various stages.

TEACHING CAREER STAGES AND PROGRAM TYPES

In broad terms, the world a teacher inhabits provides obstacles to be overcome, demands to be encountered, and almost ritualistic requirements to be met. Novice teachers must be "evaluated," growing teachers must become permanently credentialed and tenured, and veteran teachers are expected to adjust to many new policies, procedures, and innovations in both teaching and organization. These factors, all part of the environment, interact to create what might be called an "environmental press." It is from an analysis of these conditions that this typology was developed (Yarger & Mertens, 1977).

Stage 1. The Pre-education Student

Typically the pre-education student is a college undergraduate exploring but not yet committed to a teaching career. However, teaching careers can be explored by people at many different points during life. Students at this stage need to test our preconceptions regarding teaching. Their programing should help them better understand the basis of decisions they are attempting to make.

- *Introductory programing* is characterized by its comprehensiveness in introducing the student to what teaching and education are about. Not part of a professional training program, it may or may not offer college credit.
- *Experiential programing* provides the student with a chance to view on a firsthand basis the concepts that are being explored. It is almost exclusively a program of focused observations in schools and classrooms, with minimal interaction with students (if any interaction at all).

Stage 2. The Education Student

Typically college upperclassmen, students at this stage have already made a conscious decision and commitment to become teaching professionals. They need to develop basic teaching skills. The four types of programing for education students should be rigorous and demanding—the start of real professional training, leading to initial certification and a university degree.

- *Content programing* is specifically selected to help students learn what they will be teaching. Discipline oriented, it is not related to the actual instruction of students.

- *Foundational programing* focuses on the traditional foundational areas such as history, philosophy, sociology, and psychology of education. Non-instructional interactive classroom skills such as classroom management, strategies of teaching, and group processes, are also included.
- *Methodological/pedagogical programing* will help education students learn how to teach. The learning experiences will focus on the translation of content into appropriate ways of helping children learn.
- *Initial clinical programing.* Finally, toward the end of professional training, students will have the opportunity to demonstrate the interactive, methodological, and pedagogical skills they have been learning with children. Initially this demonstration should be done in a sheltered environment, e.g., microteaching.

Important though it is to distinguish at least two stages within what had been traditionally called "preservice education," it is imperative, if we are serious in our intent to provide for continuous professional development, to identify the various stages that teachers progress through as *inservice* teachers. We hypothesize that teachers progress through four distinguishable stages during their professional career.

Stage 3. The Initial Teacher

Transitioning from the relative security of a training program to the demands of being a full fledged professional, the initial teacher is faced with real problems—providing instruction to real children in real schools. Programing must help deal with difficulties typically encountered in the induction year.

- *Content programing* is discipline oriented, likely to be quite specific, and directly related to the curricula of the employing school district.
- *Additive/discrepancy programing* helps further develop pedagogical skills. An analysis of the preservice program will surely suggest training gaps that will require special programs. In all likelihood, programing during this stage will relate to acquiring an advanced teaching credential.
- *Intensive clinical programing* will aid in the transition from the sheltered environment of preservice to the complex environment of the real classroom. A significant amount of clinical help, focusing on orchestrating the rather discordant skills the initial teacher has previously learned, can be provided only within the context of a real classroom.

Stage 4. The Developing Teacher

Once the initial teaching year is completed, a novice professional still has much to learn in the second and third years of teaching. Programing most appropriate for this stage of teachers, who are usually working toward a high order credential and/or advanced degree, should include the following:

- *Content programing,* which is discipline oriented and from which teachers continue to learn about the content they teach. A master's level program in a content area is often appropriate in this stage.
- *Additive programing* is similar to additive/discrepancy programing for the initial teacher, though less focused on discrepancy programing, i.e., on closing "gaps" in previous training. The teacher at this stage will rely more on his or her own judgments to determine the appropriate type of program.
- *Adjustive programing* requires recognizing that things do change for the developing teacher. The change may be in the organization of the school, the types of students with whom the teacher deals, or even some greater change that exists within society. Regardless, programing will be needed to help teachers adjust to the changes. Although the decision to partake of the programing may be completely that of the developing teacher, the source of the change is usually viewed as external.

Stage 5. The Practicing Teacher

After 3 to 8 years of experience, teachers have demonstrated the ability to survive, perhaps even thrive, in the classroom. At this stage they are apt to have completed requirements for advance certification, tenure, and even advanced degrees. Therefore, external incentives for involvement in professional development activities are less potent. However, personal motivation may be very strong during this stage, as teachers begin to carve out areas of particular expertise or interest. Teachers who have left teaching for family reasons usually return to their careers at this stage and should receive special consideration in programing.

- *Content programing* continues to be important, necessitated by the explosion of knowledge in most content areas. Furthermore, teachers may begin to develop interest and expertise in multiple content areas.
- *Additive programing* in teaching, while no longer related to acquiring degrees or credentials, may be more specifically related to content specialties. This type of programing is probably essential in helping teachers to develop their personal styles and fortes. Additive programing for teachers who are resuming their careers after a period of professional inactivity will have to address gaps between what they once were able to do but are no longer able to do.
- *Adjustive programing* is similar to that for the developing teacher and may be required to deal with changes in the school or classroom environment. This kind of programing will be crucial for those teachers returning to teaching careers after an absence since change in circumstances is certain.
- *Career change programing* is related to preparation for a new professional role; it may or may not relate to a new credential. There are many education "specialty areas" that may be of particular interest to teach-

ers at this stage and should be addressed by a professional development program.

Stage 6. Experienced Teachers

After at least 8 years' experience, teachers may have little external incentive for becoming involved in professional development activities, since most experienced teachers have already carved out their areas of particular strength and expertise. However, if we believe that people have an innate and lifelong need to learn and to develop, then programing is certainly appropriate at this stage. Currently more teachers are at Stage 6 than at any other.

- *Content, additive, and career change programing* are similar to that described for Stage 5, Practicing Teacher.
- *Adjustive programing,* however, takes on additional importance at this stage. Since many changes in schools are incremental as opposed to dramatic, long term teachers may have to catch up with them. Conditions need to be established that will encourage teachers at this stage to engage periodically and regularly in professional assessment so that appropriate professional development activities can be devised. It is hoped that the need for comprehensive "retraining" strategies will be precluded.

Whether or not teachers will progress to successively higher levels of professional development as they progress through these career stages will depend on coherent programing that addresses the needs of teachers at each stage. (Hypothetically, a teacher may arrive at the "experienced teacher" stage with no more expertise than was possessed upon first entering a credential program, much as one can pass through the various stages of human development without progressing functionally out of adolescence.) But "appropriate programing," in and of itself, may not be enough. The teacher educator must also recognize issues in the delivery of programs that are going to impact the success of programing. Even a program that truly addresses the needs of teachers is not going to be worth much if the teachers do not become involved. Any effort to provide for the continuous development of teachers must consider that the contexts within which each of the six target populations will receive their education is dramatically different.

DELIVERY CONCERNS AND ISSUES

We could present a myriad of issues on the context within which teacher education programs are developed and delivered. Our focus here will be on *four* important issues—authority, credibility, finance, and governance. Let us examine how these issues impact on the planning of teacher education programs at the various sequential stages.

Authority

The established policies and procedures of legally constituted bodies may be embedded in requirements or regulations; sometimes they may be ad hoc. Program legitimacy is usually derived from the policies put forth by these groups. Certainly, state education departments offer authority for program development by virtue of program accreditation at the institutional level and certification requirements at the individual level.

Authority is also inherent at the institutional levels. Universities and colleges, for example, have programs that have gone through a faculty approval process; school district programs have authority by virtue of probationary requirements and tenure policies. Additionally, school districts have authority to mandate certain amounts of inservice training. A teacher educator will obviously have more clout if the proposed programs tend to be congruent with established policies and requirements. That is, programs for teachers at Stage 2, "education student," and Stage 3, "initial teacher," have more authority than those for teachers at Stage 6, "experienced teacher." Voluntary teacher involvement may be a problem in programs that do not carry the authority of legally constituted bodies.

Credibility

The extent to which a program addresses perceived needs determines its credibility. Authority and credibility are related in that both are concerned with the larger issue of a program's conceptual base; they are also distinct. In fact, programs can be credible without possessing authority, and vice versa. A program has credibility only if it appears to relate to the participants' professional life. Obviously, credibility looms as an issue in programs that do not carry authority.

Though less of an issue in certification and degree programs, credibility probably will not have impact on teacher involvement. A perceived lack of credibility will certainly affect teacher morale, however, as well as the likelihood of teachers becoming involved in voluntary teacher education programs. Teachers simply will not become involved unless they perceive that the activities address their needs.

Finances

Another major issue in teacher education is the question of who will pay the tab. As one moves from required programs, Stages 1, 2, and 3, to more voluntary programs, Stages 4, 5, and 6, the answer to that question and the stability of the program become more tenuous. Historically, a relatively stable, though client generated, financial base for teacher education programs has led to certification. Institutional support for inservice education, particularly after one accepts a teaching position, has been very limited.

In the future, higher levels of public funding will most likely relate to the question of authority, while the willingness of participants to continue to bear the financial burden will relate to the issue of credibility. Currently, since teachers are still bearing the greater amount of direct costs for teacher education, voluntary programs (most appropriate for teachers at Stages 4, 5 and 6) must be perceived to be credible, or finances will be a potent issue.

Governance

Finally, governance is a major issue in program planning in teacher education. In this case, *governance* is defined as a structure and process that is concerned with making micropolicy decisions. This type of policy decision, as opposed to macropolicy decisions, provides the most direct type of guidance for teacher education programs. It should also be kept distinct from operational decisions, as these are the realm of program managers and administrators.

Generally, the smaller the number of groups involved in micropolicy decisions, the easier the governance process. Frequently, however, there is a tradeoff; the greater the number of constituencies involved, the greater the likelihood the program will be accepted. One would suspect that the goal would be to involve all essential constituencies, at least as they relate to the potential for program success. Governance as an issue becomes increasingly complex as a function of career stages; that is, many more constituencies need to be involved in decision making at Stage 6 (e.g., teacher organizations, school districts, and institutions of higher education) than at Stage 1 which requires only the institution of higher education.

TEACHER EDUCATION PROGRAM AGENDAS

A question frequently asked by teachers prior to entering into a professional development activity is, "How much will it demand of me?" Thinking of programing in terms of program agendas will help provide that answer. In some cases, simple interest and a willingness to participate are the only commitments needed. In other cases, however, the individual participant must be committed to learning new skills and using them in the classroom. Finally, some types of teacher education programs will call for substantial restructuring of how the teacher operates.

Teacher education program agendas can also provide an answer to the question cited earlier for institutional leaders and administrators. Leaders and administrators may "support" teacher education programs with little more than a nod of the head. But when the intended effect of a program is to produce rather marked alteration in the school program, a different type of commitment is obviously called for.

Finally, this conceptual tool can provide guidelines for estimating not only the needed commitment of organizational resources, but also the necessary level of organizational tolerance for change and alteration. All too often, teachers become involved in activities that they perceive to be helpful. What they may overlook, however, is the need to invest organizational energy into creating conditions that support the newly developed skills, and into establishing an organizational tolerance for change in the way the organization will operate. Frequently, this change will challenge the status quo and security of many members of the institution, and may even move beyond the institution into the general community. Few would deny the importance of being able to estimate this type of potential impact prior to establishing a commitment for any particular program of activity.

Teacher education program agendas are essentially content free. Although more exotic content areas would probably have implications for the level of commitment, change, and tolerance that are needed, the construction of the agenda types is meant to accommodate any content area. Thus, program agendas should be thought of as being complementary to the program types presented earlier. When put together, as will be done later in this chapter, they provide an even more powerful tool for understanding program development and, hence, for understanding the role of a school based teacher educator.

Program Agenda Types

The teacher education program agenda types presented here are constructed in progressively more complex, hierarchical fashion. Although our implicit intention in constructing this brief hierarchy is to be all inclusive, we have yet to develop specific criteria for application. Regardless, these agenda types can still serve as tools to help program developers guide their thinking and planning activities.

Facilitative Programing

One kind of programing may be characterized as "goal-less," and need not even be related to school programs. It may be planned with the clear intent of exploring new approaches to childhood education or providing (facilitating) client growth and understanding in a variety of ways. One could even build a case that this type of programing simply lacks a conceptual base or is the result of poor planning. In any event, the resultant program is flexible, open, variable in quality, and may address either professional or personally derived content areas.

Program/Skill Development

The intent of this type of program is to alter the educational program or to aid educational personnel in developing new skills or improving existing ones. Typically, one can think of program or skill development programing as "fine tuning" existing school programs, or helping teachers develop new skills that readily fit into their day to day activities. It typically requires little if any alteration of either professional roles or organizational structure.

Program Modification

The skills learned in this more radical type of programing tend to be more molar than molecular, and require more individual commitment to implement. Usually though, few, if any, major organizational changes are required. In other words, although the school will look very much the same, the things that teachers are doing in their classrooms may differ in important ways.

Program Restructuring

Not only does this type of agenda call for major role changes on the part of educational personnel; it typically implies notable organizational change as well. Thus, institutional leaders and administrators must make a commitment to this type of programing in the same way that teachers must. A much wider base of role groups will participate in restructuring programs, and a thorough understanding of the effect as well as a commitment for institutional tolerance must exist. Not only will the activities in a classroom be markedly changed by program restructuring, but the organization of the school will appear different as well.

Using the Concept of Teacher Education Program Agendas

The notion of program agendas may not only allow one to understand what has occurred in teacher education but also should provide a helpful tool to program developers for planning future activities. Integrating the ideas inherent in this concept with those presented earlier (client types and program types) should provide an even greater depth of understanding. It should also underscore the complexity of the problems in program development in teacher education and allow us to start thinking seriously about the variety of roles that would characterize a school based teacher educator.

AN ATTEMPT AT SYNTHESIS

We have described several components of the school based teacher education picture and have viewed the clients of teacher education as progressing through career stages. Additionally, we presented program types and delivery concerns that are attendant to teacher education career stages. Finally, we sought to explain in detail four distinct types of teacher education program agendas.

Each component, in its own way, sheds some light on the field of teacher education. At this point, we need to relate the various components in order to develop a better understanding of the prospects and problems of school based teacher education. First, teacher education clients, program types, and agenda types will be integrated. Finally, we will try to add the impact of the delivery concerns or issues to the mix. The entire process is tremendously complicated—in fact, some of it probably cannot be well sorted. Nonetheless, one of our basic intents is to present teacher education in general and schoolbased teacher education in particular as far more complex enterprises than both contemporary and historical treatments would indicate.

The First Cut

By attempting to match up teacher education client program types with agenda types, we can begin to estimate the likelihood that a school based teacher educator will be called upon to develop certain types of programs. Figure 1 presents such a match-up graphically.

Before attempting to ascribe meaning to this figure, we should note a couple of cautions. First, a level of arbitrariness characterizes the decision to label a match-up as "weak," "moderate," or "strong." The strength of a match is far from random or capricious; rather, it tends to flow logically from the conceptualizations and definitions presented earlier. For example, reading down the program type column "career change" for the "practicing teacher" and "experienced teacher," we note that the match tends to weaken slightly at the later stage.

Career change in teaching is usually associated with the acquisition of advanced degrees and/or credentials. Teachers often enter into career change activities as they pursue the requirements for teaching certificates. Thus, career change ideas typically emerge during the developmental stages of teaching, are heightened during the practicing years, and probably become less important for the experienced teacher—though a moderate match still exists. We can use similar logic to explain the decision to weight differentially the various cells in this figure. The differential weightings are open to debate and possible change. But they are neither empirically supported decisions nor are they capricious. Rather, they reflect the current level of understanding about the field of teaching.

More program types are to be accommodated as one moves up the career stage ladder to "developing," "practicing," and "experienced teacher." Perhaps more importantly, the strength of the match between program type and program agenda increases at the upper levels of career stages, with nearly twice as many strong matches for the experienced teacher as for any other group. Thus, if a strong match-up is related to frequency of program activity development, school based teacher educators will be devoting a great deal of their time to working with classroom veterans.

The "facilitative program" agenda type is somewhat elusive because it

154

FIGURE 1

Estimate of Match Between Teacher Education Client, Program Type, and Agenda Type

Stages of Teaching Career / Program Types / Program Agenda Types

Client Stage	Program Type	Facilitative	Program/Skill Development	Program Modification	Program Restructuring
Pre-Ed Student	Introductory	+++	////	////	////
Pre-Ed Student	Experiential	+++	////	////	////
Education Student	Content	+++	////	////	////
Education Student	Foundational	+++	////	////	////
Education Student	Method./Pedagog.	++	+++	////	////
Education Student	Initial Clinical	+	+++	+	////
Initial Teacher	Content	+	////	////	////
Initial Teacher	Additive/Discrep.	+	+-	++	+
Initial Teacher	Intensive Clinical	+	+++	+	+
Developing Teacher	Content	+	////	////	////
Developing Teacher	Additive	+	+++	++	+
Developing Teacher	Adjustive	+	++	+++	+
Developing Teacher	Career Change	+	+	+	+
Practicing Teacher	Content	+	////	////	////
Practicing Teacher	Additive	++	+	+++	+
Practicing Teacher	Adjustive	++	++	+++	+
Practicing Teacher	Career Change	+++	+++	++	+
Experienced Teacher	Content	+++	////	////	////
Experienced Teacher	Additive	+++	+++	+++	++
Experienced Teacher	Adjustive	++	+++	+++	-
Experienced Teacher	Career Change	+	+	+	+

Key: //// No Match   ++ Moderate Match
+ Weak Match   +++ Strong Match

is so open and participant dependent, with the relatively greater importance for the "experienced," and to some degree the "practicing" teacher. These teachers tend to be credentialed and have enough hours and/or degrees to be at the upper levels of the salary schedule. Therefore, as teachers move up the career stage ladder, fewer and fewer external motivators will elicit involvement in teacher education programing. Thus, the involvement of "experienced" and "practicing" teachers in inservice programs will depend much more on their interest and on their opportunity to explore and check out various opportunities. We see implications here for the school based teacher educator, particularly with regard to how one solicits input, develops activities, and presents program activities to potential clients.

Finally, a glance at Figure 1 will verify intuitive sense that the bulk of the programing in schools will be of the "program/skill development" and "program modification" variety, which require less in the way of institutional commitment and tolerance than does "program modification." Hence, school based teacher educators will have different roles to play, depending on the program agenda type. In general, fewer and weaker match-ups come with "program restructuring;" schools don't change very much.

Another way of interpreting Figure 1 is to focus on one stage of the teacher career continuum. For example, looking at "initial teacher," it becomes readily apparent that the strongest match-ups come in the area of "program/skill development." Since the "initial teacher" will be receiving a great deal of external direction in the selection of inservice programs, he or she will likely have fewer "facilitative" type opportunities. Additionally, the "initial teacher" will be concerned more with development of skills to meet the day to day press of the classroom, and consequently will be less interested in "program modification" and "program restructuring" activities. Nonetheless, "initial teachers" may well find themselves placed in a school environment where some type of change has been mandated. No "career change" column is included for the "initial teacher," as it is doubtful many first year teachers are looking toward a different career in education. We strongly suspect that their primary interest will be in mastering whatever challenges confront them that relate to becoming a good classroom teacher.

Looking at the "practicing teacher," however, we can paint a somewhat different picture. More emphasis on "program modification" activities is now likely to occur, because "practicing teachers" with more experience will likely be soliciting ways to improve their instructional programs for children. The day to day press of survival, although present, will be less intense. At the same time, as has been previously pointed out, more matchups in the "facilitative program" area are likely to occur, because as the "practicing teacher" matures there will be less environmental press for involvement in inservice activities. Thus, the "practicing teacher" can probably be characterized as a more mature learner, seeking ways to improve instruction, and having to respond less to external motivators for involvement.

The Plot Thickens

Although our exploration of the match-up between client program types and agenda types may have provided some insight, the program development problems in teacher education are still more complex. The next step is to attempt to integrate the delivery concerns (issues) with the match-ups presented earlier. Figure 2 graphically presents this three dimensional concept.

Each issue or delivery concern is differentially weighted, depending on the client and the program agenda type. In one instance, authority may be an issue of major concern; in another, it will be of no concern at all. This weighting will certainly differ from site to site. An analysis of the three sets of components suggests some principles likely to apply regardless of site specific considerations.

For example, suppose we wanted to construct a "program/skill development" activity for an "education student." Speculate about what issues we would encounter. First, authority would be no problem, as the "education student" is operating in a program that, in most cases, has state authority through the mechanism of an approved program. Credibility is not likely to be bothersome, as students at this level are usually meeting requirements and are anxious to develop skills that can be used with children in classrooms. Financial considerations are probably covered with tuition costs and/or the institutional budget. Governance, however, has changed in recent years. Historically, governance of teacher education programs for preservice teachers was exclusively the domain of the university or college. In recent years, however, a variety of other constituencies have become interested and involved. Thus, the school based teacher educator would have to consider the governance problems relating to a "program/ skill" development activity for an "education student."

The task of school based teacher educators, then, is to be aware of the differential importance of the issues via-à-vis client group and program type. Additionally, they must be able to anticipate the importance of these issues and to take them into account in the planning and developmental process. Ability to perform these tasks will likely lead to more successful and trouble free programs. Although the issues suggest only minor problems in programing for the "education student," such is not the case for teachers at other career stages.

To clarify more fully the complexity of attempting to integrate the delivery concerns (issues) with teacher education client program type, two extreme examples should prove helpful. These examples are graphically presented in Figure 3.

FIGURE 2

A Model for Integrating Stages of Career, Program Agenda Types, and Program Development Issues in Teacher Education

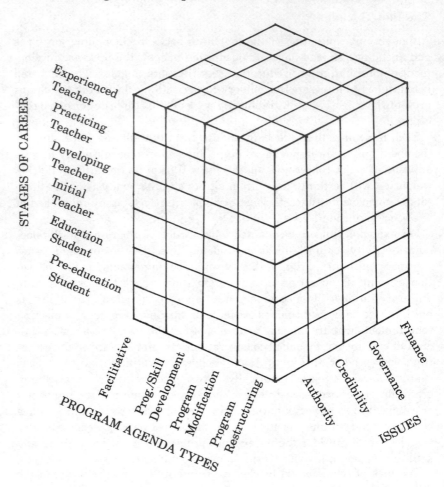

Example 1

A teacher educator wants to put together for college sophomores a series of structured classroom visitations over a 3 week period. The experiences are part of a career decision seminar to help the student decide whether or not to go into the field of education ("facilitative programing" for "pre-education students"). How would the issues interact in this instance?

Authority would probably be little problem at all. Since sophomores are students enrolled at the university, the career decision seminar as part of

FIGURE 3

**The Differential Importance of Issues by Stages of Career and
Program Agenda Types—Two Extreme Examples**

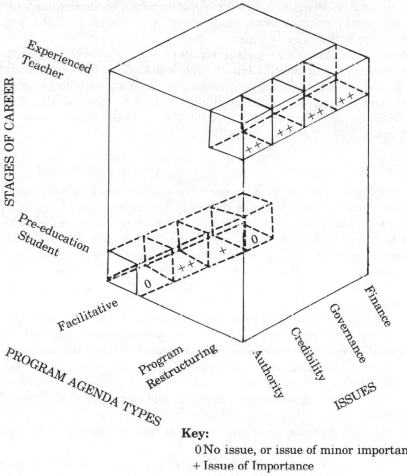

Key:

0 No issue, or issue of minor importance
+ Issue of Importance
++ Issue of Major Importance

the university's education program would not be part of a "certificate"
problem—thus, it requires little authority. Credibility, on the other hand,
would be an issue of major importance, inasmuch as one intent of the experience is to serve a recruiting purpose. Additionally, the attendance at
the visitation sites is at least partially voluntary, suggesting that the students must perceive them as potentially helpful. Finance would be a prob-

159

lem of some importance, though probably not major. Any time an institution offers a program activity that transcends the traditional need for classroom space, thus consuming more resources, the problem of who is going to pay the tab becomes more important (e.g., travel, staff time). Finally governance would not be considered a problem of importance. Few of the constituents involved in teacher education would be against providing experiences for college sophomores designed to help students make decisions about teaching as a career.

Because the students themselves are not part of a constituent group, the tendency is to treat them as fairly unimportant. Thus, it seems that the program developer must be most concerned about the credibility factor, with some concern over the financial aspects of the proposed activity. Governance and authority would not consume much of the planning and developmental effort in this instance.

Example 2

A school based teacher educator wants to lead a school to a new type of organization that includes team teaching, flexible use of allocated time, and even a school policy making cabinet. The average teacher in the building has been teaching for 11 years—a clear cut instance of a desire for "program restructuring" for experienced teachers. In this instance, *all* of the issues would be of major importance. The school based teacher educator will have a huge investment of time and energy if this program is to be pulled off successfully.

In the area of authority, not only would the program likely require school district approval and commitment, but the administrative staff and the teachers' organization would have a crucial interest in how that authority is generated. The program would obviously require a great deal of new instructional as well as organizational behavior; thus, credibility becomes an issue of importance. Because successful implementation of this type of a program would require a great deal of work over a long period of time, the promise it holds for improving the school must be perceived to be very great.

Finances would also be an issue of major importance. Not only is there the problem of released time for training, but also of the support to actually garner the needed instructional resources. Also, because of the nature of the proposed program we can assume that it is a long term activity that will require resources over a period of time. Finally, governance is also an issue of major concern, even after the appropriate authority has been generated.

In this case, then, many different constituents will want to have a major voice in making the day to day, programmatic decisions. In fact, many of the decisions may relate directly to the contract that exists between the teacher organization and the school district. And, just to cloud the issues

160

a little, it is entirely possible that the trainers and inservice instructors may have ideas that differ significantly from those of the teachers and administrators. Thus, it is evident that the school based teacher educator is going to have to invest a great deal of time and effort over a long period of time even for planning this type of a "program restructuring" activity for "experienced teachers." Unless the points raised in the issue analysis are handled effectively, chances for successful implementation of the new school organization are slim indeed.

The kind of analysis presented in the two examples can be performed for any type of teacher education client and program. Importance of the various issues changes dramatically as one changes the situation in which to consider them. Such an analysis, when carefully performed, can not only save a teacher educator time and effort, but can also insure that the appropriate conditions exist for program implementation.

EMERGING ROLES OF SCHOOL BASED TEACHER EDUCATION

We have argued that teacher education is a far more complex activity than its historical treatments would indicate. In fact, the complexity of the field requires that we talk about the *roles* rather than the *tasks* of school based teacher education—recognizing that no single person can perform all of an elongated list of specific teacher education tasks. The background, experience, and training any single person brings to the role of school based teacher educator will obviously have a direct effect on how he or she plays out the role. In fact, background can be a curse as well as a blessing. It is a blessing if the school based teacher educator carefully and sparingly integrates his or her own particular background, training, and expertise into the performance of the professional role—it is a curse if that is all that they do. Thus, perhaps the first role of the teacher educator is to recognize that the position requires the fulfillment of different roles than those associated with other education positions.

Any articulation of roles to be fulfilled by a school based teacher educator makes some assumptions. First, the school based teacher educator is assumed to possess a high level of familiarity with the site(s) to be served. This familiarity can occur by virtue of having worked on site in a different position. Or it may require that the school based teacher educator, newly assigned to a site, take the time and put forth the effort to become familiar with the salient characteristics—those presented earlier. Doing so should make the role easier because familiarity with the characteristics of the site will allow the school based teacher educator to obtain a more realistic sense of the possible.

Second, little on the educational horizon today would lead one to the sanguine assumption that a school based teacher educator will be present

161

in every school building. A more likely scenario would place a school based teacher educator between groups of three to six buildings, much as curriculum consultants are available in schools today.

With this in mind, at least four roles emerge to characterize a school based teacher educator:

1. *Analyst.* To a very large degree, the school based teacher educator must be a problem solver. Problem solving will occur by virtue of analyzing the different types of clients and program agendas that have emerged, and the interaction of these with several different delivery concerns or issues. This analytical procedure should allow the school based teacher educator to understand the process of developing program activities in a new, more powerful way.

2. *Planner.* We probably should add to this role the adjective "realistic." Once the variety of program components are delineated, they must be understood in relation to each other. Planning of inservice program activities, then, would successfully relate to the analysis previously performed. Putting the pieces together in synthesized program configurations can be referred to as planning.

3. *Resource Finder/Integrator.* Many school based teacher educators do not possess many of the requisite skills and resources to achieve program goals. Obvious roles to be performed, therefore, are finding the variety of needed human and material resources and integrating them into a coherent program activity package. This role demands a great deal of administrative skill. It must, however, occur within the context of understanding and wise planning; or it will turn out to be little more than random activity, with hit or miss results, a condition that characterizes much of school based teacher education today.

4. *Facilitator.* What makes program activities occur is the facilitating role, which calls for administrative skill, and often relates to the school based teacher educator paying careful attention to details and logistics. It also requires interpersonal skills, an understanding of physical environments, and a sense of knowing what will work and what will not. Although there may be an element of trial and error in fulfilling this role, to many it will be the bottom line of success for the school based teacher educator.

Again, we have consciously minimized the actual implementational or "doer" role for the school based teacher educator. The latter may teach workshops and seminars, supervise either preservice or inservice teachers, counsel teachers, and even perform research. However, we must always remember that ability to perform these tasks will relate to the training and experience of the individual, and will have to be exercised with great care. Instead of being just another specialist or content expert in the schools, the school based teacher educator should be a leader with the ability to put programs together from scratch and to make them work. This can only occur with careful attention and a great deal of sensitivity to the politics of the situation, the continual use of interpersonal skills, and the maintenance of credibility with the various role groups. These are probably best thought of as characteristics of a potentially successful school based teacher educator, however, and not as roles to be fulfilled.

SOME LEFTOVER PROBLEMS

Assuming that a school based teacher educator could fulfill with excellence each role described in the last section of this chapter, some important problems are left dangling. Since a school based teacher educator is a new role in established institutions, we can expect some problems with the "goodness of fit." Established institutions have established professionals performing established roles and tasks. The school based teacher educator will not only be performing new tasks associated with new roles, but will assume some tasks previously performed by others. Acceptance and "fit" are not assured.

The following areas are explored more for the purpose of understanding the problem rather than for offering a solution. Regardless, they are problems of importance and will have to be dealt with if school based teacher education is ever going to occur at the levels implied in this chapter.

Institutional Belongingness

This problem is really simple to understand—it focuses on the institution to which the school based teacher educator is affiliated. Are they school district staff or college faculty? Do they attend faculty meetings at the university or do they go with the school administrators? Or with the teachers? Although this may sound fairly insignificant, unless a clear cut institutional placement is found for the school based teacher educator, the likelihood of being viewed as an "outsider" will persist; and the ability to achieve real program success will be limited.

Professional Isolation

Whom do school based teacher educators view as their peers and professional colleagues? With whom do they lunch when they want to play off new ideas and solve problems? Any evolving or newly formulated professional role is faced with this significant problem. Nothing could lead quicker to school based teacher educator "burnout" than having to work in professional isolation in an institution and society that values professional delineation and affiliation. Think for a moment about the problem of spending a professional week attempting to "credible" your way in, and having no one to talk with who understands the forced smiles and required patience.

The Juggling of Priorities

Whose priorities are most important? Does the school based teacher educator listen first to teachers? To school administrators and board members? To university based teacher educators? To community representatives? These are difficult questions to answer. Can credibility be maintained if the predominant priorities belong to the superintendent and administrative staff? Can the role and the programs survive in a system if the predominant priorities belong to the teachers and the teachers' organization? If the role can be institutionalized— if belongingness can occur—then some direction will be offered for dealing with a variety of constituents and their priorities.

To Be or Not To Be Certified?

Will certification standards make it more difficult rather than easier to train and employ school based teacher educators in professional positions? Whether or not a school based teacher educator can become a mainstay in the field without certification is a problem of major importance. An intelligent analysis of the field would suggest that it will probably be an institutional necessity, but perhaps a functional liability.

Surely other problems can be raised concerning the viability of the role of school based teacher educator. Although we cannot anticipate what these problems might be, they will likely boil down to such questions as: Is there a career in the field of school based teacher education? Who would want to have such a career, i.e., what is the motivation?

These questions are both exciting and frightening at the same time. They are exciting because they make clear that school based teacher education is a new role offering much promise of improved programing for teachers, and thus for children. They are frightening because they suggest that developing this new role might not be as easy as many would hope. Regardless, the excitement, promise, and fear will all probably interact to keep the idea alive and to allow serious teacher educators the time needed to work toward the development of a new and valuable professional role.

REFERENCES

Broudy, H. S. *A critique of performance-based teacher education.* American Association of Colleges for Teacher Education, 1972, PBTE Series (4), 2–26.

Sawhill, J. C. Lifelong learning: Scandal of the next decade? *Change,* 1978/79, *10*(11), 7; 80.

Yarger, S. J., & Mertens, S. K. About the education of teachers—A letter to Virginia. *Issues in Inservice Education.* Syracuse: National Council of States on Inservice Education, 1977.

9

Staff Development Issues Relating to P.L. 94–142: A Local Education Agency Perspective

ELIZABETH DILLON-PETERSON

This chapter will consider issues in designing appropriate content and delivery of staff development or inservice education for educational personnel at all levels involved in implementing P.L. 94-142. We will review the issues primarily from the perspective of a local educational agency (LEA), focusing on a number of elements that make for successful implementation of all educational programing (including staff development) or that militate against it. Implied is a recognition that while special education must necessarily be viewed as a distinct entity, it is also similar to and should be integrated with the rest of the education program.

This chapter is intended to deal more with pragmatic concerns related to effective program implementation than with theoretical or philosophical issues, although consideration of philosophy and theory always underlies the operation of any program. Without attempting to be exhaustive or comprehensive, we hope to represent some critical elements of current practice. No priority is intended by the order in which statements are made.

We will use the terms *inservice* and *staff development* interchangeably, defining terms as follows: all those professional growth activities in which educational personnel within the local district (administrators, resource teachers, teachers, and classified personnel) engage during their careers and that provide them with skills, knowledge, or attitudes to enable them to provide more competent instruction for students.

ASSUMPTIONS

This chapter is based on the following general assumptions:

1. Effective programing for special education students is more like that for *all* students than different from it.
2. Inservice education of any kind, with particular focus on special education inservice needs, can be considered most effectively in the context of total instructional programing for meeting the needs of all students rather than as a separate activity.
3. Effective instructional programing and execution (including most staff development) can best be carried out at the local school building site, under the supervision of the local building administrator, *if* appropriate guidelines, resources, and support services are provided.
4. The level of competence of building administrators is crucial to the success of all programs under their jurisdiction.
5. A well trained, experienced special education teacher is an effective on site staff development leader for personnel directly involved with students, provided he or she is also skilled in working with adults.
6. A developmental, coordinated scope and sequence of continuous preservice/inservice activities is essential to provide adequately prepared resource persons with varied levels of expertise in the special education areas.
7. Effective implementation of special education programing is enhanced by expending the least possible amount of time in meeting bureaucratic requirements.
8. The increasing requirements that students be precisely categorized and labeled militate against providing services for students with specialized needs that cannot currently be diagnosed, prescribed for, and remedied without danger of stigmatization, which often results from the current complex procedures involved in placement.
9. More viable instructional options are available when there is a continuum of service for all students in which less seriously handicapped students may receive "first aid" at an initial level, and more concentrated, in depth, sustained attention if initial attempts are not successful.
10. Individuals who work with a broad range of children have many skills that are also applicable to "first line" work with special education students.
11. Mainstreaming students can be a very useful process if appropriately managed. It can provide for a more positive self concept for special education students; growth in empathy and understanding for "regular" students; and breakdown of isolation for special education teachers, as well as of special education programs in general. It is not, however a panacea and is not good for all special education students.
12. Staff development for special education resource teachers, regular

classroom teachers, and others connected with the program is most effective when focused on real educational problem solving. It may, then, include such concerns as normal child development (particularly behavioral development), overall classroom management, effective use of time, and differentiating responsibilities as needed to deal with learning problems, rather than with unarticulated skill training such as behavior modification.

13. Teachers who work with special education students at all levels of the school system, and with any level of handicap, will achieve better results when reasonable expectations are adequately, but not restrictively, defined—both for them and for the students with whom they work.

14. The fact that demands of comprehensive special education programing require a number of levels of expertise in a variety of areas makes it difficult to provide adequate training for staff members to be effective within the prevailing organizational structure.

15. Any total programing/staff development effort should view the special education program as a part of the "ecosystem" of the school, and should consider the impact of the special education program by and upon regular students, parents, and the broader community as well as professional, paraprofessional, and classified school personnel.

16. The total programing/staff development effort will be more effective if it is correlated with, and makes use of, other community agencies whose services are directed toward the target population.

CURRENT CONCERNS OF LEA'S REGARDING IMPLEMENTATION OF P.L. 94-142

Demands on individual classroom teachers have increased dramatically in the past several years, particularly in relation to accountability. Even though all levels of the educational establishment are affected by these demands, ultimate accountability rests with the regular classroom teacher. Teachers appear more and more apprehensive about their ability to deal adequately with day to day teaching, without including a plethora of other responsibilities.

Staff developers and administrators of special education programs who are concerned about morale as well as staff development are made aware of these pressures when they perceive that capable, conscientious teachers flock in burgeoning numbers to sessions (which they have requested) titled, "Relax Your Body, Relax Your Mind," or "Coping with Stress."

Protests against mainstreaming on the part of such organizations as The National Education Association (NEA) may be more an evidence of general protest against the continuously greater demands on teachers than a lack of professionalism or desire to meet the needs of students.

167

As one excellent teacher said, "I *never* did as good a job as I wanted to—even at best. Now with all the new things I'm expected to do, I often go home with a feeling of near panic. I'm not sure how long I can deal with the expectations—my own as well as others—without leaving teaching. I really love teaching and I don't want to do that, but I'm never able to forget about it or leave it behind."

LIMITING EFFECTS OF FEDERAL REQUIREMENTS

A proliferating tendency to categorize students with special needs into ever tighter, more precisely defined categories is of great concern to school administrators, especially because the school is expected to provide adequately for an ever broadening range of students within a relatively unchanged educational situation.

This restriction is both physical and psychological. Regulations actually prevent integration of special needs and regular students due to the specific provisions that must be made for individual categories of students. It is difficult enough to provide a comprehensive, focused, manageable, program that seriously attempts to individualize for students at best, without edicts from outside sources. Many individuals who make the regulations appear to have little real understanding of the extent of the demands currently being made on the schools and, ultimately on the "regular" classroom teacher. In too many cases, categorization may widen the gap between "regular" and "special" rather than narrow it.

Certification Requirements

Parallel to the categorization problem is the requirement for different certification for different personnel who work with various classes of special needs students. Although some specification is necessary to insure that appropriate services are actually provided for certain students, school districts conscientiously attempting to provide for all their students as part of a comprehensive, overall design can be seriously handicapped by too much specificity. New certification requirements have sometimes discouraged sensitive, intuitive, effective teachers from "doing what comes naturally" (and successfully) with special needs students because they do not have the proper credentials and, thus, feel inadequate.

Unless care is taken, narrow certification requirements may actually remove valuable services from students who need them rather than provide additional ones. Effective teachers often elect, or are selected, to receive further training to fill some role other than classroom teaching. They may become special resource teachers, central office administrators, or state/federal agency personnel, having less and less contact with students and the real problems of the classroom.

168

Administrative Requirements

Traditionally, when programs are organized and/or mandated at the state or federal level, they require that each have an administrator to direct and monitor the program. Ostensibly, their purpose is to help implement the requirements effectively. In fact, they often represent a double layer of bureaucratic reporting, which takes valuable time and energy from the actual task of providing services to students. The layering can result in infighting or turf problems between the special programs and the regular program, creating a special difficulty for the local building principals who should best be able to monitor and orchestrate all the educational activities under their jurisdiction.

Separation of Programs

Frequently, different programs involve some of the same students. However, because of current regulations, it is very difficult to comingle funds from the various sources in order to provide cost effective service. Management theory suggests that when those responsible are genuinely involved in decision making, effective implementation of the program is more likely, particularly for "knowledge workers" such as those involved in education. It also indicates that program implementation is most effective when responsibility for the program and its planning are placed closest to the level of implementation, with a minimum of outside monitoring intervention.

Separation of programs causes difficulty not only in using resources prudently, but also in coordinating with and being reinforced by the regular program. Ironically, the enforced specialization of the program by federal and state requirements actually makes it more difficult to implement the mainstream philosophy. Extensive care must be taken to verify that appropriate services are delivered to particular students and not to others. Moreover, personnel required to keep the necessary records must be paid from funds that could be spent for improving services to students.

In some cases, a special program requires proof that efforts made in it are separate and different from the regular program so that supplemental services can be verified. This very fact makes it impossible in the local school district to transfer many specially funded programs or activities found to be successful to the regular program. The act of such transfers prevents their continued funding in the original target population, since they then are no longer "supplemental" or "different" in the eyes of the project officers.

Some respected educators argue that the best way of assuring a better education for special student needs would be to provide an enriched learning environment for *all* students. The special education student, then, would profit along with other students and the total level of achievement would rise.

General Human Needs

Institutions can no longer ignore the needs of the human beings who work in them—whether in giant corporations that operate for profit, or in the complex sets of human interactions of "regular" or "special" education programs. Although we have referred to the personal/social needs of adults and students in prior paragraphs, we want to consider now some areas that have not been mentioned in detail.

Staff Member Needs

Insufficient attention is given to identifying and providing for the personal needs of staff members who are expected to assume new responsibilities or who move into new roles and responsibilities. Too often, mandated programs fail to consider the significant personal difficulties most individuals encounter in connection with any change process (particularly one that may raise personal value questions).

One of the best ways to improve attitudes in staff development is to pay attention to Maslow's higher order needs for affection, respect, and the opportunity to make a meaningful contribution (Maslow, 1954). Few organizations provide sufficient opportunities for input from those expected to implement changes or for leadership respecting their judgment as competent professionals.

If the individual needs of all students are to be met, organizations must be restructured to allow and encourage personnel who serve them to work together in new and different ways. Such restructuring obviously requires a different level of human relations skill than does teaching in a self contained classroom.

Administrators quickly revert to a security need level when asked to implement policy that has been handed to them without their input, or without sufficient opportunity to determine what difficulties will accompany the implementation. Not only are they always highly concerned by the administrative details of implementation and management, but in addition their personal leadership competence may be threatened, at least temporarily. If undue personal trauma is to be avoided, and the tasks involved in the change are to be accomplished expeditiously, adequate orientation and skill building must be provided for administrators.

Student Interaction Needs

The role of regular students, in relation to special education students, is usually not adequately diagnosed and planned for. One supposed benefit of mainstreaming is increased understanding of special education students on the part of regular students; but unless managed appropriately, it is not likely to happen.

170

In fact, the mainstreamed student may become more and more isolated when moving through the educational system and less and less able to cope with the material being presented to agemates, if careful provision is not made. School districts are already experiencing some backlash from parents who feel that mainstreaming has lessened the opportunities for the successful adulthood of their children rather than increased it, because of the loss of the more concentrated, more individualized time apparently available in the separated situation.

Organizational Change

Too often local school districts and individual school buildings are not seen as total social milieus within which the change or implementation is to take place. Without assessment of the potential effect of the change on the organization of its parts, no change will have substantive impact.

And no organizational change takes place without affecting the individuals in the organization. Only when the personal needs of the individuals in the organization are most closely in harmony with the organizational goals does a healthy, productive working climate result.

Support Services

As we mandate or incorporate new programs, we need to identify and provide support for successful implementation. For example, very few curricular changes are accompanied by adequate staff development programing, even in school districts that have a heavy commitment to it. Often materials are not in place at the time implementation is to begin. On site assistance to those implementing the program is seldom available, and almost never at the time and place when difficulties are actually encountered. Planning time may be inadequate, particularly in situations where several people need to work together to provide for the needs of a group of students as a team. Practical research information is seldom available for those involved in implementing an education program. Even less often is there a clinical center where special problems can be referred for more specialized attention.

IMPLICATIONS FOR LOCAL SCHOOL DISTRICT PROGRAMING/STAFF DEVELOPMENT

If the foregoing assumptions are accepted, and the concerns expressed are valid and typical, some implications for the local school district program might be:

1. Programing for special education students and related staff development will be part of the district's comprehensive educational program planning, implementation, and evaluation.

2. Accountability for the special education program will be the same as for all other educational programs, resting with the central and/or local building administration.

3. Day to day implementation and responsibility for the program will be delegated to local building administrators, who will direct all programs situated in their buildings within guidelines established by the central administration of the school district and in accordance with state and federal requirements.

4. The program will provide for the identification of (a) special needs of a broad range of students, to include EMH, DLP, etc. , and (b) of resources matched to those needs, as well as (c) flexibility in assignment of services and designation of target populations.

5. Emphasis on comprehensive building level planning and management of the total education program will necessitate improved planning and human relations skills on the part of all those involved with the program. Priority will be given to staff development for building administrators, targeted at development of proficiency in managing a variety of programs designed to meet needs of a broad continuum of students.

6. Consideration of required special services will necessitate the training of certain individuals for certain tasks, but within a context where each individual's expertise is shared and recognized—not isolated. Suggested is the desirability of some form of team operation.

7. A process will be organized for diagnosing, prescribing, and implementing special programing for all students who need it, involving all those staff members who have direct contact with the student through staffing/planning meetings.

8. A personal/social development program for both staff and students will grow out of the educational problem solving related to the individual student needs. Planning will be based on organizational development concepts.

9. A network of collaborative relationships will be established between the local school building, the school district, the institution of higher education, action research organizations, and community agencies. For example, each might contribute to a building based diagnostic and prescriptive learning center, or a clinical research/consultation center, depending on the level of expertise and function.

10. School districts, through these collaborative relationships, will actively lobby for better ways of providing coordinated, substantive services to students with special needs within the context of total effective education programing for all students.

172

COMPONENTS OF AN EFFECTIVE STAFF DEVELOPMENT PROGRAM TO SUPPORT SPECIAL EDUCATION PROGRAMING

In light of these implications, a school district (and its collaborating organizations) might consider the following as key components of an effective staff development program designed to support program implementation.

Audiences

The staff development/inservice program would be organized to assist a wide variety of target audiences. Included should be all personnel involved with the special education program (perceived as part of the total education program of the district/school rather than as separate from it).

Central office administrators need increasingly sophisticated political awareness and higher levels of management skills—especially planning and communication skills. *Building administrators* need to learn better ways to orchestrate the multiple programs existing in their buildings, and to communicate with the various publics they serve. Useful would be group process skills in conflict resolution, problem solving, and consensus building.

Special education resource teachers need to be very knowledgeable about their particular areas of expertise. They should have a repertoire of human relations skills that will enable them to work not only with the target student population, but also with their colleagues and to be able to provide leadership without the trappings of power.

Classroom teachers need to acquire a general, nontechnical, mystique free understanding of the special needs of mainstreamed students. They also should have highly developed classroom management skills and behavior management competence. They must understand curriculum requirements and have basic skills in curriculum adaptation to meet individual needs. Knowledge of mediated materials will help them extend their own capabilities. Human relations skills will enable them to assist students in working together with understanding. Cooperative planning skills will facilitate their collaboration with colleagues to find different ways of grouping students so as to reduce the student/teacher ratio. Called for is staff development in teaming, differentiating responsibility, and techniques for student diagnosis and prescription.

Levels would vary in depth and sophistication according to the audience being addressed. Table 1 shows an example.

Content

The content of the staff development/inservice program would focus primarily on educational problem solving (diagnosis and prescription) and educational program management, in an articulated program based on ac-

173

TABLE 1

Audience/Level Variations

Levels	Audiences
Orientation/awareness	Community, parents of "regular" students; "regular" students; classified personnel (such as bus drivers, food services, office personnel)
Moderate, introductory level of understanding for generalists involved with the program, and for those who use initial or primary intervention strategies (such as regular classroom teachers in a mainstreaming program)	Regular classroom teachers, central administrators (i.e., subject matter consultants, parents of special education students)
In depth, long term, comprehensive clinical or semiclinical intervention strategies. Training to be a trainer of generalist colleagues	Resource specialists for each area of special education; teaching team members who assume responsibility for a particular area of special education in a differentiated staffing/team organizational structure. Personnel who staff in-building learning centers.

tual identified needs of students to be matched with appropriate resources and intervention strategies. Some key areas of emphases might be:

1. General education program design and improvement processes, including needs assessment, program planning, and goal setting (based on a diagnostic/prescriptive model), implementation, evaluation, and revision; group process, human interaction, and change. Particular attention would be paid to the special needs of (a) principals and (b) other staff members providing leadership (i.e., team leaders, special education resource teachers, department chairpersons, staff members with differentiated responsibilities focused on a specialization).
2. Human development, including behavioral development.
3. Specific programing for special education students in each target area, to include (as examples) (a) general description of characteristics of students in each identified group related to total educational program, (b) appropriate diagnostic/prescriptive techniques, (c) individualized pro-

graming, goal setting, and curriculum selection/modification, and (d) Assessment/evaluation techniques.

Delivery of Staff Development/Inservice Program

The following characteristics would enhance the delivery of staff development programs:
1. Have them primarily building based.
2. Focus on identified goals and expectations for special students and teachers as a part of total building efforts for all students.
3. Conduct programs by trained practitioners with assistance from consultants, or outside resource persons as appropriate.
4. Build around a practicum format focused on real student problems with on site assistance as needed in a laboratory or clinical setting and including resources from IHE and community agencies.
5. Articulate with preservice training.

Quality Control

The following criteria would help to insure quality performance:
1. Base programs on clearly stated outcomes for students and competencies needed by teachers to produce those outcomes, developed with substantial input from those expected to implement the learning program.
2. Provide for evaluation and critique in a nonthreatening, supportive, collegial environment through appropriately selected on site resource persons who work as members of the team.
3. Provide continuous reinforcement and review of skills to insure internalization and successful practice, with immediate, on site assistance as needed.

Outside Resources Needed

Although we suggest that the local school district, if moderately large, can supply much of its expertise from within, we believe it can be substantially assisted in its efforts through judicious collaboration and use of outside resources.

Two examples of such assistance are shown in Table 2.

NEED FOR A COLLABORATIVE APPROACH

Because the average classroom teacher and local school administrator are so heavily engaged in the day to day business of the school and its ever increasing demands, they have insufficient time to consider better ways of providing for the varying needs of all the regular and special students they

175

TABLE 2

Functions of Outside Resources

Problem Solving Support System

Local Site Team (Local building/central office team)	*Cooperative Research Team* (Appropriate university personnel at least part time based on site)
1. Identifies learning problems	1. Participates in "staffings" on site to work up student learning problems
2. Participates in staffings to clearly describe the problem and identify outcomes to be achieved	2. Gathers data from research that might apply to the problem, or develops a research design and recommends intervention strategies
3. Works with cooperative research team members to provide data, understand strategies, give feedback, apply intervention strategies	3. Applies the intervention strategies in collaboration with the on site team
4. Assists in evaluation of intervention, planning for changes	4. Evaluates the success of the strategy in collaboration with the on site team. Restructures or changes the process as necessary
5. Acts as dissemination unit as needed	5. Communicates through a practical report for use of other teams

Communication Support System

| *Purpose:* To help local school districts communicate with a wide variety of audiences about the nature of special education programs | *Regional Laboratories*: Develop "kernel" communication kits that could be adapted to the local situation and designed to provide basic orientation and awareness to a variety of publics including the general community, service clubs, central administrators, building administrators, parents of regular students, regular students, etc. These would be most helpful if |

176

TABLE 2 (Continued)

Functions of Outside Resources

Communication Support System

they included copies of printed materials to be used, suggestions for group process to accompany the activity. Each should be general enough to allow the school district to localize them, but specific enough to enable the district to use them in a step by step, cookbook fashion. Before broad distribution, these kits should be field tested in a number of localities to determine their effectiveness and should probably be prepared by noneducators who could interpret the program in lay language after extensive consultation with educators who have approved the final product.

serve. On the other hand, staff members of institutions of higher education are often accused of being out of touch with the day to day operation of the school. Both these needs may be met through the following.

Cooperative Learning Benefiting both the University and the Individual LEA

University personnel and school district personnel have long supported the need for collaboration, but circumstances have not rewarded them substantially for working to achieve it. University staff members should have opportunities to work regularly as a part of a school staff in order to understand fully problems encountered at the interface of the program and the student. These university representatives are valuable resources of information and skill as well as of theory based objective insights. On the other hand, many highly capable teachers and administrators are successfully coping on the job with the increasing complexities of schooling today and have valuable practical insights to share with university personnel. Both audiences can learn from each other through joint problem identification, demonstration, observation, feedback, collaborative planning, and implementation.

177

Meaningful Combination of Learning Theory with Practical Application

Teachers repeatedly say "Don't give me a lot of theory—give me something I can use in my classroom." They are sometimes criticized for having such a pragmatic attitude. Experience has shown, however, that teachers who are treated as colleagues in educational problem solving become skillful in action-research, if it is seen as applicable to their own situations. The Far West Laboratory is currently engaged in a project demonstrating that "garden variety" classroom teachers can and do make astute observations and conduct sophisticated research when given opportunity to work collaboratively with trained theorists.

Some practical application needs that might be addressed from a collaborative research base are:

1. Development of techniques for identifying characteristics or mental levels of special (student) learners, tied directly to what could be done to accommodate those levels within a flexible, low visibility local situation context.
2. Development of techniques for assessing the developmental levels of teacher-learners and techniques for modifying/matching staff development techniques and materials to those levels.
3. Development of techniques for working with parents such as (a) basic human communication techniques, (b) techniques for helping parents to help students meet educational objectives, and (c) ways to develop commitment and genuine involvement.

Application of Organizational Development Concepts

Since significant program improvement is unlikely to occur without some degree of organizational change, it is important to identify and provide training in:

1. Techniques for identifying organizational tasks to be accomplished, both within the LEA and the university, and together, in relation to P.L. 94-142.
2. Planning skills for accomplishing those tasks.
3. Strategies for identifying and providing for the personal needs of the individuals in congruence with the accomplishment of organizational goals.

Leadership Training

Despite widespread belief that the quality of most programs is no better or worse than the quality of leadership, little organized coherent effort is being made to enhance the skills of those currently in leadership positions. From the point of view of the local district, these are needed in all program improvement efforts, but particularly in relation to P.L. 94-142:

1. Identification of tasks to be accomplished at the district site.
2. Planning and organizing to accomplish the tasks.
3. Techniques for collaborative management.
4. Human development processes as applied to students and adults.
5. Communication skills, including verbal, nonverbal, written, group, and individual.

ORGANIZING FOR COLLABORATIVE STAFF DEVELOPMENT EFFORTS

A jointly developed and conducted staff development effort might be organized in the following way:

Target Audiences

The five primary target audiences are: university teacher-trainers, central office administrators, building administrators, building resource teachers, and regular classroom teachers at all levels (subdivided when appropriate by levels, e.g., primary, junior high).

Curriculum

All participants would participate together in the initial overview orientation block, made up of such topics as the following:

Phase I

Phase I would cover (a) federal requirements, (b) minimal introduction to categories of identification, (c) analysis of local situation, district, building in terms of student population, (d) setting objectives, (e) identification of roles and responsibilities, and (f) general planning to include assignment of staff, instruction/curriculum modifications, and staff development activities.

Phase II

Following the general block introduction, each target audience would participate in specialized blocks focusing on their particular staff development needs in relation to their assignments or roles as identified in Phase I, and to prepare them to operate successfully as leaders in the site specific Phase III.

Phase III

The next phase of the training would involve building based training sessions in which a project team made up of the university teacher trainer, the building administrator, the resource teacher, and the representatives

179

from the building teaching staff and central office would go through the analysis process modeled in the first overview-orientation block, but targeted at the local building situation, using actual building data for the work. A followup might be a full staff training program, ideally prior to the involvement of the total staff in the mainstreaming effort.

Phase IV

The final phase would be a continuous monitor/review/revise process based on the experiences of the operation. Formal and informal assessment by the project team and the total staff would take place regularly throughout the initiation stage of the project.

REFERENCE

Maslow, A. H. *Motivation and personality*. New York: Harper & Row, 1954.

Part 5

THE FUTURE DIMENSION

10

P.L. 94-142 and Suggested Areas of Competence for Teacher Educators

AUDREY SPRINGS ANDERSON

The Education for All Handicapped Children Act of 1975, Public Law 94-142, has already had tremendous impact on countless numbers of children, parents, teachers, administrators, teacher educators, and other educational personnel. As parents of the handicapped seek free appropriate educational placement for their children, teachers are confronted with implementing individualized education programs and questioning the extent of their responsibility, while local education agencies (LEA's) and state education agencies (SEA's) strive to comply with the provisions of the law.

BASIC TENETS OF P.L. 94-142

What is the fundamental requirement of P.L. 94-142? The law requires a free appropriate education in the least restrictive environment for all handicapped children, ages 3 to 18 by September 1, 1978 and ages 3 to 21 by September 1, 1980 (*Federal Register*, August 1977). *Appropriate* is not defined specifically, but derives its meaning from individual assessment and the individualized education program (IEP) developed for each pupil. The educational environment for a handicapped child can vary, e.g., residential programs, special day facilities, self contained special education classrooms, regular classrooms with or without resource support. Some concern has been voiced over the possible placement of severely and profoundly handicapped students. The appropriateness of integrating the handicapped with the nonhandicapped and the degree of integration is to be determined individually for each student. The law does *not* say that the regular classroom is most appropriate for all handicapped pupils; however, the governing objective is that *handicapped children will be educated with nonhandicapped children whenever appropriate for the individual child.*

183

The law further requires that an individualized education program be developed for each handicapped child. The following individuals must be involved in the formulation of the IEP: parent or guardian, teacher or teachers, someone qualified to supervise the provision of special education, and, whenever appropriate, the child. The content of the written statement must include information about:

- The child's present level of educational performance.
- Annual goals, including short term instructional objectives.
- Specific education services to be provided.
- The extent to which the child will be able to participate in regular education programs.
- Projected dates for initiation and anticipated duration of such services.
- Appropriate objective criteria, evaluation procedures, and schedules for determining, on at least an annual basis, whether instructional objectives are being achieved (Torres, 1977, p. 6).

Complete procedural safeguards must be afforded all handicapped children and their parents in regard to identification, evaluation, and placement. If a parent or guardian should be unavailable for a due process proceeding, the SEA or LEA must assign a surrogate (The Act, Sec. 121a.500-121a.514).

P.L. 94-142 also seeks to guarantee racially and culturally nondiscriminatory testing and evaluation. Sec. 121a.532 provides that:

(a) Tests and other evaluation materials:
   (1) Are provided and administered in the child's native language or other mode of communication, unless it is clearly not feasible to do so;
   (2) Have been validated for the specific purpose for which they are used; and
   (3) Are administered by trained personnel in conformance with instructions from the producer;
(b) Tests and other evaluation materials include those tailored to assess specific areas of educational need and not merely those which are designed to provide a single general intelligence quotient;
(c) Tests are selected and administered so as best to ensure that when a test is administered to a child with impaired sensory, manual, or speaking skills, the test results accurately reflect the child's aptitude or achievement level or whatever other factor the test purports to measure, rather than reflecting the child's impaired sensory, manual, or speaking skills (except where those skills are the factors which the test purports to measure);

184

(d) No single procedure is used as the sole criterion for determining an appropriate educational program for a child; and

(e) The evaluation is made by a multidisciplinary team or group of persons, including at least one teacher or other specialist with knowledge in the area of suspected disability;

(f) The child is assessed in all areas related to the suspected disability, including, where appropriate, health, vision, hearing, social and emotional status, general intelligence, academic performance, communicative status, and motor abilities.

Additionally, the law reaffirms the need for confidentiality of data. The SEA is responsible for notifying parents of policies and procedures for recordkeeping—including storage, disclosure to third parties, retention and destruction of personally identifiable information (The Act, Sec. 121a.561). Essentially, the provisions for this section are contained in The Family Educational Rights and Privacy Act.

IMPLICATIONS OF THE LAW

Depending on the role (parent, child, regular teacher, special educator, teacher educator, administrator or related personnel), specific concerns with the implementation of the law will vary. Most educators, however, are faced with a common problem—that of gaining sufficient training to support and assist in the implementation. Personnel preparation aimed at providing appropriately trained individuals to implement P.L. 94-142 is considered a high priority by the Bureau of Education for the Handicapped (Harvey, 1976).

The regular classroom teacher (one without training in special education) is now more than ever in need of a variety of techniques, methods, and procedures that will allow him or her to accommodate a wide range of variability in the classroom. The skills needed for implementing individualized education programs for mildly handicapped children are consistent with those skills deemed necessary for individualizing instruction for non-handicapped students: diagnosing student needs, prescribing instruction, adapting curriculum, and ongoing evaluation. We believe that the conceptual skills and strategies effective with nonhandicapped children will also be effective with handicapped children. Rather than calling upon teachers to demonstrate a new repertoire of competencies, the law asks them to demonstrate competence in areas that should prove beneficial for all children.

DESIRED COMPETENCIES

This chapter will explore the question, "What are the general competencies needed by a regular classroom teacher who is working with handicapped and nonhandicapped students in a regular class setting?" In an attempt to minimize the usual debate that occurs when competencies are specified, we will focus on general areas of competence as identified by different constituencies affected by P.L. 94-142.

Competencies Identified by Deans' Grants

For the purpose of assisting Deans' Grants Projects in curriculum development, Rader (1978) conducted a comprehensive search for teacher competencies relative to integrating handicapped students in regular classrooms. As a result of surveying all the Deans' Grants Projects, Rader identified 13 competency categories through content analysis:
1. The nature of mainstreaming.
2. The nature of handicapped pupils.
3. Attitudes.
4. Resources.
5. Teaching techniques.
6. Learning environments.
7. Learning styles.
8. Classroom management.
9. Curriculum.
10. Communication.
11. Assessing students' needs.
12. Evaluating student progress.
13. Administration. (Rader, 1978, p. 295)

A number of Deans' Grants had as their purpose the development of a competency based program for teachers; e.g., Project PREM (Preparing Regular Educators for Mainstreaming) and The Ohio Deans' Grant (Mainstreaming Preparation for Regular Educational Personnel) among others. Individual learning packets, modules, and other materials have been field tested and are available (Peterson, 1977).

Competencies Identified by Regular Elementary Teachers

Redden and Blackhurst (1978) surveyed elementary teachers from four Kentucky communities who were in at least the second year of mainstreaming. They asked teachers to identify specific occurrences of three effective and three ineffective behaviors relative to the instruction of handicapped pupils who were being integrated into a regular class environment. Based on the response of 184 teachers, 828 critical incidents were identified and compiled into 6 broad functions and 32 competency statements. A panel of judges documented the reliability of this process. The authors cautioned that further research would be necessary to determine the validity of these competencies, as well as the addition or deletion of items.

186

The following competency statements complete the stem (Redden & Blackhurst, 1978, pp. 616–617):

In order to effectively teach mildly handicapped students who are integrated with regular students in a mainstream elementary classroom setting, the teacher must be able to:

Function 1.0: Develop Orientation Strategies for Mainstream Entry

1.1 Participate in schoolwide planning for mainstreaming activities.
1.2 Set up a training plan that will provide supplementary instruction in areas necessary to teach effectively in a mainstream setting.
1.3 Participate in parent and community orientation programs on mainstreaming.
1.4 Seek out consultative relationships with specialists or school staff.
1.5 When appropriate, develop a program to prepare the special student for entry into a regular class.
1.6 Prepare members of the regular class for the entry of special students into the class.

Function 2.0: Assess Needs and Set Goals

2.1 Gather information to determine the educational needs of each student.
2.2 Evaluate each student's present level of functioning.
2.3 Determine for each student in the class individual goals that are appropriate, realistic, and measurable.
2.4 Determine group goals for the class as a whole and for subsets within the class.
2.5 Involve parents in setting goals for their child and for the class as a whole.

Function 3.0: Plan Teaching Strategies and Use of Resources

3.1 Design a system of teaching procedures that provides for individual differences in students.
3.2 Specify and prepare a variety of activities that will involve the entire class in grouping patterns that are varied and flexible.
3.3 Develop and design a variety of alternate teaching strategies.
3.4 Develop a plan for use of human and material resources.
3.5 Develop a flexible time schedule that provides for the learning, physical, and social needs of each student.
3.6 Provide an optimal classroom climate through appropriate arrangement and adaptation of the physical properties of the classroom.

Function 4.0: Implement Teaching Strategies and Use Resources

4.1 Select and use a variety of individualized teaching methods to instruct each student within the student's level or capability of functioning.

187

4.2 Develop, schedule, and maintain on a regular basis a variety of grouping patterns that provide opportunities for students to reach class goals, both social and academic.

4.3 Use the efforts of the special education resource staff with the special students' classroom activities.

4.4 Acquire, adapt, and develop materials necessary to achieve learning goals.

4.5 Plan and maintain a system to use the assistance of volunteers (other students, parents, etc.) to reinforce and supplement classroom activities.

4.6 Develop a plan to use the talents of parents in supporting the learning activities of their child and those of other students in the class.

Function 5.0: Facilitate Learning

5.1 Identify and differentiate between a variety of behavior management techniques and develop skills in selecting appropriate techniques to manage individual and/or group behavior.

5.2 Select and apply adequate behavior management techniques and measure to meet the learning goals set for the class and each individual student.

5.3 Acknowledge appropriate behaviors in each student in order to stimulate continued effort.

5.4 Conduct class activities in a way to encourage interaction between and among students.

5.5 Provide ample instruction and practice for each child to develop and refine adequate coping strategies.

5.6 Plan with class for systematic appraisal and improvement of the psychological climate of the class.

Function 6.0: Evaluate Learning

6.1 Organize a system to collect and record data by which to evaluate student progress toward goal attainment.

6.2 Develop a feedback system that will furnish continuous data to student, teacher and parents on goal attainment.

6.3 Use evaluation data to assess goal attainment in order to measure terminal outcomes and set new goals.

Competencies Identified by Teacher Educators

Haisley and Gilberts (1978) of the University of Oregon concurred with the opinion of this writer when they stated, "If P.L. 94-142 is to be implemented successfully, educational personnel need to acquire certain basic knowledge and teaching skills—competencies good teachers have used for some time" (p. 30).

They developed checklists—one for knowledge and another for skills—to assist educators in focusing on the major areas of concern (see Tables 1 and 2). The authors recommended that the inclusion of the stated competencies

TABLE 1

Checklist 1–Knowledge Base

What teachers need to know about P.L. 94-142	What level of competence do you expect of your trainees?		
	Can identify source	Can define	Can elaborate
1. Knowledge of laws regarding the handicapped.			
2. Knowledge of handicapping conditions.			
3. Knowledge of P.L. 94-142— terminology and definitions (e.g., "least restrictive environment," "free appropriate public education").			
4. Understanding of appropriate instructional settings for the handicapped.			
5. Knowledge of child evaluation procedures.			
6. Knowledge of procedural safeguards.			
7. Knowledge of IEP (individualized education program) development and implementation.			
8. Knowledge of state and local guidelines for implementation of 94-142.			
9. Knowledge of least restrictive placement possibilities.			
10. Knowledge about related services and their availability.			

Note. From "Individual Competencies Needed to Implement P.L. 94-142" by F. B. Haisley and R. D. Gilberts, *Journal of Teacher Education*, 1978, 29(6), p. 31. Copyright 1978 by American Association of Colleges for Teacher Education. Reprinted by permission.

in both preservice and inservice training courses should ensure at least minimal personnel preparation. The authors did not include information on the derivation or validation of the items chosen for inclusion in the checklists.

TABLE 2

Checklist II—Individual Skills

Skills required by elementary and secondary personnel	Does your program include opportunities for personnel to reach competence?		
	No	Somewhat	Yes
The ability to:			
1. Use resource room materials and staff.			
2. Use peer tutoring, teacher aides, and volunteers.			
3. Use diagnostic and prescriptive techniques.			
4. Participate in, design, and implement IEPs.			
5. Communicate with peers, parents, and pupils.			
6. Monitor individual student progress.			
7. Gather and interpret data about student performance.			
8. Select appropriate curricular materials.			
9. Adapt available curriculum.			
10. Provide small group instruction based on identified student needs.			
Additional skills for elementary educators			
The ability to provide:			
1. Early identification of student needs.			
2. Individualized direct instruction techniques.			
3. Effective organization of the classroom for instruction.			
4. Effective assessment of student strengths and weaknesses.			

190

TABLE 2 (Continued)

Checklist II—Individual Skills

Skills required by elementary and secondary personnel	Does your program include opportunities for personnel to reach competence?		
	No	Somewhat	Yes
5. Effective classroom management skills.			
Additional skills for secondary educators			
The ability to:			
1. Teach the underachieving student.			
2. Use peer tutoring procedures.			
3. Modify strategies to reach content area goals in the areas of materials, expectations, instruction, and student performance levels.			
4. Participate in team approaches to instruction.			
5. Use effective questioning strategies.			
6. Assess student modes of response.			
Additional skills related to IEPs			
Teachers should be able and expected to:			
1. Screen: Identify students with possible problems.			
2. Refer: identify students who may need special support services.			
3. Comply with the law requiring nondiscriminatory testing and parent permission for individual evaluation.			
4. Compile information related to students' educational, emotional, and physical functioning.			
5. Ensure that due process procedures have been met in determining child's eligibility for special services.			

(continued on next page)

TABLE 2 (Continued)

Checklist II—Individual Skills

Skills required by elementary and secondary personnel	Does your program include opportunities for personnel to reach competence?		
	No	Somewhat	Yes
6. Meet with parents to share assessment and evaluation data.			
7. Participate as a team member in the development of IEPs.			
8. Provide goals, objectives, and minimal competence criteria appropriate to a child's needs.			
9. Implement the IEP developed by the school team for students in the classroom.			
10. Monitor student progress to ensure that goals and objectives are appropriate and being carried out and that progress is evident.			

Note. From Haisley and Gilberts, 1978, p. 32. Reprinted by permission.

Competencies Identified by a Special Educator

Philip H. Mann, Director of The Special Education Developmental and Technical Assistance Center at the University of Miami, has developed a comprehensive self assessment competence inventory (Mann, Suiter, & McClung, 1979). This inventory identifies five areas: diagnosis-student assessment, curriculum-instruction, educational management, behavior management and special education. A total of 60 competency statements are grouped under the five broad categories. Trainees would rank the competencies in each area based on their self perceived needs. *The Mann Self-Assessment Competency Inventory* was specifically designed to prioritize need for training when working with students exhibiting variability or special needs or students who are gifted and/or talented.

Competencies Identified by a Local School District

The Houston Plan uses a core of master teachers working in a demonstration training center to develop the necessary competencies needed by educational personnel working with handicapped students in regular class settings. The philosophy underlying the Houston Plan is that each child is unique and that all education should be special education (Meisgeier, undated, p. 77).

The intent of the Houston Plan is to provide personalized learning programs, with individualized instruction and continuous progress curriculum for all children. Through the Teacher Development Center, teachers and other school personnel can develop their skills through the use of 21 self paced modules in the areas of applied behavioral analysis, multiple learning centers, peer and cross age tutoring, strategies for individualized instruction, and continuous progress curricula (Meisgeier, undated, p. 79).

SEA Inservice Training Priorities

P.L. 94-142 requires a comprehensive system of personnel development (CSPD) at the SEA level to ensure the availability of appropriately trained personnel to carry out the provisions of the law. Rude (1978) conducted a review of the plans submitted by each SEA to the Bureau of Education for the Handicapped for the purpose of identifying nationwide trends and priorities for inservice training. Although the intent of this survey was not to identify competencies as such, the information does provide an overview of what SEA's consider to be priority topics for training. Rude (1978, p. 173) has provided a rank order of topics on a nationwide survey of SEA's (See Table 3).

In response to the federal mandate, the Maryland State Department of Education (MSDE) has developed a personnel development plan to facilitate

TABLE 3

Rank Order of Highest Priority Needed Training Topics Nationwide

Rank Order	Topics
1	Instructional procedures/classroom management
1	Curriculum/programing/materials/resources
2	Individualized education program
3	Identify, locate, refer handicapped children
4	Child evaluation procedures
5	Least restrictive environment
6	Implementing Public Law 94-142
7	Communication
8	Coordination of services

training efforts at both the preservice and inservice levels. MSDE (Jacobs, Peck, & Flynn, undated, p. 18) identified and prioritized the following 10 training areas:

1. Development and implementation of IEP's in special education programs.
2. Implications of P.L. 94-142.
3. Assessment and delivery of services for handicapped students in regular classrooms.
4. Programing in secondary education (including vocational education) for handicapped students in regular and special education.
5. Strategies for transportation of handicapped students.
6. Effective programing for severely/multiply handicapped students.
7. Methods for behavior management.
8. Program evaluation for administrators, supervisors, and program planners.
9. Methods for the development of motor skills.
10. Parent education (training for professionals relative to educating parents).

Areas of Agreement

It has been inspiring to note that educators with different frames of reference could agree independently of one another on what general areas of competence a regular educator would need to work with mildly handicapped students. A cross tabulation of competency areas yielded the following:

1. Knowledge of the law—federal and state
   a. Least restrictive environment
   b. IEP's
   c. Due Process
2. Nature of mainstreaming
3. Characteristics of exceptional children
4. Individualization of instruction
   a. Assessment of student needs
   b. Learning styles
   c. Diagnosis-prescription
   d. Adaptation of curriculum
   e. Evaluation
5. Educational, physical, social, and emotional development
6. Behavior management
7. Human relations
   a. Communication skills (peers, parents and pupils)
   b. Attitudes
8. Resource and support systems—using resource personnel (special education personnel, aides, tutors, parents)

9. Classroom organization (establishing environment)—physical and learning

With the exception of the first three categories, these competencies would be expected of any effective teacher.

Implications for Training

As a result of the limited nature of the research, the preceding statements on competencies should not be interpreted as a definitive position, but rather as a point of departure for those involved with training regular educators involved with mainstreaming. Before any training is begun, we recommend that a needs assessment be conducted at each site. The identified competency areas could then be used as the framework of the needs assessment, allowing for teacher input and involvement in determining training priorities as well as providing a basis for evaluation.

REFERENCES

Education for All Handicapped Children Act of 1975 (P.L. 94-142). *Federal Register*, *42* (163), August 23, 1977.

Haisley, F. B., & Gilberts, R. D. Individual competencies needed to implement P.L. 94-142. *Journal of Teacher Education*, 1978, *29*(6), 30–33.

Harvey, J. Future trends in personnel preparation. *Exceptional Children*, 1976, *43*(3), 148–150.

Jacobs, L. J., Peck, C., & Flynn, P. B. *Maryland State Department of Education Division of Special Education Comprehensive System of Personnel Development*. Baltimore: State Board of Education, undated.

Mann, P. H., Suiter, P. A., & McClung, R. M. *Handbook in diagnostic prescriptive teaching* (2nd ed.). Boston: Allyn & Bacon, 1979.

Meisgeier, C. S. The Houston plan—Retraining of regular classroom setting. In P. H. Mann (Ed.), *Mainstream special education issues & perspectives in urban centers*. Reston VA: The Council for Exceptional Children, undated.

Peterson, R. L. *Mainstreaming training systems, materials and resources: A working list* (4th Ed.). Minneapolis: National Support Systems Project, University of Minnesota, 1977.

Rader, B. T. Competencies for mainstream teachers: An analysis. In J. K. Grosenick & M. C. Reynolds (Eds.), *Teacher education: Renegotiating roles for mainstreaming*. Minneapolis: University of Minnesota, 1978.

Redden, M. R., & Blackhurst, A. E. Mainstreaming competency specifications for elementary teachers. *Exceptional Children*, 1978, *44*(8), 615–617.

Rude, R. Trends and priorities in inservice training. *Exceptional Children*, 1978, *45*(3), 172–176.

Torres, S. (Ed.). *A primer on individualized education programs for handicapped children*. Reston VA: The Foundation for Exceptional Children, 1977.

11

The Future: Creating the Conditions for Professional Practice

DEAN C. CORRIGAN
KENNETH R. HOWEY

No significant changes will take place in teachers or in the teaching profession until the situation in which teachers work is changed. This is the most vivid truth that emerges from our analysis of teacher education. Reforming the "setting" is a thread that runs through all of the chapters in this book. This is the primary reason for using the term *school focused* inservice education.

School focused does not imply that colleges or departments of education will be excluded from the process of inservice education. Educational change must move in both directions—to colleges as well as to schools. Indeed, if colleges and departments of education are to be the training and development arm of the profession they must become partners in reforming the schools so that the knowledge and skills learned in programs of continuing professional education can be *used* in the schools. If the content of teacher education cannot be used in the teacher's work place then colleges of education will be viewed as out of touch and obsolete.

WORK SITUATION AND PROFESSIONAL PRACTICE

As Scheffknecht, the noted adult educator, said in his report on continuing education:

> The effectiveness of inservice education depends far more on the quality of the situation in which it is to be used than on the quality of the learning situation . . . Training of a teacher to use active methods or

a worker to express and investigate problems or a technician to handle statistics or a local resident to use a videotape recorder has no sense unless he can apply what he has learned in his place of work or residence . . . As a result, we cannot neglect the different factors that condition education at this level. It has been found, for example, that strongly authoritarian structures, absence of participation in choosing objectives and of full or partial responsibility for action, absence of the right to err, or to oppose or discuss measures affecting us, etc. are factors which restrict possibilities for personal development and substantially weaken what is generally known as the motivation for learning . . . By the same token, a social system which strengthens such motivation gives education its justification since it enables it to be used. (Scheffknect, 1975, p. 13)

It is now abundantly clear that the educational system will not improve by merely changing teacher education programs at colleges and universities. If we prepare teachers with the latest knowledge and skill and then place them in a work situation where they cannot use this new knowledge and skill, we merely exacerbate the situation.

As Howey pointed out in his review of *Educating a Profession*,

The critical point is that by and large the favorable set of conditions called for in the report do not exist widely, either physically or psychologically. The overriding goal of quality individualization, let alone personalization, of instruction is not reality in most schools. If the current dominant operational models of schooling continue, then in some ways teachers are "over-trained" already. More intensive and sophisticated initial preparation combined with more formalized transitional internships could very conceivably exacerbate already existing role conflicts, unless expectations for and conditions surrounding teachers are changed as well. It is imperative that new directions in teacher education be embedded in and consonant with equally innovative directions in school renewal. Major reform in one cannot occur without concurrent major reform in the other (Howey, 1977, pp. 81–84).

The same message is true for the larger profession of teaching. We will not improve the professional status of teaching by merely expanding the knowledge and skill base of teachers. These are essential but not sufficient factors in achieving professionalism. The aim of teacher education must be to change the *setting* for teaching and learning as well as the teacher.

After a comprehensive review of the characteristics of professions in America, the *AACTE Bicentennial Report* said:

The question of status within the hierarchy of professions is a false or non-issue. Status is a consequence of important conditions rather than an important condition in its own right. What the teaching profession needs is a set of conditions which are favorable to the delivery of professional level educational service to the society and its communities. (Howsam, Corrigan, Denemark, & Nash, 1976, p. 39)

Up to now, for reasons that are complex and obscure, both the instructional processes of education and those of teachers have retained large elements of conventional wisdom and craft orientation. The failure of education to advance beyond this stage of development is largely responsible for the failure of schools to meet the educational challenges of our time. The rapid pace of social change has placed unprecedented demands on schools and professional educators.

The most recent dramatic example is Public Law 94-142, The Education for All Handicapped Children Act of 1975 (*Federal Register*, August, 1977). When the current state of our educational system is examined in the light of the requirements of P.L. 94-142, it becomes clear that massive reforms will be needed not only in the kind of teachers who staff the schools but in the nature of the schools themselves.

Schools have not been designed to achieve the objectives of P.L. 94-142 and our teachers have not been prepared for the responsibilities it expects of them. Such complex educational functions cannot be performed without a high level of professional knowledge and skill, and the setting in which to use them.

This chapter presents a view of the kind of schools needed to implement "appropriate education" for all children and some concepts to consider in the development of inservice programs to create the conditions for professional practice.

A CALL FOR A NEW KIND OF EDUCATION

Because it will require fundamental changes in the school setting, P.L. 94-142 could be the most important piece of legislation in the history of the country. Furthermore, since it calls for a new kind of teacher education to produce a new kind of teacher for schools that must meet the learning needs of *all* children, it could be the vehicle through which teaching emerges as a "real" profession.

P.L. 94-142 received overwhelming support in the Congress of the United States. It was passed by a vote of 404 to 7 in the House of Representatives and 87 to 7 in the Senate. Educators can pursue the purposes of P.L. 94-142 knowing they have a clear mandate to do so. Since, as previously stated, this Act is a piece of civil rights legislation as well as educational legislation, it cannot be fully understood except from this perspective. Review of the Congressional testimony on P.L. 94-142 indicates that the basic rationale in support of providing access to equal educational opportunity for persons with handicaps is that they are *human beings* living in America and, therefore, have a right to *access* to equal educational opportunity, *even if it costs more to provide it.*

Roots of P.L. 94-142

The roots of this Act can be found in the civil rights movement of the 1960's. The same rationale behind the Supreme Court decision of 1954, *Brown* v. *Board of Education*, influenced the thinking of advocates for the handicapped. Central to that rationale is the notion that segregation has harmful effects on both the person who is segregated and the person who does the segregating (Friedman, 1969).

The educational philosophy that produced P.L. 94-142 was expressed by Dr. Edwin Martin, Chief of the Bureau of Education for the Handicapped and Associate Commissioner of Education.

> To improve education for *all* children, the dichotomous constructs existing at all levels of the educational system and in society, in general, must be eliminated. If human rights is to become a reality in America, the notion that handicapped children or black children or any such group are very different persons and should be set apart in different categories, must be rejected . . . all children are more alike than different in their basic human nature (Martin, 1974).

P.L. 94-142 has shifted the focus of concern from children's handicaps to their learning needs, and changed the educational setting from segregated classrooms and institutions to "appropriate" education in the "least restrictive environment."

Extending the Educational Concepts in P.L. 94-142

In the end, if the zero reject principle, the individualized education program, the due process requirement, the parent involvement directive, and the integration imperative of P.L. 94-142 are implemented for handicapped children, they will be extended to all children. Thus, in the decade ahead, *special education* could become general education and *general education,* special.

Zero Reject Principle

P.L. 94-142 calls on educators to eliminate isolation of the handicapped and the prejudice and discrimination that isolation breeds, and the mockery that this isolation makes of the fundamental right of *access* to equal educational opportunity. American schools must now be based on the principle of "no rejects," based on the firm assumption that every human being has a right to be treated as a person—not an object, or a symbol on a chart, or a category in a student grouping structure. The labeling and classification

200

of children and the social stigma that this labeling produces must be eliminated. It is not the purpose of American schools to be the sorting station
for society's other institutions, or to perpetuate social Darwinism—the
"beat the other guy before he beats you attitude."

Least Restrictive Environment

P.L. 94-142 identifies the regular classrom as the "least restrictive environment" unless another setting is prescribed as more "appropriate" to
meet the child's special needs. If other settings are used, movement to such
settings must be justified. The implications of using the regular classroom
are enormous, not the least of which is that all educators—regular classroom teachers, counselors, administrators, and other support personnel—
must now be educationally prepared to work with persons with handicaps.
This will call for a change in roles of all education personnel and especially
a change in the role for special educators. They will become members of an
instructional team in which they will share their expertise with other members of the team as well as with students.

Continuous Progress Evaluation

Ultimately, the individualization mandate will require a continuous progress reporting system with diagnostic profiles describing each student's
human variability, exceptionality, and intellectual-personal growth. The
marking system and the illegitimate comparisons it makes, the pressure
it creates, and the failure it produces will have to go the way of all outmoded
practices. It will do little good to place children with handicaps in regular
classrooms and flunk them, or deny them a high school diploma based on
standardized competency tests.

It will be necessary to develop new evaluation systems. These systems
should include criterion or domain referenced evaluation practices in which
the concepts of expectancy and capacity are related more to access to competent teaching in educational settings than inherent individual learner
traits. The current overreliance on normative testing and the misinter-
pretation and misuse of intelligence, achievement, and aptitude tests must
be corrected. Also, under P.L. 94-142, parents must be notified that the
evaluation instruments that are used by the schools will not in any way
discriminate against the child on the basis of race or culture.

Parent Relationships

A goal discussed for years by educators is parent involvement. This Act
requires a sign off by the child's parent, guardian or surrogate on the IEP
and consultation at each step of the process of identification, evaluation,
and placement into an "appropriate" setting. If parents are not notified,

they have the right to obtain an impartial due process hearing with regard to these various steps. They must first be notified of the time and place of the hearing that they request and of all their procedural rights. The parents may be accompanied and advised by counsel and by individuals with special knowledge or training with respect to handicapped children.

The parents also have the right to present evidence at the hearing and to confront, cross examine, and compel the attendance of witnesses. They must be supplied with a record of the hearing including the written findings of fact and a clear written statement of what the decision is and the basis for reaching it.

Finally, parents also have the right to appeal the hearing. The ways these child-parent-teacher relationships are developed, starting with "child find," will be critical in achieving the goals of this Act and restoring the public's confidence in its schools. If these procedures are implemented wrongly they will produce antagonism and adversary relationships. If they are developed effectively by competent educators they will produce a new constructive parent-school partnership beyond any that has existed in the history of American education.

Reducing Class Size

In order to develop the kind of individualized-personalized relationships between teachers, students, and parents called for in P.L. 94-142, we must eliminate overcrowding and the resulting class loads, easy anonymity, and shallow teacher-pupil-parent contacts.

Goldberg (1977) provided documentation that current class size is a 4th century invention:

> The profound insights of the 12th century philosopher, physician and theologian, Moses Maimonides, including many education matters, are detailed in the *Mishnen Torah*, a 14 volume codification of law and tradition which he started to compose at age 16. The standard translation into English of the "Code of Miamonides" is published by Yale University Press.
>
> The passage on class size from Maimonides reads as follows:
>
> > "When a community has twenty-five children, they are to study under one teacher. If the number in the class is twenty-six, but not more than forty, an assistant should be placed with him to help with the instruction. If there are more than forty, a second teacher should be appointed."

This commentary on class size did not originate with Maimonides. It is attributable to regulation 21a of the Talmudic Tractate, *Babe Bathra*, written in the *4th century*, 800 years before Maimonides. The classic translation of the work published by the Soncino Press of London reads: "The number of pupils to be assigned to each teacher is twenty-five. If there are forty, we appoint an assistant, at the expense of the town" (Goldberg, 1977, p. 15).

After all these years the basic configuration of the classroom must change. Recent research (Glass & Smith, 1978) proves once again what good teachers have always known: class size makes a difference in student achievement because teachers have the time and space to differentiate instruction and use personalized approaches. In the future, if the public will not provide the resources for smaller classes for a full day, schools may be better off to have children go to school for half day with 10 to 15 in a class than a full day with 25 to 35 in a class unless an aide can be provided for the larger class. It will be fruitless to add more specialists to collect diagnostic data on children unless teacher-pupil ratios are provided that permit teachers to use these data in developing differentiated approaches for each child.

Individualized Plans for Each School as Well as Each Child

It is critical to note that P.L. 94-142 addresses individualized programs and plans, not just individualized instruction. Even though it is not stipulated, one realizes that this legislation views the total setting in the school and the classroom as well as the individual interaction between teachers and students as being educative. The "milieu" of the school will especially affect the attitudinal learning of students and educators, such as developing an understanding and respect for individual differences and working with other persons in the community. The plan for mainstreaming includes consideration of the total learning environment. Given that each school has its own subculture, it would seem feasible, therefore, to consider "individual plans" for each school as well as for each child.

Academic Freedom for Students as Well as Teachers

Academic freedom in a learning environment is reciprocal. The nature of academic freedom is such that it cannot exist for some members of the community and not for others. We must develop the kind of interactions between teachers and students in which students are free to say right out loud what they do not know as well as what they do know—a relationship based on the realization that responsibility and freedom cannot be learned without having the opportunity to make choices and deal with the consequences. The "right answer syndrome" that discourages values clarification and risk taking activities must go. We must give students an opportunity to ask their teachers and classmates questions as well as answer them. Cooperative procedures should be used to help everyone in the environment learn to develop a sense of responsibility for assuring the human rights of others, as well as learn to read, write, spell, and do math and science.

Civil Rights in the Schools

Our schools should exemplify the humanity we explicate in our most visionary human rights documents. Students should not have to give up due process and other civil rights when they walk into a school. We must abolish the cruel, outmoded, unreasonable, professionally demeaning practice of corporal punishment. Children learn what they live and will not learn such values as love, compassion, and justice if the schools make a sham of them. No college of education offers a course on how to beat children—it is an unprofessional act. Teaching will only become a profession when it stops using outmoded regulations to accommodate the inadequacies of some of its members and starts using professional ethics, knowledge, and skill in teaching and learning to guide and judge professional performance.

Differentiated Instruction

The educational setting must be organized so that students know what they can do to achieve a *success* experience. The methods used to differentiate instruction should be neither exclusively behavioristic nor cognitive; child centered nor discipline centered. They should be purposefully eclectic. Curricular tracking that fosters a caste system, and the grade level lockstep that ignores what we know about the ways unique selves develop, must be eliminated. The school must develop ways to use the individual's own rhythm, learning speed, style of learning, and exceptionality.

Expanded Resources, Flexible Time and Space

The inflexible and nonvariable time schedule and the conformity it demands must be changed. The school should be integrated into the community and be an integrator of the community. The paucity of curriculum options and the boredom it creates must be replaced by using the world outside as well as inside the classroom through direct experiences in communities as well as by old fashioned poring over books.

Linking with the Human Service Delivery System

The beneficiaries of P.L. 94-142 are approximately 12 % of the human beings in the United States between the ages of 3 and 21 who have a handicap, as defined in the Act. During the past year "child find" and services to children aged 5 to 18 were undertaken. Now all states will be asked to extend services to persons ages 3 through 21. Some states have gone beyond this age group already and in their enabling legislation have started the "child find" of children age 1 and have extended services beyond age 21. Since many agencies work with these age groups, school personnel must now view themselves as part of a human service delivery system rather than a school system. New means of linking with these agencies and new systems of preservice and inservice training to bring about better collaboration among all roles involved in the human service delivery system must be developed.

Differentiated Roles for Teachers

The career option grid in education is presently too flat; it does not foster uniqueness. Differentiation of roles both in schools and in a variety of human services settings should characterize teaching, and support systems should be established in which teachers share their specific knowledge and skills with other human service professionals. We must change the stereotyped view of teachers as people who perform the same role 40 years after they start their careers as they did when they began. Teachers must have the opportunity to move in and out of a variety of teaching settings during their careers. Only when educators reflect an enlarged view of the settings in which teaching is a vital function will the profession of teaching reach its full maturity.

Fostering Global Awareness

The school curriculum must also reflect the new realities of a changing society and a changing world. Schools must foster global awareness with the view that all children of the present population will live in a mobile, international community solving problems with ideas and technology we cannot imagine, in a world as different from today's as today's is from that of the first settlers in this country. Provincialism and the lack of opportunity to speculate about the unknown must be eliminated.The school must help this generation of Americans learn how to shape the future, not just accept it.

INSERVICE EDUCATION AND PROFESSIONAL PRACTICE

A new kind of teacher education will be needed to produce teachers who can create the aforementioned school of tomorrow, today. To add a sense of urgency to the task, Reynolds (1978) reminded us that events and needs relating to P.L. 94-142 are already running far ahead of the necessary changes in training programs—literally hundreds of thousands of teachers and related professionals are being required, at this moment, to undertake duties for which they are unprepared. Unfortunately, the precious time being squeezed out of the educational system for inservice education to meet the educational imperatives of P.L. 94-142 has thus far focused primarily on how to "fill out the forms" for the IEP's and set up the mechanisms of due process hearings. The lofty educational purposes for which P.L. 94-142 was created are in danger of getting lost in the paper shuffle. Reynolds described the current response to P.L. 94-142 as follows:

> About half of my special education friends these days seem to be out giving lessons to the masses on individualized educational plans (IEPs). Without even trying I have been shown at least six sets of transparencies, listened to endless audio cassettes on the requirements of Public Law 94-142, and I have been guided through several versions of "sure fire" forms to satisfy all the new regulations.
> What I see and hear seems well designed to keep teachers out of jail—to comply with the law, that is—but usually I sense little vision of how people might come together creatively to design environments for better learning and living by handicapped students and their classmates.
> . . . The danger is considerable, I think, that some communities will go through the motions on IEPs, and consume a great deal of time and resources, but will advance the cause of the handicapped by little or not at all. In the name of due process they may well undertake more process than is due, letting bureaucratic machinations overtake and mutilate the lofty purposes and enterprise envisioned by the makers of P.L. 94-142. (Reynolds, 1978, p. 60)

A New Strategy

The strategy for improving the schools has been to prepare new professionals with the most recent knowledge in their field, and send them out as crusaders to improve the schools. In a large part, this strategy has *failed*— the new recruits and their ideas were swallowed up by the system. The experienced professionals, those in the field who are 40 to 45 years old with 20 to 25 years of service left, are the "career" professionals. Unless we reeducate them right along with the new professionals, the schools will not improve significantly.

A new strategy is required that brings together preservice and inservice teachers in the same training program in a team relationship. The program should have as its primary goal the improvement of all aspects of education in school and nonschool settings. Training should be developed as a by-product of a joint search for better ways to improve the delivery of educational care to people of all developmental ages and stages. From this cooperative school-college community commitment to the larger end in view, *creating healthy human communities*, the training program will receive its relevance and vitality.

If our educational institutions are to become the kind of powerful instruments for social progress as called for in P.L. 94-142, we will need a new design for teacher education. Central to this new design is recognition of

206

the fact that teacher education, schools and other educational community agencies, and colleges themselves, are interrelated and interacting components of one system. Schools, their communities, and colleges are unnecessarily isolated from one another, to the detriment of all. We must replace our present disconnected approach with a new partnership that provides an interlocking process of educational improvement and training at all levels of the educational spectrum, including the training of "career" teachers in the kind of school focused inservice teacher education programs described in this book.

School Focused Inservice Education

A number of assertions that have emerged from our study and experience with school focused inservice teacher education are summarized here for consideration in future planning.

School Focused Reform

Inservice education must be easily accessible, school focused, and evaluated by its impact on learning environment of the school, not just the individual teacher. Where professional growth is concerned, changing the behavior of a group often is easier than changing the behavior of an individual. The school, the work setting, should be the focus for reform and all in it should be participants—either participating as *innovators*, or agreeing to at least not be *blockers*. Because inservice education must be related to the work situation to be useful, it is by its very nature a "political" process as well as an educational process. Policies to guide continuing education of teachers must start from this basic premise or they will be ineffective in dealing with the conflict that effective inservice education will produce as adult learners seek to *use* the knowledge and skills they are taught as instruments to reform the system in which they work and live. Each student in the inservice program is a potential change agent and must be treated and supported accordingly.

Changing the Work Situation

Inservice education must be based on knowledge of the teachers' *work situation*. The schools will not improve by just giving teachers more knowledge, skills, and values. The conditions in the work situation must change to permit them to use this training. Teachers are already overtrained for some of the settings in which they are expected to work. Inservice teachers understand the realities of the work place. They process formal experiences in teacher education in terms of those realities. For example, teachers will not be interested in individualizing instruction if they believe that in the community in which they teach individualization is not possible, valued, encouraged, or even permitted. Nor will they plan continuing education or

207

other professional activities after school if they must suffer large classes and heavy burdens every working day. Teacher education institutions serve the teaching profession and the schools best by helping create conditions favorable to professional practice as well as professional study.

Career Long Preparation

In the making of a teacher, it is highly probable that inservice education is infinitely more important than preservice education. However, they should not be viewed as separate entities. They should be viewed as interlocking phases of a *career long* preparation program (Phases: initial, induction, inservice). The first 2 or 3 years of a teacher's experience are the most critical and the supportive environment provided by the principal is a key to success. Teachers function according to the various "representations" of their role (their own perceptions, the perceptions of the pupils, parents, administrators). Their view of themselves depends on the professional context in which they operate.

Variety of Places and People for Inservice

Practicing teachers who are good adult educators as well as good teachers of children are often excellent "cotrainers" of other teachers in the work situation—they have "credibility." Also broadening the definition of *expert* to the local setting decreases the probability of discounting the "outside" expert and keeps the responsibility with individuals in the setting to achieve their own goals—scapegoating is lessened. The emerging role of the university teacher educator is to be a good trainer of school based cotrainers. This multiplier model extends the impact of the colleges and provides backup support for the"onsite" trainers.

Teachers are not the only people in need of growth. Teacher educators, principals, custodians, secretaries, parents, aides, etc. must be included in inservice plans. It should be a "we" process not a "they" process and this applies to "partners" from the university. Inservice will be quite different according to the case of a variety of clients. Some clients will want and need specific knowledge, others will want and need specific skills.

The general aim of inservice training is to relate theory to improved practice in the teaching-learning setting. Theory of swimming does not teach people to swim. Theory of surviving does not teach people to survive. It is not necessary for all inservice activities to be held "on site" in order to be school focused. Training can be offered in a variety of sites and institutions, including schools, teacher centers, community agencies, and colleges.

Roles and Competencies of University Inservice Educators

Some university professors may not be prepared to teach adults inasmuch as they view their role as primarily the dissemination of specialized subject matter without reference to its uses. This is an obstacle in working with another adult since adult education serves other purposes than injecting knowledge. The role of the adult educator includes being a colleague, consultant, and advisor, as well as subject matter specialist and researcher.

The adult educator of practitioners is also expected to demonstrate enough understanding of the work place in which the knowledge is to be used to be viewed as credible. College personnel need organized personnel development. Anyone who has worked in continuing education programs for adults knows that many college professors cannot do the role. They do not know how to teach, and especially how to teach working adults who come to them to learn how to be more effective in their work.

Some professors are so narrowly specialized as to appear virtually illiterate to mature experienced men and women. Concretely, this means that colleges must expose professors to the challenges of teaching and research work outside of their own specialities; to teaching and research with different kinds of students who are at different development stages and cycles in their lives; and to opportunities for learning, especially learning about teaching adults. This same message holds true for "onsite" teachers who intend to teach their colleagues in inservice programs.

Cooperative Decision Making

Involvement of adults in self management of training is a way to bring meaning to what is studied. If the role of teachers is to carry out orders— to be "executors" rather than persons who can make a difference then teachers will not want further training. Motivation for inservice is directly connected with the potential opportunity to change practice. If they have autocratic managers there is a complete difference in motivational factors for being a better teacher.

The hierarchical structure of schools must be changed. The current approach to administration and supervision is contradictory to professionalism and has too often inhibited what teachers were able to do with the education and experience they already possessed. Teachers have been trained (or even not trained) to implement innovations conceived by supervisors or outsiders, but very rarely have they been trained to manage the system themselves. In the future the source of professional authority should be expertise, not title or position. Constructive peer relationships and cooperative learning and decision making should pervade the school administrative structure as well as the classroom. Teachers will act like professionals when they are treated like professionals.

Using Adult Learning Theory

Inservice education must use knowledge of adult learning theory. Movement from one stage of personal and professional development to the next occurs through cycles of challenge and response, cognitive dissonance, cultural discontinuity, differentiation, and integration. It occurs when a person confronts situations for which old ways are not adequate, which require new ways of thinking and acting. The experience may be upsetting and uncomfortable; coping with disequilibrium, learning new skills, assimilating new knowledge, resolving value conflicts, does not always happen simply and smoothly. The trick is to achieve that optimal distance between where the student is and what the new situations require so that the student is challenged but not bowled over, so change is possible without provoking trauma, entrenchment, or flight. This means that a very diverse array of resources, school based educators, field experiences, instructional materials, and learning alternatives must be available if a diversity of adult learners are to be appropriately served in inservice teacher education programs. Professional growth, particularly when it involves the exchange of old habits for new, breeds considerable insecurity. It may well be that we have greatly overestimated teachers' psychological resistance to change. However, we now know that if we fail to attend to teachers' emotions as well as to their minds, we will again blunder. Professional development is both an affective and cognitive process.

Teacher-Educator as Mentor

Teachers are more likely to identify a person than a course or program as a key influence on their intellectual-personal lives. Though such persons are sometimes called "advisors" for program planning purposes, they actually function as mentors. The mentor-student relationship is a unique one, exemplifying an acceptance and friendship well beyond narrow academic consultation. The mentor is a model not simply of a variety of teaching modes and subject fields, but of the humane professional. Mentors are needed in inservice as well as preservice teacher education programs. There is a vast range of difference between good teachers and poor teachers. We should build our training models on the skills, knowledge, and values possessed and demonstrated by the *good* ones. Also inservice teacher educators should be models of effective teaching. They should exemplify what they explicate.

Creating a Milieu as Inservice Education

Any school can, if it wishes, arrange for professional growth of its faculty and administrators as a regular part of the work load. The most ideal inservice program would be where the "milieu" of the teaching setting is such that living and working in it is in itself educative. The best sign that an institution is an educative one is the fact that the emphasis is not placed on "going to" training. It means that a dynamic training team is permanently questioning itself about its day to day practice; the basic learning tool to be taken into consideration is the day to day work in the school.

Inservice education is virtually useless if the objectives of training programs are not valued and *rewarded*—by the power structure of the school system.

The Potential of the Teacher Center Concept

Teacher centers possess great potential as school focused continuing education centers as well as collaborative governance mechanisms. They can be designed to deliver college and community resources, get professionals together, and form a network of available educational services. Neither the public schools nor the colleges can live in splendid isolation. All partners in the education process can cooperate in the operation of a teacher center: (a) teacher education; (b) the schools; (c) teacher organization; (d) the university; (e) the school board and the community; (f) the state or intermediate agencies. Any less than a high level of interchange of experience and expertise among schools, colleges, and communities will widen an already considerable gap between what is and what could be.

Inservice Education as an Instrument for Social Progress

Although private purposes and individual self interest are powerful motivators, significant amplification occurs when those interests are linked to active engagement with larger human and social concerns (e.g., P.L. 94-142). Experiences that occur when one works to understand and deal with a significant social problem have great developmental power and foster many kinds of learning. The profession itself takes a "quantum leap" forward when it looks outward for purposes as well as inward.

THE CHALLENGE: PUBLIC AND PROFESSION

The professional status of teaching and teacher education will be recognized when the corpus of validated knowledge and skills to which teachers and teacher educators subscribe is clearly identified and the public recognizes that the teaching profession possesses the skills and knowledge to perform a service that is a matter of life and death to this society and its people. Implementing the concepts in P.L. 94-142 would constitute such a demonstration.

In 1980, education has reached the end of an era. Society now demands a new breed of teacher for a new breed of school—a well prepared, highly motivated professional, capable of understanding a broad range of learning problems and of designing and implementing curricular and instructional strategies to solve them. If the school of the future is to become a vehicle for social progress then a sense of social purpose must pervade every level of the educational system and the teaching profession.

In this book, we have proposed a school focused approach to the education of experienced teachers and school reform. We hope that the concepts presented will serve as a guide to *action* as well as thought.

211

REFERENCES

The Education for All Handicapped Children Act of 1975 (P.L. 94-142). *Federal Register, 42*(163), August 23, 1977.

Friedman, L. (Ed.). *Argument: The oral argument before the supreme court in Brown vs. Board of Education of Topeka, 1952-55*. New York: Chelsea House, 1969.

Gilhool, T. K. Changing public policies: Roots and forces. In *Mainstreaming: Origins and implications*, 1976, *2*(2), 9.

Glass, G. V., & Smith, M. L. *Meta-analysis of research on the relationships of class-size and achievement*. Report for the Far West Laboratory for Educational Research and Development, San Francisco: September, 1978.

Goldberg, H. The day after tomorrow in education. Keynote Address at Conference on New Directions, Washington, D.C., George Washington University, 1977. (Mimeographed)

Howey, K. A bicentennial commission plots the path to professionalism: A review essay of educating a profession. *Journal of Teacher Education*, 1977, Fall, 81–84.

Howsam, R., Corrigan, D., Denemark, G., & Nash, R., *Educating a Profession: Bicentennial Commission Report on Education for the Profession of Teaching*. American Association of Colleges for Teacher Education, 1976, pp. 15–138.

Martin, E. W. An end to dichotomous constructs: A reconceptionalization of teacher education. *Journal of Teacher Education*, 1974, *25*, 219.

Reynolds, M. Basic issues in restructuring teacher education. *Journal of Teacher Education*, 1978, *29*, 25–29.

Sarason, S., & Doris, J. Mainstreaming: Dilemmas, opposition, opportunities. In M. C. Reynolds (Ed.), *Futures of Education for exceptional students: Emerging structures*. Minneapolis: University of Minnesota, National Systems Project, 1978.

Scheffknect, J. J. *The tutor*. (Supplement, section 2.2.2) Strasbourg, France: Council of Europe, 1975.

Weintraub, F., Abeson, A., Ballard, J. & Lavor, M. L. (Eds.). *Public policy and the education of exceptional children*. Reston VA: The Council for Exceptional Children, 1976.